Tell the Truth & Shame the Devil

THE LIFE, LEGACY, AND LOVE OF MY SON MICHAEL BROWN

LEZLEY McSPADDEN

WITH LYAH BETH LeFLORE

Regan Arts.

NEW YORK

Regan Arts.

65 Bleecker Street
New York, NY 10012

Names and identifying details of some of the people, events, and places portrayed in this book have been changed.

First Regan Arts hardcover edition, April 2016.

Library of Congress Control Number: 2016932844

ISBN 978-1-942872-52-8

Interior design by Nancy Singer
Cover design by Richard Ljoenes
Cover photograph by Mark Seliger
Front endpaper photography © David Goldman/Associated Press

Printed in the United States of America

10 9 8 7 6 5 4 3 2 1

Equal rights, fair play, justice are all like the air;
we all have it, or none of us has it.
That is the truth of it.

—Maya Angelou

To my children . . .
If I had to choose between loving you and breathing . . .
I would use my last breath to tell you
I LOVE YOU . . .

—Anonymous

To my four children Michael, Déja, Andre, and Jazmine who
didn't ask to be brought here. God blessed me with you and I
vow to honor, respect, and love them for all my days. I never
thought I'd be someone's mother, or be called "Mama."
Thank you God for showing me love, how to love another, and
what being loved feels like.

CONTENTS

FOREWORD

Myrlie Evers-Williams

My general impression of today is that we are filled with sadness, but also with hope for the future, and that we will learn from what has happened to Michael Brown. Of course, my history goes back fifty years ago when my husband, Medgar Evers, was shot down in front of our home, with my children and I there watching and rushing out to him.

Since then, there have been many positive changes, but how much does what has happened to Michael Brown say to us about the spirit, the hope, and the belief in America and where we are today, particularly when it comes to the health and welfare of young African-American men?

It is a tragedy that we are still dealing with this racially motivated hatred. After my husband was shot, I found in my life that I had to have a purpose. I had many purposes really, but one was to see that Medgar Evers's killer was tried and convicted. It took thirty years for that to happen, but you don't give up on these things. You don't give up on the American dream. You don't give up on the rights that we as Americans have, and should have freely in this country. To see our young people taken down as they are, says something not only to the African-American community but also to the whole country. Where are our values? What do we do? What can we do to keep this from happening again?

Michael Brown was lost to us. What about all the other young men who are out there? What can we do to preserve their lives and their future? It makes me recall an old saying: "We must keep our eyes on the prize."

As a mother, I say to Lezley, sometimes you pick up the pieces slowly; other times your progress seems to come fast, fueled by anger, even a degree of hatred. How do you overcome that? You find something positive. Like Lezley, I had children to take care of. I had to go back to school. I had to work. I had to develop careers. I had to be a community activist, all of which was a little difficult for me.

One of the things I think is critically important, though, is that my family and I involved ourselves in activities that spoke to the needs of our communities. What I want to say to Lezley and to all the other loved ones of people we've lost to hate is, do not give up. Hatred serves as a motivator, but you can't live and grow with hate.

We should speak loudly, strongly about our beliefs, about these issues, about the need for change. Not doing so is not just a black problem; it's a problem for all Americans. How dare we tell the rest of the world how to live when we don't embody our message within ourselves. Be strong, stand up, be firm, and try to embrace all people in this area of justice and equality, but particularly our young black males.

There are various organizations throughout this country that focus on youth and their development, helping them find jobs and instilling them with a sense of pride. But these organizations are not one-stop shops for handling these issues. They need to be addressed day to day in our places of worship, in our schools, in our homes. This is not just a black problem; all races need to be able to address our issues of justice and equality.

It's tragic that we have to have our young people taken away from us in the manner in which they are. It is tragic that our law enforcement officers and our communities don't get along better. It's tragic that the civil rights organizations and other community organizations have not come together and developed a plan of action that we can take beyond just our particular cities.

My heart bleeds for Lezley, and the other mothers and families who have lost their children. We have to take the bull by the horns and say, "This will change, and I will be a part of the change, and I will find within my community ways in which I can be involved and bring others into that involvement too." It is up to us to find those ways and to act on them, not only in one moment, but also in an ongoing way throughout all of our lives.

MOTHERS AND SONS

By Common

Everything I know in life, my experiences of life, and what I know to be love and life came from my mother. She is the most consistent form of love I can identify beyond God and the first person that I really got to know fully and deeply. I didn't have the blessing of growing up with a father at home or a male figure to truly sit there and take the time to teach me life's truths. The stuff I learned about being a man, both the beautiful and the ugly, I learned from my male friends and the men in my neighborhood. But my mother taught me how to live. She did her best to teach me how to be a respectable, strong black man.

I remember there was a time when I was a teenager and I talked back to my mother. I even had the gall to raise my hand once. Man, she hit me and I hit the ground. My mother knew about the street, coming from the Southside of Chicago, the Chatham area. She also knew how to flow with the corporate world. I can recall the first time I heard her talking "proper" on the phone. She was selling products for the Gillette Company and I asked her, "Why are you talking like a white person?" She turned to me with a glare full of complete resolve and said, "Look, you gotta be able to adjust to all worlds." That statement has always stuck with me and it was just one of the many lessons about life I learned from her.

My mother is still a rock for me. When I'm dealing with some deep emotional challenges and life gets really tough or it's time for something important to happen, I still go to her. The mother-son connection, I believe, is one of the strongest connections in existence. When it comes to most mothers with their sons, they don't know anything but to love them. That relationship is unbreakable.

That's the place I drew from when I first heard about Mike Brown's death. Of course, this was not the first time I had heard of young unarmed black men being pointlessly shot and killed. The country had only recently mourned the senseless death of Trayvon Martin. Still, there was something about the Mike Brown case that hit me hard, something that pulled at me more than the other cases had in the past. It wasn't just that he was unarmed, or that he had just turned eighteen. That sounded ridiculous enough. But hearing that his body lay there, in the street, for over four and a half hours? It sounded unreal, out of control. How was such a thing possible in a land dedicated to treating all people equally under the law? Where was the respect for the sanctity of human life?

Shortly thereafter, I saw his mother, Lezley McSpadden on television. I later read about a question she had posed to the media: "Do they know how hard it was to raise a young black man?" This woman had not only lost her child, but she had lost him to the searing bullets of someone who was supposed to protect him. Unless you've felt the devastation of seeing your baby's soul leave this earth, I doubt anyone can begin to comprehend the magnitude of that emotional distress.

Soon after I met Lezley for the first time, I could sense that her pain was especially profound, a deep lasting hurt I've rarely witnessed. You could feel her sorrow dangling in the air. When I looked into her eyes, I could feel the weight of her son's life being ripped from her. She was occupying space, but not completely. Her mind and spirit were elsewhere, dealing with the loss of her child, trying to process how to make that empty hole she was feeling have real meaning.

As we stood facing each other, there was a moment when she suddenly became present and gazed at me. I could see a powerful, insightful woman, eyes wide open, taking things in, thinking things through. She clearly had a warrior's spirit and energy, but was also warm and generous. She was a woman who had worked hard and had done her best and was *still* doing her best. She was in a place of indescribable grief, but she understood that all she could do now was what she had always done all her life: fight, and fight hard. As we spoke, I could feel a surge of strength behind her agony. It was clear to me that this was a woman who was never going to give up, and that this incident was not the end of her story. That same strength she used to raise Mike was going help her survive. Out of the most difficult situation you could ask a parent to endure, she was determined to make the world a better place. Her words, her demeanor, and her quiet strength were undeniable and, at the same time, inspiring.

What happened to Mike Brown was probably the darkest thing that Lezley has ever and will ever experience. Yet, in the darkest of places, light will eventually come and when that light comes, it will erupt with the force of a thousand suns. The more you recognize it, the brighter it gets. Lezley McSpadden is putting her light out there for the world to see. She's communicating with others who've experienced unspeakable loss, and even those who will never experience what she has. She is showing how bright and purposeful Mike's life was and is. She is tirelessly working to eliminate the ignorance that led to her son's untimely death and to keep the flame alive that will forever honor his legacy.

Mike Brown is the Emmett Till of this generation. Emmett Till's story changed my life. I remember as a kid first reading the story and studying the pictures of him after he had been found in a river, head swollen beyond recognition. He was just fourteen, killed for the sickest of reasons, for simply whistling at a white woman. He was from Chicago, just like me. My body tingled with fear as I felt like that could easily have been me. I did not understand how anyone could hate another enough to do what those men had done to Emmett Till. Though he had died before I was born, I could feel the power of his spirit moving through me, motivating me to make a difference with my life. Mike Brown, like Emmet Till, has a strong spirit. His death awakened me again. It also ignited the world.

We won't ever be able to feel what Lezley McSpadden feels. However, we can at least try to bring value or some type of positive results from such an excruciating experience. We have to look at the bigger picture. What can we do right now that's going to improve the world? How can one young man's life better the lives of all people, particularly black and brown brothers and sisters? We may not have all the answers, but we do have the heart, motivation, and spirit to demand that Mike Brown's life be valued. It is a cause in which Lezley finds unending hope and inspiration. A mother, after all, stays with her son, no matter what, until the day she dies. Hopefully, we can all hold hands with her in her quest to begin to bring change to the world long before then.

PART ONE

INTRODUCTION
MY TRUTH

First off, I don't tell lies because I can't keep up with them. My grandmother always said, "Don't lie. Tell the truth and shame the devil." She considered a lie a curse word and would be like, "Believe what you see and none of what you heard." Your word is what you still got when you don't have any money. That's why if I give you my word, say I'm going do something, or tell you I got you, then I'm ten toes down. Anybody who knows me for real knows that. Feel me?

So that's why I have to say this to the world, and I want you to hear me loud and clear. Never mind what you've heard or think you know about Michael Brown, or about me, for that matter. You don't know about Mike Mike. You don't know about me. Now, you might know something, some snippet, some half a moment in time, but you don't know my son's life and what it meant, and an eighteen-second video doesn't tell you anything about eighteen years.

See, before the news media and the nation first heard the name Michael Brown, he was just Mike Mike to me. That's what we called him. Everybody thinks he was a junior, but he wasn't. Even though he had his daddy's first and last name, his full name was Michael Orlandus Darrion Brown. I wanted my son to have his own identity, so he did.

From the moment Mike Mike was born, I knew my life had changed forever. I was sixteen years old with an infant. I didn't know what kind of mother I was going to be. But when I held him in my arms for the first time and felt his soft skin, he opened his eyes, and I could see my

3

reflection in his little pupils. I suddenly wasn't scared anymore. It was like we were communicating with each other without words. I was saying, "I got your back, baby," and he was saying, "I got yours, too, Mama."

I can't just say he was mine, though. When Mike Mike was born, he was adored, doted on, and loved by me and his daddy, my siblings, and his grandparents on both sides, who helped with his rearing. He was our beautiful, unplanned surprise—my first son, a first grandson, and the first nephew in my family.

And then, one day our Mike Mike was shot and killed by a police officer on Canfield Drive in Ferguson, Missouri, and suddenly his name was being spoken everywhere: Mike Brown Jr., Michael Brown, or just Brown . . . but never Mike Mike, never our family's name for him, the name that marked him as special to us and those who knew him for real.

Pastor Creflo Dollar asked me what I thought about all the people out there on Canfield Drive when I got to the scene the day Mike Mike was shot. I turned, looking directly at him, and as sure as the breath I'm breathing, in a very matter-of-fact way, said, "I didn't see those people. That day, I was looking for one person: my son. Nobody else mattered."

I think I kind of shocked Pastor Dollar. I was respectful, of course, but I had to tell it to him straight up. I was just keeping it real. You see, because as a mother when your child is hurt, scared, or in danger, *you* hurt, you want to comfort them, and you will protect them from harm, even if it means laying your own life down. That day out on Canfield Drive, I had tunnel vision. Nothing and nobody was more important than getting to Mike Mike and helping him in any way I could.

It wasn't until days later, when I looked at the news and people showed me pictures from their phones that I saw the crowd of folks that had been out there. So the only way I can really describe that day is to compare it to the day I had Mike Mike. Bringing him into the world was almost the same feeling as when he left here—a lot of people making noise and milling around, and my attention just glued to my new baby boy.

I'm not going to lie; I've been wanting to get mad and just go fuck the world up, because my son being killed has messed my whole life up.

No way should my son have left here before me. But I have to stop myself every time my anger begins to build like that. If I look at it that way too long, I'll find myself in trouble, doing something out of rage and revenge. That would be out of my character, and Mike Mike would never want me to do anything like that.

It's so hard sometimes, but I have to find some type of something to keep myself calm so I can be a good wife and a good mother for my other kids. That's why, looking at my son's death today, I try to see it from more of a spiritual standpoint. God let me have Mike Mike for eighteen years. He wouldn't let me have him longer because He had other plans for us. Those plans are still being revealed to me, but I believe a big part of His plan was to wake people up to some things in the world that need changing. I'm ready, though, for whatever He has in store.

What I do know for sure is that I was just a kid when I had Mike Mike. I made a lot of mistakes when I was young, but in raising him I got stronger, wiser. What we endured together, especially in his years as a small child, is a story that only his mother can tell. One that I have held close until now.

The naysayers and judgers and haters wrote me off when I had my baby, saying things like, "She ain't gonna do nothin' with her life," but I never gave up. I had to develop thick skin to get through those scary and confusing days, but I was determined to make it for my child, to do right by Mike Mike.

I never finished high school. It was once one of the most uncomfortable and embarrassing facts about my life. Of course, I wanted my high school diploma. I even thought about going to college, but at the time, it was about providing and surviving—and I didn't know how to do that and finish school. It was a hard choice, but life is hard sometimes, right?

I was raised in a single-parent house and watched my mother work hard on jobs she should have been paid more for doing, making sure my brother, me, and my sister had clothes on our backs and food on the table. I knew what her struggle had been.

I've worked for years barely making minimum wage, sometimes at two jobs, to put clothes on my children's backs and shoes on their feet, even Mike Mike's size 13 feet. I've even received public assistance, because a mother will put her pride to the side and accept help from others to make ends meet and care for her children.

As my firstborn, Mike Mike saw my struggles the most, and I know that motivated him to accomplish the dream I had of finishing school. Same for my other three kids who came after Mike Mike. I *know* they can go farther and do better than me and be successful in this life. So on May 23, 2014, when Mike Mike received his high school diploma, just a few months before he was gunned down, I was able to live my dream through him.

Every day is rough for me, but like Maya Angelou said, "Still I rise!" Amen! I find a way to smile because my baby had aspirations and dreams. That really gives me comfort on the low days. That's why I got to clear things up, because folks out here got it twisted: Mike Mike wasn't a criminal who deserved to be shot like a dangerous animal. He was a good boy who cared about the right things, and family and friends were at the top of his list. He didn't have a police record. He never got in trouble. He was a techie, in love with computers. He loved his mama and was proud to be headed to college and of the things he knew. The whole family was proud of him, too.

When my son was killed, everybody had his or her own version of how everything went down. Cops with their version of the facts. People living in the Canfield Apartments with another. The television and newspaper people, EMTs, firemen, old people, young people, black, white, you name it—everyone with a different story that was supposed to be the truth about my son's last minutes on earth.

My son was dead on the street in front of the world, and everybody except Mike Mike was busy telling his story. Even in the months since that horrible day, people still haven't stopped talking, from Twitter to Facebook to Instagram, in the beauty shop and coffee shop, everywhere.

Well, let me just say this: I wasn't there when Mike Mike was shot. I didn't see him fall or take his last breath, but as his mother, I do know one thing better than anyone, and that's how to tell my son's story, and the journey we shared together as mother and son. So I'm about to give it to you.

This is the truth of it.

CHAPTER ONE

FOUR AND A HALF HOURS
TOO LONG

The deli at Straub's where I worked had been jumping since I got there. Straub's is a kind of cozy gourmet market. It's in a suburb called Clayton, where you got mini glass skyscrapers; little cafes with that chichi, froufrou food, you know those kind of restaurants where the menu be making basic stuff like a house salad sound like a foreign language; and boutiques that be selling a T-shirt for fifty dollars just because it's got some high-end designer's name on it, and I could go right over to Dots or Rainbow and get a shirt that look just as good for fifteen.

The county court was just down the block, so we got a lot of lawyers, judges, and businesspeople coming in to buy lunch. But we also got some of the regular, everyday folks that worked in the offices around there, like county clerks, DMV workers, secretaries, basically the people who do all the work for those high-paid people.

Then you had your white soccer moms and a lot of rich old white people who came in to do their weekly shopping. Mixed in, there are a handful of black professionals. I was so proud when I saw a brotha come up to my counter, representing with his Brooks Brothers suit on, showing them white folks that we had it going on too.

One of my best customers was Mrs. Hirschfield, a little Jewish lady who was real cool and always came directly to me. One day I saw her coming in the door and figured I'd make her my last customer before my break.

"Hi, my favorite customer!" I called out, giving her a warm smile.

"Good morning, Lezley! I just love you!" She smiled back. She was a petite woman in her sixties, a little homely, she wore large glasses, and her hair was curled and poufy.

A few of my coworkers rolled their eyes. Everybody said she was annoying, probably because she couldn't always make up her mind about what she wanted, but I thought she was sweet.

The first time I met her, I was working one of the store's private tasting parties upstairs. As I was roaming the room with my serving tray, I kept making eye contact with this plain-dressed woman. Each time I passed by with a reloaded tray, she eagerly tapped me and whispered, "Can I please have another?"

My coworker joked, "Damn, she asking for more?" I got a kick out of it. Hell, I encouraged her to take two and three at a time. Why not? They were free! To this day, Mrs. Hirschfield will sample the whole deli display if you let her. And I always do.

So, even though I was anxious to dip out, I didn't mind squeezing her in at all.

"I'll take some artichoke dip and a pint of chicken salad," she said, smiling.

"No problem, I'll have everything right up for you. You made it just in time before my break."

"In that case, I'll take a Lezley too!" She gave me a wink.

Customers be begging for a Lezley. That's a sandwich they named after me. It isn't anything but roast beef, but I guess it's how I make it.

I laid out two pieces of soft wheat bread like I was about to perform surgery, smeared some brown mustard on, and gently placed the roast beef on it, sliced not too thick, not too thin. Then I laid the Swiss cheese on it, then topped it off with pickles, banana peppers, and onions.

To me that sandwich isn't anything special, but like all the food I make—eggplant Parmesan, grilled artichoke, all that chichi, froufrou stuff we sell there, to good old down-home soul food—I make it with love. When you have a gift to "burn," as my granny said, you can make any and everything.

I checked the time and quickly took my apron off before the stiff-looking man standing behind Mrs. Hirschfield could order. *Break time!* Before anybody could blink, I had slipped out and walked across the broiling parking lot to sit in my car, determined to make my few moments of peace matter.

I lit a cigarette, inhaled deep, and let my breath out slowly. Another hot-ass day in the Lou. I turned my key in the ignition and felt the *whoosh* of warm air from the car's vents before the AC started to cool it down.

I took another puff from my cigarette, closed my eyes, and started to have one of them good old Calgon take-me-away moments. But right then my cell phone rang. *Dang, so much for gettin' a moment to myself.*

"Hello," I answered, half interested, letting out a cloud of smoke. I didn't even look at the caller ID.

"Lezley, somebody been shot on Canfield, and he just laying here," the man's voice on the other end said in a panic. His voice was quivering and didn't sound right.

I quickly straightened up. It was Mario, a coworker who lived in the Canfield Apartments in Ferguson, Missouri, a mostly black area in the suburbs a few miles away. That was the same complex my mother lived in. My son Mike Mike had been visiting her for the summer.

I took a nervous puff. "Mario, please describe him to me," I said, beginning to shake all over. I took another puff and got out of the car, my hands trembling now.

"I'm trying to get near, but it's so many people out here," he said.

I swallowed, my mouth was all of a sudden dry, and I felt a dull thud fill my chest. It got faster and faster as I got out the car and began to pace the Straub's parking lot, back and forth.

Just then my call-waiting clicked.

"Hold on! Hold on!" I shouted, trying to stay in control, but my hand holding the cigarette was now shaking uncontrollably.

"Nette . . . Nette Pooh!" It was my sister, Brittanie. Let me just say this: She isn't really a frantic person. It's like something could be bad, but she always stays calm. She's the kind who holds it together enough to tell you what's going on in a crisis. But her words were choppy, and she couldn't get nothing else out before she broke down moaning and sobbing. It was weird she wasn't screaming or nothing. Her crying was different than I'd ever heard it before.

Between her sobs, she was able to get out eight words: "Nette Pooh, the police just shot Mike Mike."

I heard her, but my mind wasn't trying to understand nothing like that. I quietly started gasping for air. What she had just said was trapped between my ears like some muddy standing water.

I didn't ask her if he was still alive. I didn't even want to think about that. A gust of wind shot through my body, and then like lightning, I just started running back toward Straub's. I don't even know if I said bye to Brittanie and Mario or not. All I could think was, *Oh God, I gotta get to my son, make sure he all right.*

Tears exploded from my eyes as I burst through the narrow front doors of the store.

"I need to get to my son! The police just shot my son!" I frantically shouted.

Everyone in the store turned around. I didn't care who heard my screams. I just needed somebody to help me. Erica, one of my coworkers, came running out the bathroom and burst into tears, her screams as loud as mine. I grabbed hold of her.

"Get me to Ferguson, please!" I yelled, collapsing in her arms.

Moments later, we were on our way, racing down Clayton Road onto Interstate 170 toward Ferguson. I wrapped my arms around myself and kept rocking, trying to hold it together as Erica drove. Now I was trembling all over, my stomach churning. I blinked several times, trying to clear up my vision. I was crying so hard everything was cloudy and out of focus. I took a deep breath in and then slowly let it out. Deep breath in, slowly out. In, slowly out.

This is a bad dream, I was thinking, *and when I wake up, everything's gonna be back to normal, all good again.* I tried to imagine Mike Mike's smiling baby face and him leaning down to me, giving me one of his cuddly hugs. My son was big for his age, six-four and barely eighteen, but still just a kid. Here I was just five-five, and I swear I don't know how my baby grew up to be that tall. He had even outgrown his daddy.

I took another deep breath, exhaled slowly again, and kept rocking back and forth. I rubbed my stomach, trying to calm all the flip-flopping it was doing. I needed to get there, and it was taking too damn long.

I closed my eyes real tight, and as the tears gushed out, my mind flashed back to Mike Mike as a newborn. It was the first time I laid eyes on him. A mother never forgets that day, that moment. I looked into Mike Mike's little brown eyes, barely open, thinking, *Wow, I've been waiting all these months to see, kiss, hug, smell, and take you around to show off, little man. This is what everybody wanted me to leave behind and get rid of? No, you here now, and I got you forever.*

A slight forward jerk of the car snapped me back into the moment. Traffic ahead was bumper-to-bumper and at a standstill in one of the lanes. My friend's car was creeping along at a stop-and-go pace. My nerves kicked into overdrive. I began wringing my hands. Normally, it's a short twenty-minute ride between Clayton, where I work, and Ferguson, where my mama lives. Why the hell was it taking so long? Where was all this traffic coming from? It felt like all of St. Louis was sitting in they cars. I was getting so worked up I wanted to bust out the car, leap over all the traffic, and run to where my son was.

I spotted a female highway patrol officer and flagged her down. "Please, Officer, help us get through. I gotta get to my son," I begged.

"You're just gonna have to make it through the best way you can," she replied in one of them flat, authoritative tones. Before I could think to tell her that I had to get to Mike Mike because he had been shot, she had moved on, and got into her car.

Beads of sweat formed on my forehead, my heart racing, pounding through my chest. I was shaking all over. I could feel myself about to go off, and I didn't care about her being the police. The officer must've known it had to be something serious, maybe even felt a little bit of sympathy. I don't know, but whatever it was, she suddenly blared her sirens and horn. The cars in front of us gave us a small clearing, and we started moving again. It all got foggy at that point. I lost track of everything, and the world felt like it was whizzing by. I just stayed focused on getting to Mike Mike. I knew he was scared and needed me.

We finally got to the corner of West Florissant and Canfield Drive, a few blocks from my mama's apartment complex. The local traffic was just as thick and congested as the highway was. The streets were cluttered with what seemed like a sea of police cars. We pulled to a stop, and I saw my son's father, Big Mike, getting out of his car a few cars away. We were on opposite sides of the narrow, two-lane street. I couldn't think about saying nothing because I could feel that gust of wind shoot through me again. I took off running. Me and Big Mike were both running across from each other, in between the lanes, on the sidewalks, wherever we could get through, neck and neck, in sync. Something we hadn't been in a long time.

The street was thick with people, and I fought my way through the big blur of everybody. I caught a glimpse of Brittanie and my brother, Bernard, standing in a small grassy area about six feet away. Suddenly, there wasn't any sound, just the hard pounding of my heart. I had tunnel vision on one thing: getting to my son.

I slowed to catch my breath, tears streaming down my face, my chest heaving, like I was going to hyperventilate. Brittanie rushed over, trying her best to console me, but she was tore up herself, tears pouring out of her bloodshot eyes.

"Naw, man, not Mike Mike! Not my nephew!" I could hear Bernard shouting. I saw him in my peripheral vision, pacing, shaking his head.

Everyone else around kept fading in and out. I rushed toward the yellow tape the police use to mark crime scenes but was stopped in my tracks by the chest of a towering white officer. I looked around him, and what seemed like the whole damn Ferguson police force had formed a human wall, keeping everybody back.

I started pushing my way past him. Somebody behind me grabbed me to hold me back, but I was still shoving, kicking, and yelling, "Somebody! Somebody! I need to get to my son!" I couldn't get through. As far as my eyes could see, white men dressed in blue uniforms were standing in my way.

I caught a glimpse of a blood-covered white sheet laying over the form of a motionless body stretched out on the ground and screamed, throwing my arms into the air, "Naw, naw, naw, that ain't my child! It can't be!"

I was sweating and lightheaded. Brittanie had been so certain on the phone that the police had shot Mike Mike, but she had to be wrong.

I could kind of see a hand and one foot wearing what looked like a yellow sock on it. Mike Mike had a pair of yellow socks, but still, that didn't prove it was him, did it? Then I saw a red Cardinals baseball cap resting on the ground several feet away. Mike Mike had that same red baseball cap.

I tried pushing my way past the wall of cops again, but they pushed me back. "Oh, God, please!" I pleaded. I just wanted to run over there, lift up that sheet, and hold my son, comfort him, then he'd be all right. I could get him to wake up. He needed his mama.

"Let me see my son! Why ain't he off the ground yet? Do anybody hear me?" I begged, frantically running from officer to officer. Didn't these fucking police understand? I said, "Do anybody hear me?"

They just stood there like a stone wall. None of them would speak to me.

I felt like I was being swallowed up, my feet sinking into the pavement like it was quicksand. My head was pounding. More people had gathered and filled in a row in front of the police. I mustered the little strength left in my body to push through the crowd to find a closer view. It looked like a finger poking from underneath the bloody sheet. Mike Mike was trying to point something out to me, tell me something about what happened. Who had done this?

I closed my eyes. "Mama, I need you, I'm scared." I could hear his voice.

It was my son under that sheet, my son's yellow sock sticking out, my son's red Cardinals hat, my son's finger. All at once, it hit me that what Brittanie had said was true. Mike Mike was dead. I tried to open my mouth, but my words were stuck, trapped in my throat.

My husband, Louis, suddenly appeared at my side and held me up as my knees gave way. I tried to reach for Mike Mike, but it was like trying to grab air. I opened my mouth, and a moan broke loose.

"Who the hell did this? Who did this to my son?" I demanded, sweat pouring over my body. I could taste the salt of my tears flowing into my mouth.

"The police," Brittanie gasped, putting her shaking hand over her mouth like she was trying to stop the words.

Anger shot through my body. "The police? They 'posed to be protectin' us, protectin' my kids, my son. How they do some shit like this?" I stormed up and down the sidewalk. "Where is he? Where's the one who did this to my child?" I got closer to one of them whose face had a permanent scowl carved into it. He stood over me. "Y'all muthafuckas gonna have to answer to this," I challenged, looking up at him, square in the eye like I was every bit of the giant he was.

"Well, we some good motherfuckers," he growled, then threw up his middle finger.

What he did knocked out the last bit of wind I had in my lungs. My heart was beating so fast I thought it was going to jump out of my chest.

I stared him down, trying to cut him up with my eyes, and the harder I looked, the redder his face got. It was like I was daring him to come at me, and he was doing the same. So what, was he going to shoot me like the other one had done to my son?

I exploded in a rage, punching the air, swinging in all directions like I was fighting him to the finish, then all of a sudden I was overcome with exhaustion. I fell to my knees, weak, drenched in sweat, and cried out, "Why, God?"

My tears erupted like a volcano. My baby boy was gone, stolen from me, lying dead under a sheet, surrounded by police, in the hot summer sun.

CHAPTER TWO

THE TWELVE-YEAR-OLD DREAM AND THE LITTLE RED SUITCASE

My whole name is Lezley Lynette Bingo McSpadden. Don't ask me where they got that Bingo part from. Family and friends from around the way call me Nette Pooh. Auntie Bobbie, my mama's younger sister, said she came up with that name. Mama's big brother, Uncle Cleo, said he gave it to me. Uncle Cleo even put a little extra on it, calling me *Netty* Pooh. My daddy and everybody on his side just call me Nette, from my middle name.

It's funny, I never felt like I was a favorite to nobody, but I guess you gotta be pretty special to have a nickname. That's why I'm always making up nicknames to call kids. I want them to know how special they are. When I was a little girl, the person who made me feel special the most was my daddy. I wasn't around him that much, but when I did see him, he was my whole world, and in my mind I was his.

I remember when I hit puberty, I made up what I called the Twelve-Year-Old Dream. I would hear my favorite love song or watch a music video or see a movie and put together every character I had seen to create an image of the man of my dreams that I'd have when I grew up. I imagined looking for him at school, at my job, in the mall, or at the park. But one day I'd find him and we'd live happily ever after.

I had that dream, but it never involved me having a baby at sixteen.

. . . .

My mama met a guy I called Mister at a birthday party her sister, my aunt Evelyn, had. In the short time he started coming around, he never showed my mama much respect and acted like he didn't even like Brittanie and me too much.

When she got with Mister, it made me wish things had worked out better for her and my daddy. Maybe they could've got married, but all they did was just spend a bunch of years going back and forth, on again, off again, in their relationship. It was like that as far back as I can remember. When I was a baby, up until I was probably preschool age, Mama and me even lived with Daddy and his mama, my granny, in the Clinton-Peabody housing projects, also known simply as the Peabody, in the Darst-Webbe area of the South Side of St. Louis.

My daddy was way different than Mister, though. He was one of them easygoing dudes. He wasn't a bad man. He just wasn't any good to my mama because Daddy's downfall was women, lots of them.

One time, when I was a toddler, Daddy actually took me around one of his ladies. I was little, but I could talk good and I was smart. The lady leaned in to me and smiled real big.

"Aww, look at how pretty she is!" she said, pinching my cheeks.

"Nette, this is Miss Rose," Daddy said.

Maybe at that point he kissed her or touched her in some kind of way. Whatever it was, I knew that he was doing what he was doing like he did to my mama.

"Baby, you can call me 'Mama,'" Miss Rose said, pinching my cheeks again. I pulled away behind my daddy's leg.

When we got back to where we lived on Rucker Lane, Mama had one of them nigga-I-know-you-been-up-to-no-good looks on her face.

"Nette Pooh, where y'all been?" she said, pulling me close.

"Over to my mama's house," I said innocently.

Next thing I knew Daddy had snatched me up and dragged my little ass into another room. He whipped out a wire hanger and began whuppin' me. My cries got louder and louder each time that wire landed on my skin. When he finished he went and sat down in a chair that faced me. I was delirious from crying so hard, and my eyelids were heavy like somebody had put little weights on them. I let out a few sighs in between the sniffles and went on to sleep. When I woke up my daddy was still sitting in the same chair looking at me.

"Go back in there with yo' mama, Nette Pooh," he said in a low voice.

I got up slowly and my little feet tiptoed away. Every few steps I'd turn and look back at him, trying to understand what had just happened. Daddy never whupped me again after that.

Not long after, Mama and me moved from there. Mama would still take me down to visit him every now and then, though.

When I was about six, I remember how geeked up I'd be the whole drive just thinking about seeing my daddy. As we drove down Highway 70 East, leaving North St. Louis, we'd pass the gigantic cylinder-shaped towers of the Pillsbury factory. The smell of fresh-baked dough hung in the air like a thick pastry cloud, making my stomach instantly start to growl.

As the car coasted farther down the highway, there was the smell of old, dirty water coming from the Mississippi River. I perked up because that meant we were getting closer. We zoomed through downtown St. Louis, passing the gigantic Gateway Arch, high-rise buildings, and Busch Stadium, and all the Cardinals baseball billboards and banners.

North City, where we lived, is a whole different-looking part of St. Louis. It is not only a mostly black area, but over there we got churches practically on every corner, and you can almost guarantee it's going to be a barbecue joint or barber or beauty shop next door, or a corner Chinese joint.

The South Side, or South City, was known more for having mostly white people, but it was a weird mixture of poor white trash and a few white people with some money sprinkled in. They got neighborhoods called Dogtown where the Irish at; the Hill, where you got the Italians; and then the Germans in Germantown. I guess where I grew up you could divide it up like, "OK, here the block where the Crips be at, and here the block where the Bloods be at." My point is we were all just black.

Once we hit the bridge into South City, I could barely contain myself. I knew we were getting close because the blocks of old, boarded-up brick buildings were fading behind us. My heart was beating faster and faster. My face was starting to hurt from my smile being so big. As we pulled up, the high-rise project apartments stood like giant hood guards, overshadowing the lower-level complex, which was made up of redbrick two- and four-family flats. My granny and daddy lived in a two-family.

As Mama pulled up, I could see Daddy in the doorway of their house; his smile matched mine. He looked like a cool, hood comic-book superhero, standing tall and lean, with a full mustache that made him look important. Daddy's Kangol hat was cocked a little to the side. Mama had barely stopped the car before I jumped out, my two pigtails flopping on top of my head. I threw my little arms around his legs. Daddy scooped me up in his strong arms, swung me around, and I laughed until I was dizzy.

Seemed like the drive over took longer than the visit, and then it was time to say good-bye.

"No, I wanna stay here," I begged, tears streaming as Mama pried my arms off Daddy's leg.

Maybe we had just come over for that hug, or for my daddy to give my mama a little bit of money. It didn't matter. It was the fact that I got to see him. I was a daddy's girl. I never wanted to leave him, because I didn't know when I was going to see him again. Those visits started to stretch out to weeks and months and, eventually, years in between. For the first few years, when I saw him I would go right back into feeling like I was his princess again. But as I got older, that feeling of excitement started to fade.

When I was seven, I asked for Daddy's phone number. I still remember slowly punching out the numbers on the telephone pad. I wanted to make sure I didn't make a mistake. It was the number to my auntie's house, my daddy's sister, who lived in the projects too. Daddy was living with her by that time. The phone just rang and rang. No answer. I was determined, though. I called every day until somebody answered one day.

"Daddy! It's Nette Pooh! Where you been, Daddy? I wanna see you."

"Hey, baby!" Daddy sounded so excited to hear my voice. "Oh, I just been workin', Nette Pooh. Look, I'mma come get you for the weekend. OK?"

Friday after school I burst through the front door after Mama picked me up from the bus stop, and run right to my room. My mama had bought me a little red suitcase, and across the front of it read: GOING TO GRANDMA'S. I packed everything I could think of into that suitcase. Then I sat on the couch and waited. I looked for him and looked for him some more, but still no Daddy.

"Nette Pooh, don't get your hopes up too high," Mama said flatly.

"Naw, Mama, he said he was comin'," I said, taking another look out the blinds.

Daddy never came.

"Fuck it! C'mon, Nette Pooh! Get in the car!"

Mama was fed up with Daddy's lies and seeing me hurt. So we jumped in her car and made that long drive to Peabody.

For as long as I can remember, all Mama's cars were a little piece of a car. She never could afford a new car. They ran good enough to get back and forth to work, but they'd be old. But it was what her money could buy. She'd get them from somebody she worked with or who knew somebody who was selling a car. She even had an old Chevy Chevette one time that every time we stopped, we had to put a quart of oil in it. But Mama would say, "Hey, it's gonna get me around, it's mine, and I ain't gotta depend on nobody."

I smelled bread, then old, nasty water, then I saw the projects up ahead.

"Nette Pooh, you crazy 'bout that muthafucka, and he don't give a damn about you," Mama said with a blank expression, her eyes glued to the road.

"Well, I don't care, Mama. I'mma keep tryin'." My mouth was twisted and I was gripping the handle of my little red suitcase.

That time we didn't even find my daddy. I guess he had forgot he was supposed to get me and was out somewhere. When I finally got him on the phone again, he couldn't give me a good explanation.

By the time I was twelve years old, I was tired of him lying to me. Anger was shooting through my body as I pressed each number on the keypad. All I could think about was how he never took me to school or met me at the bus stop or came to see me in a play or sat me down and told me about boys. Nothing! He didn't even just call to say hi. I didn't even give him a chance to say hello before I lit into him.

"Why you be lying to me? You ain't never here for me! I hate you!" I shouted recklessly. I didn't care. I slammed the phone down. The tears poured down my face and I closed my eyes tight, wishing I had one of them corny daddies on television who wore a colorful sweater, smoked a pipe, and sat in a big easy chair reading his newspaper. He'd be waiting for me to run in and jump on his lap. Then he'd kiss me on my forehead and call me his princess. But that was just a dumb dream.

My mama never made a lot of money working in food service, but cooking for people is what she loved to do. She worked her own schedule cooking food for a small senior citizen center. She even worked catering at a few other hotels. The only other place she cooked for a long period of time was the Hilton Hotel, where she wore those black-and-white checkered pants and the white jacket. It was tight financially with her being a single mother. My brother, Bernard, who is five years older than me, stayed mostly with my mama's mother, who I called Granny, and my mama's older sister, Aunt Bobbie, but that was cool because she had a son, my cousin Chevelle, and him and Bernard were around the same age. Bernard eventually left to go to college and then got a place of his own. My sister, Brittanie, is four years younger than me, and Mama kept us with her.

Now no matter how tight the money was, we had clean clothes on our backs, food in our stomachs, and a nice roof over our heads. Mama's always been a woman who worked hard and had her own. That's why I never understood why she got hooked up with Mister. He moved in with us and he didn't even bring a couch, or a TV, or a chair, not even a plate or fork, *no nothin'*. He walked around our house like he was some kind of king.

Mama always liked having company over. She'd cook up a pot of neck bones and beans or spaghetti, and friends and family would come over for good food and a good time. She wasn't really the type to show a lot of emotion, but when she was happy, you knew it. One night she was wearing a wide, toothy smile, and a few of her girlfriends were over for game night. Mama was busy working the room, making sure everybody had a beer or ice in their glass.

I usually ignored Mister, but that night it was hard because he seemed to get agitated just because Mama was enjoying herself.

I liked seeing Mama in a good mood and looking good. Mama had a little thickness to her, but she was tall and shapely, and that night she was fresh from the beauty shop with her hair curled up, and that made her slanty eyes that were deep-set in her slim face stand out.

Bernard, Brittanie, and me got them same eyes, too, even though we each got different daddies. That goes to show how strong Mama's genes are.

I tiptoed out of our room to fix Brittanie and me a plate of snacks. I was moving fast because Mama and about four of her girlfriends were sitting around the dining room table, and we were always taught that grown-folk time is grown-folk time. Mama took a sip from her beer and a long drag off her cigarette, then picked a card from the deck and spun the wheel on the board game.

"What would your dream man be like?" Mama laughed, reading the question out loud. Her friends all busted out laughing and I giggled to myself, but Mister jerked his head back and gave her a menacing look.

A few hours later the party was over and Mama had already cleaned up and was walking back in the front door from dropping off one of her girlfriends. I was in my bed and Brittanie was sound asleep in her bed across from me. Mama's shadow slid into her room, then I heard Mister's booming voice.

"Aw, what, you got anotha man?" he demanded.

Whop! Crash!

I heard the loud, dull sound of a body being hit by a heavy fist, followed by glass smashing on the floor. I ran out of our room and into the hallway. Mama was hunched over on the floor still clutching her purse.

Mister was standing like a giant above her. I didn't wait for Mama to get up and fight him back.

"I'mma call the police!" I shouted, running into the kitchen, grabbing the phone off the wall. My chest was heaving and I was out of breath.

"Li'l girl, you ain't calling nobody," Mister said, snatching the receiver out of my hands.

I sat in my bed, holding my knees to my chest, rocking back and forth. I heard Mama's bedroom door slam. My daddy may have been a lot of things, but I never saw him lay hands on my mama. The tears welled up in my eyes, but I refused to cry. I made up my mind right then and there that I wasn't ever going to let a man treat me like Mister had done my mama.

CHAPTER THREE

GRANDMA'S HANDS

Mama told us that Mister went to jail. I didn't ask why because I didn't care. I was just glad he was gone and the house was peaceful. Things seemed like they were looking up for us as a family, too, because Mama had found a cute little three-bedroom house to rent over on Emma Street in the Walnut Park area of North St. Louis, and now we'd be living closer to my grandmother, Mama's mama. I called her Granny too, just like my other grandmother, but I saw her way more often.

I sat on the brick steps of our new front porch, with my back against the iron rails, itching to walk around the neighborhood. Our house was near the corner of Emma and Mimika, and I could see houses on both streets. Each one was different. Some were all wood with wooden steps leading up to houses that looked like shacks down in the Deep South or something. Then some houses were all brick and two stories, like ours; some had balconies, and others were just one level. Most of the houses were separated by a narrow gangway leading from the front to the back-yard.

It was only a matter of minutes before I felt the weight of two sets of eyeballs checking me out.

"Hey, you just moved over here?" the short, dark-skinned one with two gleaming gold teeth in the front of her mouth asked as she ap-proached. I could tell she was sizing me up. "Well, what's your name?"

"Everybody calls me Nette," I said confidently.

"Well, I'm Stacey and this is my sister, Casey. So how old are you?

You must go to Clark Middle, huh?" Casey kept firing questions but I couldn't stop focusing on the gold teeth. I was wishing I had just one of them, but I bet not even think about asking Mama to get me no gold.

Stacey was older than me. Turns out six years older. She had short hair, and it was in a fly cut. It looked like she had just got her hair done, the way each bump of a curl went from small to large, from the middle of the back of her head to the top of it. Casey, who looked around my age, had long hair, was a shade lighter and tall.

"Well, we just checkin' to see who movin' in. If you need somethin' just let us know. We two doors down." Stacey had done all the talking. Casey just agreed. Then they went on back to their house.

I made up my mind from jump that living on Emma was going to be the bomb. I was only thirteen, but I could already see myself kicking it with them.

• • • •

When Mister got out of jail he came straight to Emma Street. I couldn't believe my eyes when I opened the front door. Hell naw! I almost dropped my schoolbooks on the floor when I saw that fool sitting on the couch. I marched straight to Mama's bedroom.

"Mama, what he doin' in there?" I demanded.

"I told him he had to ask y'all if he could come back, Nette Pooh," Mama said softly. Suddenly I didn't even recognize my own mama. Mama wasn't supposed to be no weak woman.

"What? Well, that's a no for me. Why would you want him back?" I asked, folding my arms across my chest. Usually, grown people quick to check you when you be making a comment about something you see them doing but now for the first time, Mama was putting me in an adult position.

Then, just like that, Mama switched the tables on me again. "Look, don't be fuckin' questionin' me, Nette Pooh! And let me tell you somethin': What happen in this house stay in this house. Don't be out tellin' ya granny and ya cousins about nothin'!"

We didn't talk about it anymore. But Mama warning me about not telling Granny or anybody else didn't just have to do with him putting his hands on her. It applied to a situation where even if my mama was gone and I knew where she was, and somebody called asking, "Well, where she at?" I better not tell anybody. Mama made it clear that our business at home was our business. That was house rule period.

• • • •

Mama and Mister were fighting again.

He hit her with a plastic mug, and blood exploded from her face. I saw her sliding down the wall, I felt my heart sinking. I wanted to scream and yell, "Take your damn hands off my mama!" I wanted to hurt him bad, just like he had done her. But I didn't do anything. I held my tongue and all my anger inside.

For me, it hurt too much to watch this happen again. I couldn't take it anymore.

"Nette Pooh, if you can't respect Mister, you don't have to be here," Mama said, looking me squarely in the eyes.

I waited a few nights to make my great escape. I didn't have much of a plan, but I knew I couldn't go to a place Mama would go looking first. Stacey let me crash at their house.

"Yeah, I found yo' ass!" I was awakened with a big whack to my head. Mama was standing over me with her hands on her hips. Turns out Casey accidentally told her I was at their house after Mama had been combing the neighborhood all night. I'm sure she had been worried sick, and now that she knew I was alive, I was sure she was going to beat me to death.

"Get yo' ass up!" she said, dragging me out the bed, down the stairs, and out the door.

Mama made me feel like having Mister with her was more important than me. So I was sent to live with my granny.

• • • •

Ecclesiastes 3:7 says, "There's a time to be silent and a time to speak." But my granny would simply say, "There's a time for talkin' and a time for keepin' your mouth shut!" She wasn't a real religious woman. I can't even say I ever seen her get ready for church on a Sunday, let alone go. But I know she could put the fear of God in you when she told you to do something. Growing up you just knew you'd better listen, and you'd better not ask no bunch of questions. Granny isn't big on fussing either, because she feel like if your mama alive, then it's her business to discipline you. But she is a whoop-yo'-ass grandma if you at her house and do something you haven't got any business doing.

My granny had eight kids, and pretty much built the life she had from nothing, proof how strong she was. Shoot, you have to be to have all them kids. She moved to St. Louis from West Point, Mississippi, determined to get what she wanted, and made a way for all her kids. Making her way also meant making sure the family had that one place that you could always go to if you were in trouble or sad, to have a good time on holidays, or just to know you were loved.

For as long as I can remember 6335 Albertine had been her address, and it was the biggest house on the block, two stories that sat on the corner, with a backyard that was a double lot. You knew it right away when you turned down the street, because it was a wood-framed house with one of them large cement front porches and iron railings all around it. Granny took a lot of pride in her house too. She had a small front yard, but the grass was always cut and it looked real neat, and in spring she always planted fresh flowers.

When I went outside on Granny's street I knew to be on my best behavior, because at least one of her neighbors—Miss Jenkins, Miss King, her sister Miss Rogers, or a woman we called Mama Lady—was going to be sitting out on her porch ready to report.

"Nette Pooh, you really growin' up and just as pretty as you can be," Miss Rogers called out from behind her screen door.

"Thank you, Miss Rogers!" She could catch you off guard, and you wouldn't even know she was watching you; just out of nowhere you heard her voice.

"Nette Pooh, tell yo' granny to call me," Miss King, the lighter-skinned of the two sisters, instructed me, taking a sip from her glass of brown liquor. She always sported the most perfect silver Afro and had a glass of Crown Royal in hand.

"Yes, ma'am," I replied. I didn't understand why she couldn't just get up and go to Granny's instead of me having to deliver a message one door away. I always made a clean getaway before she could start rattling off all her ailments.

I quickly made my way across the street to Mama Lady's house.

"Nette Pooh, how yo' mama doin'?"

"She good. How you doin'?" Me and Lady's daughter, Nina, kicked it a lot and got real tight. In the hood we call it your ace boon coon. We been tight ever since I was real little and knew what a friend was.

"Hi, Mama! Bye, Mama! Whassup, Nette Pooh?" Nina said, bopping out the door, her weave ponytail just a-swinging. We gave each other girlfriend hugs and quickly shuffled away.

"I'm good, girl. I'm stayin' with my granny now. Mama was trippin'," I said, rolling my eyes.

"Girl, well you know we gonna kick it!" We high-fived. "I'm hungry. Let's go to the Chinamen!"

I don't know any black person in St. Louis who doesn't love the neighborhood chop suey spot. The Chinese got the hood on lock, too. They got wig shops, nail salons, and the corner Chinese food joints. I don't care how bougie or ghetto you are, you know when you hear somebody say they're going to get Chinese, they're going to get some fried rice, or a St. Paul sandwich, or some fried gizzards.

What you were going to order was one dilemma, but the other was which way you were going to walk to get there. The distance wasn't going to change, but you had to factor in whether or not you felt like walking past a whole bunch of niggas hanging on the corner, wearing oversize white Ts and baggy Tommy Hilfiger jeans, grabbing themselves in the crotch, trying to prove who was harder than the other. But soon as some girls would come by, they'd turn into a small pack of dogs.

The other option was walking down a busy street like Goodfellow and having to tolerate cars zooming by, dudes blowing horns at you, or, worse, a car rolling to a stoplight with the window down, bumping so much bass the block would be shaking. It was OK to get a couple hollers if the dude was cute, but you don't want an ugly boy trying to get at you, besides nobody wants to be bothered with that when they're walking down the street trying to go get something to eat.

Which way you walked also depended on how you looked. Either you were going to run in the house real quick and make yourself look cute, or you'd say, "Girl, forget it, I'm finna just go like this," or, "Well, I'mma give you my money and you can get mine for me."

When you decided to walk to the store, you already knew you'd be stopping and speaking with folks. You might even see some girls you into it with, and there might be a fight. You had to ask everybody on the block if they wanted Chinese or something from the store. That's just a hood courtesy.

Anytime you walk somewhere in the hood, if you don't know nobody, people are going to ask, "Well, who is you? Where you from?" Don't wear your jewelry, either, or somebody might try to snatch it off your neck. Or maybe you could just be cool with everybody, and then you'll be pretty safe. That's how our family was. And my uncle Cleo was always out in our neighborhood and Granny's, cutting grass, raking leaves, putting up Christmas lights, painting their houses. It was like, "Here come the Ewings!" That isn't my last name, but it's my granny's, and that's how we became known.

That day me and Nina were both feeling cute, hair done, clothes right, and we took the walk past the corner store. Luckily, only a couple brothers were out on the block, and they said, "Whassup?" we said, "Hey," and that was the end of it. We quickly moved past them and slipped inside the chop suey spot. The smell of fried onions and peppers hit me at the door, and I knew that steaming hot rice was going to hit the spot.

· · · ·

Granny didn't have a separate TV room or a TV in the living room, or what we referred to as the front room. Hers was in the kitchen; it was the place everybody gathered whether it was to watch a favorite show, eat some of her good soul food, or just talk, hang, and laugh. The smell of fried fish, a pot of beans cooking, collards, chicken and dumplings, peach cobbler, or, her favorite, corn bread, found its way to your nose as soon as you walked in the front door, making you want to go straight to the kitchen to see what daily soul food delight she was cooking up.

I bounced into Granny's kitchen, sat down, and started immediately running my mouth, asking a million questions a minute: "Granny, how you doing'? What you doin', Granny? Granny, what's this on TV? Ooh, can I get some of that?"

My mouth started watering right away when I saw her plate of half-ate cabbage and corn bread. Every day she made a pan of corn bread from scratch to have with every meal. I don't care if she made a pot of spaghetti; she made a pan of corn bread. Granny looked over her glasses that had slid down her narrow nose, and shook her head. She wasn't paying my interruption a mind, dipping her corn bread in the cabbage juice, taking a bite, before licking her fingers that was wet with mushy crumbs stuck to them. She liked to eat it with her hands, said that made it taste the best.

I was just about to reach for the pan of corn bread when I saw a bag of flour on the counter. "Granny, what you 'bout to make?" I forgot all about the corn bread, never giving her a second to answer the first flurry of questions.

"Nette Pooh, put this plate in the sink," she said, sucking her teeth, handing me her plate. "Nette Pooh, I 'clare, sometimes a person can just talk too damn much," she said, giving me a matter-of-fact look.

One thing she didn't do was have a lot of idle conversation. Me, I've always been talkative, but Granny was known to speak her mind and consider your feelings after—straight, no chaser.

"Nette Pooh, you thirteen now, right?" she said, looking over the top of her glasses.

"Yes, ma'am!" I said, flashing a big, proud smile.

"Uh-huh, well, you gettin' older, and it's time you learn to just listen, or you gonna miss what's goin' on in the world one day," she said, standing up, grabbing a dishcloth, wiping her hands. Granny smoothed down her clothes over her tall, thin body. A lot of people's grandmothers would wear housecoats or housedresses, dusters, and that made them look old. But Granny got dressed every day, usually in pants, a T-shirt, and a button-down shirt over it that she would leave open. She was casual but hip with her style, even down to the Jheri curl she sported.

"Nette Pooh, I bet you don't even know how to make a butter roll, huh?" Granny said, raising her eyebrow before walking over to the counter. She turned around and started sifting some flour over the bare countertop through her long fingers.

I didn't hardly get what a butter roll had to do with anything, but I wasn't about to give her no crazy look.

Granny was right, I didn't know how to make a butter roll, but it was one of my favorite desserts she made. When I saw how calm and quiet she got, sifting that flour real easygoing like onto the counter, I wanted to watch more and learn how to fix it like her. I was just about to get comfortable in a chair.

"Uh-uh, you bet not sit down because you gotta work." I was really confused now. "Nette Pooh, today you gonna learn to stop talkin' so much and listen more." She pointed at me and said, "Chile, you be in the kitchen wit me so much you should at least know how to make a butter roll. Matter fact, you should know how to make everything, but you don't. That's because you be talkin' too damn much. Now, hand me that sugar."

I reached into the cabinet with the quickness, barely looking at the bag, handing it to her, spilling some on the floor.

"See there, Nette Pooh, when you run yo' mouth, you don't pay attention, and when you don't pay attention, you can miss important details. You make mistakes."

I sucked my teeth and cracked a smile.

"Now, get me a mixin' bowl, and hand me that cinnamon, bakin' powder, salt, and nutmeg."

"That's all? What about the water, Granny? Don't you need the water now?" She gave me one of those chile-if-you-don't-shut-yo'-mouth-you-betta looks.

I slowly gave them to her one by one, watching her patiently mix together the simple ingredients. First, she poured flour into the bowl, and then she cut the stick of butter up in it and added a little salt and a little baking powder. She took the fork and mashed it all together until it turned into little balls of dough and was crumbly. Then she motioned for me to get the water. I filled a cup up and handed it to her. She added it slowly, and then mixed the dough some more until it was in a bigger ball. She put it on the counter that was covered with flour. I handed her the rolling pin and she began to roll it all out. When it was flat, she put cinnamon and nutmeg all over it and rolled it up.

Granny put the pan in the oven to bake, and then while it started cooking, she said, "Now I'mma show you a secret. She winked, pointing to the can of evaporated milk that was sitting out and the butter. I handed them both to her, watching her carefully blend them together. I was fixed on her every move.

"This gonna give it a nice coat and keep the moisture in," she said, handing me the small bowl she had mixed it all in. She opened the oven and nodded toward me. I was nervous as I carefully poured the mixture over the entire roll. Granny nodded her approval, and then, with an easy glide, made her way over to her favorite chair. It was in front of the sink, and a large kitchen window was over it. Granny would sit there every day, watching the cars going by and checking out what the other folks in the neighborhood was doing. You could see part of her backyard and the street from it too. So when her grandkids visited, she could watch us playing on the block and in her yard.

Granny ate her breakfast in front of that window, drank her coffee, dipped snuff, and watched her favorite program, *The Young and the Restless*, like today. She turned the TV dial to channel 4, and it was perfect timing. Her girl Drucilla was giving much attitude on the screen. Granny and me sat there without saying a word. I looked at her slowly sipping on her coffee with her eyes fixed out that window on catching any and all action outside.

As soon as Bob Barker called out, "Come on down," Granny opened the oven and the hot air gushed out. She smiled. I smiled back. She grabbed a pot holder and put the pan on the stovetop. That butter roll was golden brown and perfect.

Now, Granny called that butter roll a "kitchen dessert," but you could eat it for dessert or breakfast.

"Now who ain't got flour, sugar, cinnamon, and butter, Nette Pooh?" she said, breaking her silence. "Everybody oughtta be able to go in they kitchen and make this dessert without even goin' to the store," she said, cutting down into it, carefully placing a slice on a saucer and pushing it across the table to me. You could see the warmth rising from the bread. "I came up from the country, wasn't nobody rich. You make due with what you got, and when you use your eyes and ears, you learn about food, people, and everything in life." I was hanging on to her every word as my teeth sank into the sweet, soft dough, leaving my lips glistening with melted butter.

Granny wanted me to understand that there was a time for talking and a time for keeping your mouth shut, and when she set that butter roll down in front of me and looked me in the eyes like she did, I got the message just like that. She had her way of teaching you stuff, and you didn't even know you was being schooled.

CHAPTER FOUR

HOOD LOVE

When I turned fourteen and I moved back home to Emma Street, I was happy for two reasons. Mama had finally gotten fed up with Mister. She kicked him out, and he was gone for good. The second reason was because even though Mama kept a tight leash on me, worried that I'd get caught up in a fast crowd in the streets, she agreed that I was old enough to make the short ten-minute walk to Granny's by myself.

I had come around the block to see my mama and Brittanie. It wasn't like living around the way full-time, so I had to get reintroduced to my old world. I was feeling myself because I was going to be a freshman in high school in less than two months. But for now, it was still summer vacation, and the only thing I was interested in studying was Hanging Out 101. Even once high school started, unless I was doing homework, or over at Granny's, or it was wintertime, I'd be chilling on the porch.

I took Granny's rule to always look clean and neat when you stepped out the house to the next level. Taking extra time in the bathroom mirror with the curling iron to put another bump in my stack, I grabbed a small hand mirror and held it up at an angle. Oh yeah, them stacks in my hair was like perfect stair steps. I dusted the stray hairs and was out the door.

From the moment I came back on the block, I could tell right away these three girls who lived a few doors down were going to be trouble. I couldn't figure out exactly how many people lived in their itty-bitty old raggedy house. It leaned forward, looking like it was about to fall over in the dirt patch of a front yard that hadn't seen grass in I don't know how long. But I did know that these sisters lived there, each one bigger and fatter than the next one, dark-skinned, looking like a trio of the meanest, ugliest NFL linebackers you ever want to meet. Even their mama had a twisted-up, mean look on her face.

Seeing them hang outside, hair never combed, clothes dingy, wearing dirty sneakers with the tongues sticking out and no shoestrings, I couldn't believe their mama let them come out like that. My mama would snatch Brittanie or me backward before we could open the door if we ever tried to go out in public like they did.

They would test me whenever they had a chance. Like the day I was just sitting out on our porch, minding my business. I could feel their eyeballs on me, following my every move.

"She think she cute," the smallest girl out of the three said under her breath, rolling her eyes and neck chicken-head style.

I played it off, shooting back a nah-you-just-must-think-I'm-cute look.

Just then Pinky called out from her porch across the street. "Hey, Nette!" she said, waving. The girls backed off, but I knew it was temporary.

Pinky was one of the older women on the block I had become cool with, and these big girls didn't seem to mess with the older ladies around our hood. Pinky was in her early twenties and had already had a daughter and two sons.

I could see all the action at her house right from our porch.

"C'mon over, Nette!" Pinky called out again. The music was blasting.

My girl Stacey was already there in the backyard. The weather was warm but not too hot, and with no humidity. It just felt good to be outside. Another friend of Stacey's showed up just as Pinky was walking inside. It was on!

"Oh, that's my song!" I screeched when my favorite summer jam came on, but the best part was when 69 Boyz sang, "Look at them girls with them Daisy Dukes on." We put our best moves together to make a dance routine. By the time the song ended we had worked up a sweat, and as our laughing died, the deejay on the radio mixed in H-Town's slow jam "Knockin' Da Boots." I started popping my fingers, bopping my head. "Nette, have you ever gone down on a boy?" Stacey whispered, leaning into me.

"Gone where?" I asked, with a confused look on my face. Stacey and her friend bugged up.

"Naw, Nette, she mean slob a dude down!" Stacey's friend could hardly stop laughing. She made her jaw bulge out with her tongue, then raised her hand and motioned up and down.

"Girl, hell naw!" I looked around nervously, making sure nobody else had heard her.

"Look, when you do it, you gotta make sure it's clean first before you put your mouth on it, then . . ."

"Uh-uh, that's nasty!" I said, shushing her.

"Stop playin', Stacey!" Stacey's friend said, cracking up.

"I'm just sayin', it's somethin' you gonna have to do one day, Nette," Stacey teased.

"Girl, I ain't gonna be doin' nothin' like that!" I said, folding my arms across my chest.

Just then Pinky came back out with a few more of her friends. I was glad she had broke that conversation up. The music got to pumping again, and we got to laughing and kicking it, and then somebody fired up a joint.

"Y'all know Nette too young and don't smoke no weed," Stacey called out.

I wasn't smoking, drinking, *or* having sex. Hell, I never even smoked weed until I was about twenty-two years old. But I won't lie, I was a little curious, in a setting where everybody was either talking about or doing all those things, and I didn't. I was getting uncomfortable.

"I'mma 'bout to be out, y'all," I said.

But just as I was about to leave the party, everything came to a screeching halt.

"Them mothafuckas done come in my house and they stole my god-damn food stamps!" Pinky was fired up, going off.

Pinky was paranoid as hell. Like clockwork, every month she would flip out and accuse somebody, or all of us, of stealing her food stamps. It scared me the first time she had one of these outbursts, but I was used to them by now. We all played it off, but one by one folks was yawning or suddenly checking they watch or saying they had to get home. The party was officially over.

I never saw Pinky actually smoke crack. To me, it was just a rumor until one day I got proof when the little pipe fell out of her pocket, and she was quick to put that mug right back, thinking nobody saw it.

I wasn't mad at her, though, because she handled her business. She had her own house, was clean-looking, took care of her kids, kept them clean, too, cooked every day, all that.

One day she yelled over to me from her porch, "Nette Pooh, can you do me a favor?"

I did my regular and ran right over.

"Can you keep an eye on my kids? Just make sure they don't run out in the street or anything. I gotta go next door and get some barbecue."

She must've had to get to that barbecue fast because she didn't waste no time going next door. It must've been code for "I'm 'bout to go get this hit real quick!" But, I was too naive to know it then.

A few minutes later, her youngest son, who was about seven, came running up, crying, and said, "That boy next door hit me, Nette." He sniffed between broken breaths, snot running out his nose.

"Okay, yo' mama at the neighbor's. You betta go tell her," I said, pushing him along. It had just been a couple of days since my last run-in with them three sisters, and I could see them coming directly toward me. They had a little old dusty boy about the same age as Pinky's son with them.

Within seconds you could hear Pinky yelling from the neighbor's front door, "What the fuck is goin' on?" She wanted answers from any-body on the block who would give them to her. "Why the fuck you hit my son?" she said, coming outside, yelling at the little boy.

Now Pinky didn't have any railing on her porch, and it wasn't that high off the ground, only a couple of feet. So them four walked right up on me.

"That bitch Nette lyin' on me, Pinky!" the little boy cursed.

"Bitch? Who you callin' a bitch?" I said to the little boy.

"He callin' you a bitch, bitch!" I felt the heat from the biggest of the sisters' breath on my face.

Everything happened in a flash. The youngest sister straight stole on me. I was blindsided with a right hook, but I shook it off and swung back. I started punching wildly. But with every swing I made and lick I got in, each of them sisters got one in on me. I was still standing on the porch, trying to hold my own, but I was overpowered and outnumbered, too small to fight them off.

Just then I see their older brother out the corner of my eye step out onto their porch. He picked up a folding chair and threw it at me. *Craaack!* That chair knocked me upside my head so hard I was out cold.

When I came to, a crowd had gathered. My mama was standing over me, shaking my arm. "Nette Pooh, get up! Baby, you OK? Get up!"

I jumped up and must've been in shock, because I took off running like a racehorse out the Kentucky Derby gate. All I could think of was getting to my granny's house, where it was safe.

I ran past Mimika, past Era, past Troy, past Goodfellow, and when I got to the fifth block, Acme, I knew I was in the clear. My granny's house was just a few feet away, but I damn near collided with one of my brother's friends.

"What's wrong, Nette? What happened?" He grabbed me and tried to calm me down.

My nose was bleeding, my eye was swollen, and my shirt was ripped, dirty, and bloody. Between breaths I got out, "Them people down the block from us jumped me. Where Bernard?" I barely got it out before he took off running in the direction I was running from.

I knew if I could get to Bernard he could help me. I burst through Granny's front door.

Bernard rushed toward me. "Nette Pooh, who did this to you?"

"That family next door!" I shouted hysterically.

I didn't need to say nothing else. My big brother was on the phone, and all I could hear was, "Hell naw, somebody done beat up Nette Pooh!" He pulled me out to his truck and we jumped in. Bernard revved the engine on his little put-put pickup truck, smashed his foot on the gas pedal, and we burned out.

The truck's tires screeched to a halt. I could see my auntie Evelyn, in the distance with an iron car jack in her hand. My uncle Carl was on the scene, running after them girls' daddy. A full-fledged neighborhood fight had popped off, and all hell had broken loose.

Everybody was fucking that family up. I didn't feel any remorse, neither. I didn't want anybody to die or nothing, but them folks was bad news, and maybe they needed to be taught a lesson so they'd stop bullying people.

I knew people was serious about looking out for me and my family when I saw some of the local gangbangers had got the word and was on the scene. Mimika and Emma was Crips gang territory, and there was a small sea of Crips, aka the Rollin' 60s, dressed in blue and gold, who had just rolled up when we did. They gave us a nod, then rushed in with pipes in hand just as three more women and two more men came running out that shack of a house swinging bats.

The whole scene had my head spinning. Just then I saw a flash of the mama in the street fighting off two women. The daddy was running and jumped up on their porch, but all the kids had beaten him inside, slammed the door, and locked him out.

Buddy, one of the Crips who was in a wheelchair, had rolled himself up to the people's house and started throwing bricks and bottles through that family's windows. My brother and somebody else who I couldn't even make out broke a stick on the daddy's back.

The mama helped the daddy get inside, when out of nowhere, my uncle Carl leaped up on them people's porch, jumped up in the air, and kicked their door in with both feet. Within minutes we heard a car engine start in the back of the house. The entire family had piled into a long, green Buick, and all we heard was the sound of tires squealing.

When it was all over, my mama took me to the hospital, where they treated me for cuts and bruises. Funny thing is the cops never came that day. I guess when you in the hood things like a fight or even gunshots happen like the sun coming up in the morning.

The next day the neighborhood was pretty much back to normal. The city was doing construction on our street, folks were back at work, and I was headed back home when suddenly I heard *click click*. It was the sound of somebody cocking a gun. I froze in place. My heart stopped. I looked up and saw the daddy of the family who had jumped me standing on their porch with a shotgun aimed right at me.

But just like that, this dude named Stretch from around the way swooped in, grabbed me, and pulled out a Smith and Wesson. Stretch started shooting at the man, and the man started running from those bullets.

I never had another problem out of them girls or none of them, because they never came back after that night, and I never saw them people no more.

That day taught me a lesson that I'll carry with me the rest of my life, and that was, simply, whether you're ready or not, bullshit is going to come for you. The question is, how are you going to deal with it? One thing for sure, I'm not going to back down no matter what you throw at me.

CHAPTER FIVE

LADUE

"**C**'mon, y'all, get up!" Mama called out. "Get your butts up 'fo you miss that bus!"

It was almost 5:00 a.m. and still dark outside. I was barely awake, slowly brushing my teeth. I'd been doing this since kindergarten. I ought to been used to this crack-of-dawn trek from the city to the county. Me, Brittanie, and my brother, Bernard, all grew up going to the schools in Ladue. It's one of the wealthiest, and whitest, areas in St. Louis County.

We were in the deseg program, short for desegregation program, where the government pays to bus you to a school in another neighborhood so they'll have some racial diversity.

We moved a lot, but since Granny's address was never going to change, my mama used the 6335 Albertine address for us to go to school out there. No matter where we were living, Mama would get Brittanie and me up and drive us to our bus stop, where that yellow deseg school bus picked us up at 6:00 a.m.

I saw Nina on the corner waiting at her stop that was next to mine. In the mornings we'd always catch up on the latest action and gossip in the hood until our buses came.

"Hi, Miss Harris!" Nina waved to Mama. "Whassup, Nette Pooh!" she said, pulling her coat over her ears.

"Hey, girl!" I rubbed my hands together.

It was cold this morning, and the wind was howling. Nina and me danced in place to keep warm while Mama looked on from the car. Rain, shine, sleet, or snow, Mama would get us to our stop, fire up her cigarette, and wait on Brittanie and me to get off to school.

Our buses picked us both up on the corner of Lena and Goodfellow. Nina was in the deseg program too, but was in the Parkway District. That area was a little farther out in the county than Ladue, and it was mostly white too, but them white people weren't as rich as the Ladue ones.

A tall, brown-skinned girl walking fast, like she was trying to outrun the cold, waved at us. She was on her way to meet up with a small crew of girls at the end of the block.

"You remember that girl, don't you, Nette Pooh?" Nina whispered.

"Naw, not really. I was 'bout to ask who that was." The girl looked familiar, but I couldn't place her face. "She live over here?" I asked, shaking off a shiver.

"Yeah, 'round the corner on Acme. She that one girl that had that fight a few years ago and got her head busted with a lock. Some girl just took it right off her locker and stole on her with it!"

"Dang, what school was that?" I asked, cringing.

"Girl, Cook Middle School." Nina sucked her teeth and rolled her eyes.

I was horrified. But that's how it is in the hood. You might get beat down, but after you get your stitches out or your bruises heal, you just go on about your business and hope the fight ended the beef.

My bus was first, slowing to a stop, followed by Brittanie's, which took her to Ladue Junior High. Then Nina's brought up the rear. I waved to Mama and Brittanie, then disappeared behind the folding doors.

"Hey, Lezley!" April screeched as I slid into the seat next to her. She was my ace boon and BFF at school. April was petite and wiry but would fight anybody, always full of energy and popping off at the mouth.

"Heeeeey!" I said, giving her a hug. I carefully removed my hat so I didn't mess my hair up. "What you think?" I said, twirling around, showing off the blond color my big cousin Tracey had sprayed in my hair. She could do color and the dookie braids that everyone was wearing in their hair, and weave ponytails. I was happy that I had graduated from getting my hair done at Aunt Bobbie's. Me and April settled in for the long ride and the bus got quiet.

Staring out the window made me drowsy, and in between dozing off I watched as we passed old black ladies on the bus line and dudes who might've still been hustling from the night before, hanging on the corner.

I had been making this bus ride for so many years that even though I knew I was on my way to where rich people—doctors, lawyers, and business owners—sent they kids, it didn't really faze me. Sometimes, the kids I went to school with had daddies who were rich because their daddy's daddy and his daddy before that were rich. Hell, these were some white people who probably never worked a day in their lives. Their kids weren't about this life.

When I was in elementary school and junior high going to school out here, I didn't realize that my atmosphere was changing. Part of that was because my granny always lived in a big house. In the hood some folks looked at us as privileged, and in some ways we were. But now that I was in high school, I knew what my surroundings were.

Truth be told, St. Louis is really two cities in one town: one black, one white. Over here is the black side, and what they refer to as South Side or South City is the white part. You got a lot of people who live in the city who have never been out to the county or hardly ever go. It's like some unspoken rule that if you aren't white with some money, don't be hanging around in the county too long. The good shopping malls were always in the county, so you might catch us there on payday. It goes if you one of them white people with money; you're not going to feel comfortable coming down to the hood.

Each day my bus would chug its way onto the first of three highways. Life in the hood faded away, as we connected to the second highway, Interstate 170. Better and better neighborhoods started springing up in the distance. Then by the time we connected to Highway 40 the air got clearer, cleaner, fresher.

When the bus exited the highway and passed that WELCOME TO

LADUE sign, you couldn't see the mansions that were hidden behind large tree-filled areas, but I would see some of them same-looking black ladies who stood on that bus line back in North St. Louis, exiting the Bi-State bus, to go clean them big houses that the rich white people owned.

The light turned red as we were passing Reed Elementary School, my old stomping grounds. A little black girl caught my eye. She was getting off her bus and started running toward the school. Fifth grade had been my favorite year at Reed, and it was all because of Miss Zimmer. She was patient when she worked with me, like she saw something in me that maybe nobody else could see.

"Good morning, Lezley!" She would greet me each day with a smile. Miss Zimmer was younger than most of the other teachers. Every day she wore a long, blue jean skirt, button-down shirt, and a sweater tied around her shoulders. She wasn't done up with a bunch of makeup either.

"I have good news, Lezley. I'm picking you to hang the flag on the flagpole today."

"For real, Miss Zimmer?" My eyes went wide. That was a big responsibility, and I was going to make sure I was the best flagpole hanger Reed Elementary had ever seen. I was, too. Then she hugged me afterward and gave me a gold star.

When my mama got home from work I was still amped up, "Mama, Mama, I got to put the flag on the pole!" I knew my mama was probably tired, but I was wearing her ear out anyway. If it wasn't the flagpole, it was me joining the band or auditioning for a play. She was happy I was involved in activities, but hated that every time I signed up for something that meant she had to drive me all the way out to school and pick me up. Mama wasn't trying to hear about me and no flagpole right about then, that's for sure.

"Uh-huh, that's good, Nette Pooh." She went on into the other room.

Shoot, all that signing up I did got me all the top awards at the fifth-grade ceremony at the end of the year. My big smile started to suddenly fade, and for the first time I felt sad standing next to Miss Zimmer. I broke out crying, tears pouring out of my eyes like a water faucet.

"I don't wanna leave you, Miss Zimmer," I stuttered.

"Lezley, you're going to meet lots of new friends there," she said, wrapping her arms around me.

"Nobody else is going to care about me like you, Miss Zimmer."

"Lezley, you'll be fine, and there are other teachers that will care just like me at the junior high."

"But they won't be you," I sniffed.

"No, they won't, and I'll never have another Lezley McSpadden, either."

She smiled, and then I smiled back as she helped me wipe my tears. "Listen, you're bright, you work really hard, and I just know you're going to go far. And don't ever let anybody tell you anything different." For the first time Miss Zimmer was real serious. I was one of just a few black kids in her class. So it was like she knew something I didn't know about what life might have in store for me.

Junior high was a breeze, and Miss Zimmer was right. But I was a freshman in high school now and should've been thinking more about that future that Miss Zimmer seemed *so* optimistic about. I wanted to go far, I guess, but how far and where I hadn't figured out yet. I didn't really know where to start. Bernard was five years older than me. Mama told me he was going to college, but since he never really lived with us, he hadn't spent any time talking to me about school and stuff.

I knew one thing: when kids at school were talking about being a doctor or a teacher or a lawyer, shoot I can't imagine going to school for seven more years after high school! I was just trying to get through these four.

The only person who expected me to do more in life and to go back to school to finish after I had Mike Mike was my aunt Mary, Sandra and Tracey's mama. She was the only person who would be on me saying, "Nette, let me see your report card." She'd call and ask me about my grades and how school was. If she bought me anything, it would be educational.

• • • •

The deseg bus turned into the main parking lot of Horton Watkins High School, also known as Ladue High. The student parking lot off in the distance was already filling up with BMWs, Jeep SUVs, and station wagons. Most of these kids had they own cars, probably got the keys the day they turned sixteen.

My bus waited for the regular buses carrying the students that actually lived out here in the district to pull up into the large horseshoe driveway directly in front of the school. Then, like they were on cue, all the buses opened their doors and white faces filed out one by one. The white girls looked happy, giggling with each other, their blond hair bouncing and flowing. The white boys were goofy and playful. Some of them jumping on each other's backs, roughhousing.

When one of the last buses pulled in and opened its doors the faces of the students it let off were shades of brown, with just a few white faces mixed in. The girls looked like me, some with ponytails and braids, others with long hair, some with short cuts. They were just as happy and giggly as the white girls. The boys were more cool, some of them were dapping each other up, bumping fists, instead of jumping on each other like the white boys, acting all wild.

This bus had done its pickup in Indian Meadows, a subdivision on the border of Ladue and the municipality next to it called Olivette, a mostly black cluster of middle-class streets.

After the coast was clear, my bus revved up and continued on past the horseshoe around to the back entrance of the school. There was another deseg bus parked, letting kids out. When we stepped off my bus it didn't look anything like the kids in the front. We all came off one by one, anxious to get out the cold.

Being around all the white people at Ladue and seeing them with the new cars and fancy boots didn't bother me one bit. I might not have had the name-brand Timberland boots, but I had a close-enough-looking version. Me and my friends called them them Jodeci boots because they looked like them black combat boots Jodeci was rocking in their "Forever My Lady" video when they had them white walking shorts suits on, no shirts underneath, and hats to the back.

April and me got our morning whassups in to everybody. We had about fifteen minutes before the bell was going to ring, and just as everyone was starting to gather his or her bags, I suddenly felt uneasy. One black girl always walked around acting like she was all that, with her designer clothes and purse, and she hung with a group of girls that was the same type. They noses was always up in the air.

"That's so ghetto!" I heard her mumble.

She was near me, and I don't know if she was talking to me or about me to somebody else, but she had her damn nerve. We looked each other up and down.

"Humph, this bitch think she something 'cause she live out here in Indian Meadows," I snapped. She rolled her eyes. "Damn, I'm out here, too! You think 'cause you stay out here you better than me? Bitch, please!" The bell rang and that squashed anything jumping off.

That exchange had my adrenaline going as I headed off to my class. It made me open my eyes that black girls was trying to draw a line that not even no white girls did. This wasn't "he say, she say" gossip or getting mad over a boy. It wasn't even about being jealous because of what somebody else got, or because they might be a little cuter than you. No, it was about black-on-black racism.

Neither my mama nor granny had gotten me ready for this. I remember when I was in junior high and out the clear blue, Granny said, "You just as good as anybody, Nette." She was sitting at the kitchen table, dipping her corn bread in her plate of greens. "Don't let nobody call you no nigga! A nigga is an ignorant person, and you ain't no ignorant nigga."

I don't know why she said what she said that day. Maybe she had just seen something on the news about something happening to a black person, and it made her mad. I don't know, but Granny was old-school, and she knew what was up. She knew we were going to this school with these white people. Granny also made it clear that when we came out here to school that we had to be confident, we had to know that we got the same privileges as the other kids. Her philosophy was "If somebody turn a flip in that hallway, you better turn one better and straighter!"

I went on about my day and tried to forget about that girl, but as I sat in the cafeteria, I started thinking about her again, and just how the black kids from the city and county dealt with each other. There were other black kids who had the same attitude as she did. They didn't come from where I came from, and were critiquing me on not just where I lived, but also on how I looked. Sometimes we'd all get into innocent jonin' sessions, folks cracking jokes on each other if you county vs. city. But other times, just like with this girl, it would turn into something more serious like the heated words we had today.

Then I looked over to where most of the black people were sitting and saw old girl from that morning. We both rolled our eyes at each other. It was clear; this bitch was straight up judging me because I came from the city. So what was I supposed to do now that the racism wasn't coming from no white girl or boy, or no white teacher? It was coming from somebody who looked like me.

• • • •

Having that run-in at school didn't compare to what would happen back in my own neighborhood.

One day, I got off the bus, and this girl was standing at the stop with two guys next to her. The three of them were blocking my way and wouldn't move.

"Oh, that bitch stuck up! She think she better than us," she said, smacking on her gum like a cow.

"Naw, you think I'm better than you. Whatever!" I said, forcing my way past her. Suddenly, the girl pushed me from behind. I had my notebook and a couple of books in my hand, and all my papers flew everywhere. I wasn't about to get stole on or sucka punched. I bent down, pretending to pick up my papers and books, and instead picked up a stick and turned around and started hitting her upside her head with it. I didn't know who this chick was, but hell naw, I was still Nette Pooh from the hood! I wasn't about to let her get the best of me just because I went to a white school.

My boy Mike was walking down the street and saw me whuppin' that girl with the stick. Mike's family and mine were real cool, and we had grown up together around this way. He ran over and broke the fight up. I was so revved up and upset that I didn't even talk to him. I ran all the way home, and as my legs moved faster and faster, tears of anger were pouring down my face. I had won, but did I really? It was like damned if I do, damned if I don't. The black girls in the county mad because you a black girl who maybe didn't grow up on the side of the tracks they did, and they think you beneath them, but what makes them better? In the hood, the black girls were mad because you go to school in the county to get a better education to get out the hood. They want to fight you because they think you soft or that you done changed because you out with the white people.

The whole fight opened my eyes up to another reality. These were *my* people, so why did I have to prove my blackness?

CHAPTER SIX

THE PARTY . . . ROLO GOLD

"Mama, please let me get a gold tooth." I started begging Mama as soon as she walked through the door. I followed her into the kitchen. She had an armload of groceries.

"Let me help you, Mama." I smiled, trying to butter her up, taking a bag from her. "Please! I gotta get one. Key Key got two!"

"A gold tooth?" I heard a voice call out from the front room. It belonged to my cousin JoJo. "Ask Key Key to give you one a hers!" he said, laughing real loud and hard. JoJo, my auntie Mary's son, is five years older than me. He grew up with Bernard and Chevelle. He was always cracking jokes and jonin' on somebody with his tall, lanky self. I gave him one of them mind-yo'-own-business-fool looks, with razor-sharp eyes.

"Girl, if you wanna gold tooth, you'd better buy it yourself!" Mama snapped, stopping at the kitchen table and looking at me like I had three heads. She wasn't having it and didn't want to hear nothing else from me about it.

"What JoJo doin' here, anyway, Mama?" I asked through gritted teeth.

"He gonna stay here for a while until he get on his feet."

Granny let any and all of us stay at her house no matter if it was a crisis with our money or one of us needed to be there until things got better at home with our mama. My mama, my aunts, and my uncles, they all took after her, and if they was able, tried to look out for each other's kids. Just like my auntie Bobbie helping to raise my brother, Bernard.

I had Key Key's big sweet sixteen birthday jam coming up on the weekend, and I needed to be fly, and a gold tooth would set my look off. I was going to have to take matters into my own hands.

It wasn't just that Key Key and me were cousins who had grown up together or the fact that she was one of my best friends, but more than that, she was that cousin who I looked to for style. Don't get me wrong, my mama always had us dressed nice, and I knew how to coordinate, but Key Key had flava, in other words, a natural sense of style.

• • • •

I had had my party clothes picked out for days, and on Friday night I pulled out a fresh pack of Rolo candy, slowly peeled off the shiny gold paper, and carefully tore a tiny square of it off. I opened my mouth as wide as I could and neatly wrapped the gold paper around my left front tooth. I checked myself in the mirror and flashed a big old Kool-Aid million-dollar, gold-tooth smile. Aw, yeah, I was looking fly!

I needed to practice how to speak with it in my mouth. It was all in the technique.

"Haaa-peee birf-daaay, gurl!" I said, curling my top lip slightly over my front teeth, giving my lips an awkward pucker. "Whas-sup! Haaaay!" I contorted my mouth to hold my makeshift gold tooth in place. Shoot, I was good to go!

I'd be on point. I slipped on my new blue jean shirt. It had white polka dots on the back and white stripes on the front. I had a brand-new pair of jeans. To top it off, my hair was slamming. I had definitely come a long way from the days of Aunt Bobbie giving me a cute little girl style, like back when my cousins and me were kids and she would do our hair for Easter. We just settled for whatever hairstyle she decided to give us. Me, Key Key, Tonya, and Sandra might've all looked the same when we left the shop, but we had fun while we were there.

A trip to Auntie Bobbie's was an all-day adventure. Our job was to be her helpers, and we stood front and center in her shop, like good beauty-shop soldiers reporting to duty. Auntie Bobbie was all that to us. She was a female who owned her own business and had a big house.

Shoot, we thought she was rich. She always had candy or a gift for us too. She only had one son, Chavelle, so she treated us girls like princesses.

I remember one year in particular when we arrived, Auntie Bobbie was working on a customer's head, about to press it, when there was a hard knock outside the screened gate that was in front of the shop's door.

"Heeeey, Miss Bobbie, um, you got two dollars I can borrow?" The man, who was scratching his face and arms and was all jittery, proceeded to bang on the gate even harder.

"Chile, that's that beggin'-ass fool that be comin' 'round here," Auntie Bobbie's shampoo lady said. They both rolled their eyes. Auntie Bobbie was so angry she slammed down the pressing comb she had in her hand and stormed over to the door.

"Get on back, fool!" she shouted. "Before I come out there and knock you upside yo' head, then you'd really have somethin' to beg about!"

I had never seen somebody run so fast. We were in shock. To us Auntie Bobbie was this classy, sweet lady, but she could clearly handle her own. It was already hard to picture her even having this shop in the deep North Side on Union Boulevard and Terry Street.

"I'll be with y'all in a minute. But y'all can get to work in the meantime." Auntie Bobbie nodded toward Tonya to grab the broom. She always swept the hair up. Key Key passed out magazines to Auntie Bobbie's waiting customers. Sandra watered her plants. We were always happy to help out around her shop.

There was another knock at the door, and when Auntie Bobbie looked up, she motioned to me to let a stocky, gray-haired man in. He had two big bags over his shoulders.

"Hey, Miss Bobbie. I got some nice designer socks, Calvin Klein and Polo. And I got brand-new videos that's still at the movies."

A customer who was asleep under the dryer suddenly woke up and said, "How much is *House Party*? I heard that's funny as hell!"

"Gimme ten dollars for it!" the man replied.

"No, sir. I run a respectable business here. You gon' get on outta here chargin' all that money." Auntie Bobbie stopped doing her customer's hair and walked over to the door and let the man out herself.

Customers would come and go, and we'd just have to wait patiently.

"We gon' be the last people," I mumbled.

"I know. Why we gotta wait?" Tonya said under her breath.

"Are you payin'?" Auntie Bobbie's head snapped up, startling us. We all shook our heads no at the same time. "Well, then you gotta wait."

Finally, when all her customers was gone and the door was locked, Auntie Bobbie would wash our hair, plat it up, and put us under the hairdryer. The cone-shaped hairdryers faced the large wall mirror, and we were each sitting on a small stack of phone books to prop us up taller. When she turned the dryers on, we'd get a kick out of our plats swirling around up in the hairdryer.

Next it was time to get our hair pressed. The smoke would come off the pressing comb when that iron hit the hair and make a sizzle sound, like bacon frying. Auntie Bobbie would get so close to the nape of our necks, where we knew it to be called the "kitchen," that the heat felt like that iron was laying on our necks. We'd be almost in tears when she'd get down on them edges. After that came the curling iron, and then our transformation was complete. Our hair would be bouncing and behaving as we all ran up the steps to Granny's house, where Auntie Bobbie would drop us afterward to spend the night.

• • • •

I gave myself a once-over before leaving the house for the party. Baby, lip gloss was popping, hairstyle was popping, and outfit was popping. Check! I looked like I could've been in a Jodeci video, with KC singing "Forever My Lady" to me.

Key Key and Tonya stayed in a working-class neighborhood with nice single-family brick houses. They had parties all the time, so the neighbors sometimes sat out on their back porches to enjoy the music from the parties. Even the police was cool, patrolling the vicinity and keeping the flow of traffic in order.

I rushed in and barely took a moment to speak to my auntie Evelyn.

I made sure to hardly open my mouth, because I wasn't ready to unveil my golden masterpiece. The hallway was lined with decorative mirrors; I stopped to give myself a last-minute once-over. "Oh yeah, girl, you betta work it!" I opened the door to Key Key's room and shouted, "Surprise!" My homemade gold tooth was flashing in all its glory.

"Nette Pooh!" Key Key shouted.

"Look, I gotta gold tooth too!" I screeched, proudly spinning around to show off my new 'do and outfit. I was cheesing so hard I thought my face was going to break.

"You look fly, cuz! And I can't believe Auntie Dez let you get a gold!"

I was feeling myself, maybe a little too much. "It's dope, right?" I started smiling and high-fiving some more. "You like my too—" Next thing you know my fake gold tooth flew right out of my mouth. Key Key and me couldn't do nothing but laugh. We were cracking up so hard I nearly passed out. But not even my fake gold tooth flying out was going to stop my shine. I was ready to get my groove on.

The basement lights were dimmed and coming down the steps it looked like a sea of heads. The bass had the walls vibrating. Key Key and me weaved our way through wall-to-wall bodies. I was more reserved as she worked the room. Each person we passed wanted to give her a birthday hug. The heat coming off everyone's bodies made the basement air thick.

When Aaliyah's "Back & Forth" came on, I watched people dancing on the sardine-packed dance floor. Key Key came and found me dancing in place to my other jam, "Real Love" by Mary J Blige.

"Nette Pooh, somebody wanna meet you," she said with a slight attitude.

I looked up and saw this tall, dark-skinned dude dressed in Dickies pants and a T-shirt. I wasn't real impressed, but it felt nice that a boy wanted to meet me.

"Hey Nette Pooh, I'm MB." His voice was deep and low like a grown man's.

"Hey, how are you?" I said, nervously standing there.

Shai's jam, "If I Ever Fall in Love," came on and MB asked me to dance. He took me by the hand, and wrapped his arms around me and pulled me close. When the song ended we went back to standing to the side. We talked a few more minutes, and it was cool because we weren't all up on each other.

I felt special that someone had noticed me.

The party was just about over when I heard a loud ruckus and then saw what looked like a scuffle in the back of the basement. A girl called out loudly from across the room, "Aw, shit, it ain't a party if a fight don't happen!"

Folks started pushing to get out the basement. Fools were falling out the door to the yard. It was a straight-up smackdown between these two dudes. I just saw some punching and somebody on the ground. Nobody was pulling out a gun in some punk-ass move. Boys were about using they fists to show how big and bad they were and get their respect. A couple of dudes broke up the fight. So we didn't need the police that night. It was over as fast as it had started. Funny thing is, the deejay turned the music back on and the party got jumping all over again.

Laying in bed that night, I was still pumped up. My sister, Brittanie, was sound asleep in her bed across the room, but I was wide awake with a big smile on my face. *Nette Pooh met a boy and gave him her number. Maybe he will be my real boyfriend one day. Wouldn't that be a trip and a half?* I giggled out loud at the thought but caught myself so I didn't wake Brittanie up.

CHAPTER SEVEN

FIRST TIMES AND
BLUE LINES

My mama wasn't going to let me have any boy company come over and visit. The most I could do with a boy was talk on the phone, because I wasn't allowed to date yet. One time a boy at school who liked me tried to stick his tongue in my mouth, and I had to check him quick.

"Uh un. What you think you doin'?" I shouted, pushing him back with all my force. "I don't like how that feel!"

So as far as MB was concerned, things were going to go real slow in my book. Plus, I just wasn't feeling him like that, yet. I was warming up to him the more we talked and just in a couple of weeks he had quickly become my friend. MB would call me nightly, right on time. When the phone rang, I'd pick up so fast a full ring hadn't even come in.

"Hello?" I said, out of breath, trying my best to play it cool. MB's baritone voice made me smile instantly. He sounded so mature.

"Nette Pooh, get off the phone!" JoJo yelled all in my ear. He always got started when it was my turn to get on the phone, and we fought like we were both teenagers.

"Naw, you been here all day! Give me the phone!" I shouted back, grabbing the phone and storming into my room. I climbed into my bed, and the conversation was on. I didn't have any privacy, unless Brittanie was in Mama's room or the front room watching TV. Otherwise I'd talk low, under the covers if she was sleeping. It wasn't like we even had important stuff to talk about. It was just the fact we were on the phone together, and he was laying down his mack action in my ear. He finally told me that MB stood for Mike Brown. I decided I'd just call him Mike.

After what seemed like hours of talking about nothing, I'd start yawning, scared to look at the clock, knowing I'd have to be up before the crack of dawn.

"You hang up," I'd whisper.

"Naw, you hang up," he'd tease back.

"Naw, for real, hang up."

We went back and forth so much sometimes I'd fall asleep. When Mama's 5:00 a.m. shouting alarm went off, I'd find myself waking up tangled in the phone cord and with a crook in my neck from falling asleep on the phone receiver.

• • • •

It had been about a month and Mama got curious about who I was spending so much time talking to on the phone. so she gave permission for me to have company one afternoon. The first time Mike came over, my cousin JoJo was walking around with a bat as a joke.

"Nigga, you know she twelve years old?" JoJo blurted out.

"Aw man! For real?" Mike's eyes went wide.

"No I ain't, Mike!" I said giving JoJo a shove. "JoJo you play too much!"

Although, I had told Mike I was a year older than I really was when we met at Key Key's party. Now I was just busted all around.

"Mike, it really isn't that much difference 'cause I'll be fifteen in December."

Just then Mama came in the room and stood in front of us with her hands on her hips. Mike quickly got up and shook her hand. Mama didn't waste no time running down the law.

"Does your mama know you want her to be your girlfriend?" Before he could answer, she fired off another question, "Are you going to talk to her father? Are you going to be taking her to work or picking her up?"

I had to hold back my laugh, because Mama was too funny breaking him down. Her attitude was, look, are you going to help me with her since you want to be her boyfriend?

"Yes, Ma'am," Mike followed.

Between Mama and JoJo, I was officially embarrassed but still smiling and blushing as me and Mike made eye contact. He gave me one of those yo-mama-something-else looks.

• • • •

I was definitely feeling myself, and my little hormones were bubbling under about my budding relationship with Mike. I was just a freshman, so it was still all about taking things slow, even though he was an upperclassman. I had schoolwork and a job to focus on first and foremost. I had wasted no time getting a job when the school year started. My cousin Tonya was working at McDonald's got me a hookup there. I was underage, but I rigged up my own work permit, and I got the school counselor to sign off on it. Mama didn't know anything about it. It was on! I was able to buy myself clothes and I always let Brittanie borrow them.

I worked until close some nights, and Mama didn't like that part too much. She didn't want me working any place until eleven and twelve at night. So, by the time she picked me up and got us home, she was beat and went straight to her room and closed the door. That's when I started letting Mike sneak over.

Mike would insist on seeing me because that was better than talking on the phone. I'd be a nervous wreck.

"Ooh, did you hear somethin'?" I said squirming away.

"Naw, Nette, I ain't hear nothin'. Come here," he said.

"Uh-un, Mike," I said pulling back again. "You gotta go. I don't want my mama to wake up. She'll kill both of us."

He flashed a smile and then stepped back. As I watched him run back to his car, I felt like I had just been swept off my feet.

• • • •

I may not have been able to have boys over, but Mama's rule didn't stop me from going to see him. Mike lived in Pine Lawn, an area that bordered North St. Louis city and county. Even though it was a neighborhood of houses, some that were owned by people who had been living there forever, like Mike's parents, it also had a dangerous element. There were a lot of younger knuckleheads rolling through who would shoot, fight, rob, and there were known gang-affiliated streets. The police always had a presence over there.

Mike would pick me up in his daddy's clean Oldsmobile '98. It was a big car, felt like a boat on wheels. For fun, Mike would drive fast through the narrow, hilly streets of PLO and nearby areas like Beverly Hills, Velda Village Hills. The car had bucket seats and I would grip my seat cushion tight. He wanted me to meet his parents but Mr. Brown wasn't there and Mrs. Brown was in her room, which was so dark I couldn't really see her. I felt like I hadn't met her at all. We spent the rest of the afternoon hanging out by the car.

Mike's street was small but busy, with cars driving by and people outside working on their yards, kids playing ball in the street. It seemed like the whole neighborhood, and anybody coming through, was speaking, waving, or honking as they drove by. Mike was that dude on his block, repping his hood hard.

"Whassup, MB?" A dude who looked to be the same age as Mike slow rolled by in his car.

"'Sup!" Mike said, with a cool nod. "This my girl, Nette."

• • • •

One day, Mama had let Mike pick me up from work. As I was wrapping up my last order at the drive-through, I overheard my coworker out front repeating my name.

"Nette Pooh? Who? No, don't no Nette Pooh work here, ma'am." My coworker was having a confused exchange with a customer out front.

I quickly wrapped up my customer's order and raced to the front of the store. I could see an older couple standing on the other side of the counter. The woman was dark brown–skinned, had a shoulder-length

Jheri curl, wore glasses, and was somewhat matronly. The man was lighter brown–skinned, and his face was framed by a mustache, beard, and short Afro dusted with gray.

"Well, I'm Nette Pooh, but who are y'all?"

"Oh, we Michael's parents," Mrs. Brown replied.

"Well, how you doin' Mr. and Mrs. Brown," I said, shifting uncomfortably.

"Michael told us to come get you from work," Mrs. Brown said.

I clocked out and followed them to the car, torn between cracking up with laughter and fear. At that moment, as I rode quietly in the backseat of Mr. Brown's gray '98 that Mike had taken me riding in, I thought, *Dang, he must really like my butt, 'cause who just sends their mama and daddy to come get a girl from work that they just met?*

I was impressed that Mike had sent his mama and daddy to get me. Mama was too. After that, she loosened up the reins a little more and agreed that he could come by some Friday nights to visit when I got off work.

• • • •

A few months into things, Mike had got suspended from school for fighting. So he convinced me to skip school and come over to his house and hang out because his parents were going to both be gone for the day. Their house had a warm feel. It wasn't real fancy, and their style of furniture was kind of old-fashioned but comfortable. The house felt like two people who had been together for years, something I didn't have with my own parents. His daddy was former military and drove trucks. His mama worked too. I mean, they were definitely not rich, but they had stability.

He led me downstairs to his room, and we only stayed a few minutes. I was uneasy. I sat down on his bed, uncomfortably.

"We official," Mike said, wrapping his large arms around me. "You know my mama and I know yours," he said. I looked around nervously, and then he leaned in and kissed me.

Just then, we heard the front door unlocking. He quickly pushed me in the closet. I could hear Mr. Brown's voice, and he asked Mike to take the pizza he had bought for him for lunch. I couldn't believe that not only was I hiding in a closet at a boy's house, but also that this boy had got suspended from school, and his daddy was talking to him just as nice and had bought him an Imo's pizza.

I must've stood in that closet for thirty minutes or so, not moving and barely breathing, because his father was chatting up a storm. Eventually, he got me out.

"I'm never doing this again!" I said, then thought about the pizza, "And by the way Mike, you a brat. They got you straight rotten!"

• • • •

The April tree buds had gone from full bloom to changing colors and falling off the trees. Something must've been in the air, because my mama and daddy had started kind of messing around again. Daddy had been around before now, but it was his same old sketchy visits. This time it seemed like he'd stay longer. Maybe Mama was lonely, I don't know. I was just happy to see her with him. I may have had my issues with him, but he was my daddy, absentee and all, and I was still a daddy's girl.

Maybe Daddy was really trying. I mean he got paid good money as a foreman for the railroad. He been working there since I was two years old. I just hoped he'd keep his promises.

Daddy settled right in at our house. Having him, Mama, Brittanie, and me under one roof was my fantasy of a family. Looking at him and Mama sitting at the kitchen table sipping on beers, her smoking her cigarette, felt like old times. That's all I ever wanted for my mama. Her to be with my daddy and be happy.

• • • •

Me and Mike were getting more serious as the weeks and months passed. But I definitely wasn't going to share that I was considering having sex with anyone I knew. Even my mama hadn't had a conversation with me about sex.

I didn't care that I had been going around the Browns for several months, anxiety would kick in each time I walked in their house, and Mike led me down into his tiny room that had been an add-on to the house.

We would always sit on the couch in his room first. Then he'd move to his bed and try to get me to join him. Although he was trying to put his mack down and trying to make sex sound good, I simply wasn't ready. I knew we were getting closer and closer to dangerous waters.

I let things go a bit further each time. It became our new pattern to try once a week, but I'd chicken out every time. One day, I thought I was ready. I had on my favorite blue jean bibs and I thought I was looking cute. I sat on his twin bed and looked around nervously, and he turned me around, gently pushing me back on the bed.

"C'mon, Nette Pooh."

"Naw, boy, I ain't ready!" My eyes were rolling back in my head, and I felt hot all over under my clothes. He worked his large hands over my bra, pushing it up and cupping my breasts, while he sucked on my neck. I did not want him giving me no passion mark. My mama would kill me.

"Aw, girl, it ain't gonna hurt, c'mon. I love you," he whispered, sliding his hand down my torso. He unsnapped my bibs and we started kissing. I felt myself letting go but knew we had to stop. I was terrified. There was so much friction between us I thought we were going to spark a fire.

I knew he was tired of our heavy petting, kissing, and hugging. My mind was flooded with what-ifs and what-to-dos. Was this going to be magical? Was it going to hurt? He must really love me because any boy who waited seven months to get some got to love you. I closed my eyes as tight as I could. In between his grunting and breathing, I was fighting back my tears. This wasn't magical at all. I just wanted it to be over.

Later that night, it was over, and I rode home in a cab because Mr. Brown had left with the car to go to work. I walked up my house steps, feeling like a bowlegged cowboy. Sex wasn't a good feeling. It was nothing like what I'd heard. I felt embarrassed Mike wasn't a virgin. I was. I didn't even know how to have my next conversation with him.

• • • •

It was time for my period, but it never came.

"I missed my period, April," I said in a low voice, shaking my head.

"Ooh, you need to take a pregnancy test."

"No."

"Girl, don't you worry. I'mma get you one," She didn't give me a chance to answer. Oh my God, I was fifteen and my mama was going to kill me. The bell rang, and I had to get to class. I couldn't be bothered with thinking about no kind of baby today.

That night I did my best to hide my emotions from Brittanie, but the more I thought about the possibility of being pregnant, the weaker I felt. I was nauseous and dizzy, and so overwhelmed I started crying.

"Why you cryin', Nette Pooh?" Brittanie whispered, then started to whimper.

"I'm OK," I said weakly. The more I cried, the more she cried. We were so close that she even cried when I was the one getting a whuppin'.

"Please, tell me what's wrong," she begged.

"I think I'm pregnant, and I don't know how to tell mama."

"Ooh, I don't neither."

She put her arms around me.

• • • •

The next day, April rushed me between classes. "Lezley, c'mon," she said, dragging me to the girls' bathroom. "Here, take this," she ordered, shoving a brown paper bag in my hands. Inside was a Clearblue Easy pregnancy test.

"Go'on!" She folded her arms and nodded toward the nearest stall.

I was so terrified peeing on that little stick, I almost peed all over my hand.

"I can't look," I said, handing her the pee stick.

"Ooh, girl yes you is pregnant!" she announced.

After several minutes, I was able to put my words together. "How tha hell I'mma tell my mama?" I asked. April sucked her teeth as if to say, "You ain't got no choice."

We slowly walked to the pay phone in the commons. I put the money in, and then chickened out. "Here, you tell her!" I said handing her the phone.

"Hi, Miss Dez, this April, Lezley's friend." Mama was demanding to know where I was, then April blurted out, "Lezley's pregnant." Them words just fell out of her mouth so easy. I couldn't even breathe. We both put our ears to the phone to hear my mama's response.

Mama was silent for a long time before straight snapping, "Pregnant? I know this is April, and this better be a April Fool's joke!" Then all I could hear was my mama hollering. I didn't say anything. I just hung up. I was scared the rest of the day. I didn't even want to go home, but where else was I going to go.

When I got home from school, Mama was still going off. My head was spinning, but when she shouted, "I knew this shit was gonna happen! Well, yo' daddy said if this ever happened, he was gonna kill Mike!" I heard that part loud and clear.

"You gettin' an abortion! You too young to have a baby." Mama had put her foot down, and that was the end of the discussion.

That night Brittanie and me were lying in our beds talking.

"Nette Pooh, I'm so excited about the baby. I'mma be a auntie!" she said in an excited whisper, sitting up in her bed.

"Um, I don't think so," I said softly. I sat up on my elbow. My eyes started welling up with tears. "Um, Mama decided I was gonna get an abortion."

"Naw, Nette Pooh," she pleaded. "I can help you take care of the baby." I knew she was going to start crying any second.

"Brittanie, don't cry. It's probably for the best. I'm just too young. I ain't got no job like that. Babies is expensive. I gotta go to school. Uh-uh, it's for the best." My voice was quivering.

"I said I can help, and as soon as I'm old enough, I can get a job too," she sniffed.

I laid down and closed my eyes tightly. Tears trickled down my face.

In the days that followed I couldn't stop thinking about my baby that was growing inside me. I was amazed and tripping but I knew I wanted to be able to keep my baby. My head started to hurt I had so many thoughts. I hadn't told Mike yet and wanted to wait until I had it all figured out. I knew it was time to face my daddy. I feared what he was going to say or do to me. I feared what he was going to do to Mike.

A week passed, and it was the day I was supposed get the abortion. I had been fretting all day. I already loved this baby and couldn't bear the thought of getting rid of it.

Daddy got to the house before Mama. We sat at the kitchen table, and he was silent for a long time.

"What you wanna do?" Daddy asked.

"Daddy, I wanna have my baby."

"Well, when yo' mama get here that's whay I'mma tell her."

"You gonna kill Mike?"

"No but I wanna talk to him. Y'all gonna be young parents, but he gonna have to be a daddy to his baby."

Then Daddy gave me a much needed hug of assurance.

• • • •

Mama came in from work, and me and Daddy was sitting at the kitchen table again. She didn't even put her pocketbook down.

"Well, it's time. Come on, let's go," she said, standing at the door with her keys in her hand.

"She don't wanna do that. She wanna keep her baby."

"What the hell you talkin' 'bout, Les?"

"Dez, that's what she wanna do."

"Well, you know what that mean?" she said, turning to me. "You gonna have to get a job and take care of yo' baby," Mama said, letting out a deep sigh.

"I know, Mama," I said, with a shaky voice. "But it's what I want."

"Well, Nette Pooh, ain't no more skatin'!"

"I ain't gotta skate," I said, swallowing hard and digging up my strength.

"Ain't no more hangin' out with yo' friends. All them days is over."

Mama kept going down the ain't-no-more list, and I was blinking a lot, trying to take in all the stuff she was saying. But I was standing firm by my decision. She gave me a look as if to say, "This yo' last chance, girl." I didn't blink. She threw up her hands, grabbed a beer out the fridge, sat down at the table, and lit a cigarette. Daddy joined her. I walked out to the porch, looked up to the sky and thanked God that conversation was over. Then I smiled. I could officially be happy about having my first baby.

• • • •

"Okay, Nette Pooh, how you think yo' baby gon' look?" Brittanie giggled.

"I think it's gonna have my eyes. If it's a boy, I just hope he tall like his daddy, instead of short like me. But if it's a girl, ooh, I can't wait to put her in all them pretty dresses!" Now we were both giggling. "Hey, I'mma name my baby after you if I have a girl, and Bernard if I have a boy!"

"For real, Nette Pooh? Well, one day when I have my baby, if it's a girl I'mma let you name her, then!"

"Deal!" It was the first time in days that I had smiled. We had made a sister pact right then and there and pinky-swore on it.

• • • •

Later on Mama had calmed down, and it was time to tell Mike about the baby. I didn't know how he was going to feel, but I was already thinking about things like how my baby was going to look, how it was going to talk, and walk. It was early, but I started getting excited. Mike came to visit me at my daddy's house. We sat out on his front porch. He wasn't going to stay long, and had left his car running and Jodeci's, "Forever My Lady," was pumping softly from the car speakers. I was building up my nerve to break my news to him. But before I could say anything, he shocked me, opening up about his feelings.

"I really care about you Nette Pooh, and one day I really want you to have my baby."

I guess the song had inspired him. But little did he know, I was really going to have his baby.

"Well, Mike I actually am pregnant!"

He gave me a big smile and hugged me, before leaving.

My aunt, who was upstairs, had her window open, and came outside to tease me as he was pulling off.

"I heard you and Mike talkin' 'bout 'is you gonna have my baby,' and you said yeah."

"I know you probably thinking I'm too young but I'mma have my baby, and I'mma finish school."

My aunt raised her eyebrow, and gave me a look of surprise, before backing away into the house. At that moment, I felt complete with the thought that no matter what anybody said, I had made the right decision, and my baby was going to be special.

CHAPTER EIGHT

GOD BLESS THE CHILD

"Lez-lee! Hello, I am Dr. Ekunno!" Dr. Ekunno had a heavy African accent. He greeted me with a big smile.

"Just relax, OK?"

"OK." I was nervous, laying back on the exam table with my feet in the stirrups. My head was spinning trying to keep everything you have to do when you're expecting in order. I had gone from seeing the pediatrician to having an obstetrician.

"You are great," he said, helping me to sit up. "Lezley, I want you to eat well, take vitamins, and get sleep!" He sounded more excited than me, and I was the one having a baby.

When I got home later, I stood in front of the mirror looking, and wondering what new change my body was going to make. I smiled at my reflection, just thinking about the fact that another human being was in there.

"Lezley? Lezley, wake up!" A classmate had to shake me a few times, because I had fallen asleep again in class.

"What's wrong?" I asked groggily.

"Girl, them girls over there are pointing at your belly." She was known as the school gossip. I looked across the room, and a cluster of about three girls was definitely sneering, looking at me like I was some kind of disgrace.

I was too tired to even be offended. I was just at the start of sophomore year, and I had a whole lot of weeks to go before I had this baby. I had just thrown up before class. My eyes were so heavy and I needed sleep. And I was having a hard time with morning sickness. So I wasn't in a mood to argue with anybody.

It was close to the end of the day, and I couldn't wait to get home. I raised my hand and excused myself from class to go to the nurse's office. I had tried not to make my pregnancy a big deal at school, because the teachers and my principal had been so nice once they found out I was pregnant. In my early months they even adjusted my schedule so that my first period could be spent resting in the nurse's office. I wasn't about to let no petty-ass girls upset me.

I only had a little bump, but word had gotten around that I was pregnant. Being the only pregnant girl at school *and* black made it an even bigger deal. I didn't regret my decision, but the more stares I got the more reality set in—I was so young and feeling real uncertain about my future.

I soldiered through the pregnancy, and by the beginning of my second trimester, it was wintertime and I was sick, throwing up twenty-four hours a day. I was used to my new routine, and Mama had come around.

"Nette Pooh, you hungry?" She had always cooked, but now she'd even started cooking my favorite meals and foods I was craving.

"Yeah, Mama!" I was dozing on the couch, but my ears perked up at the mention of food.

"You gotta keep yo' strength up with that baby. You know you got that ultrasound tomorrow."

Mama slid a steamy plate of baked chicken and potatoes and vegetables in front of me before sitting down across from me, and I went to town on that food. For a moment Mama and me locked eyes, and I knew she was really in my corner. Brittanie sat down next to me at the table, and in between bites, I showed off the samples of baby products that had started to arrive in the mail.

• • • •

"Lezley! Hellooooo!" Dr. Ekunno squeezed some warm gel on my belly and pressed the ultrasound wand against my skin. "Aha! Look at here!"

"Look like a big black blob to me," Mama said, squinting at the screen.

"Uh, naw, Dr. Ekunno, I don't know what you talkin' 'bout. Mama, I can hear a bunch of water crashin' around, and that don't look like a baby," I said, stretching my neck around the doctor to see the computer monitor. All I could make out was a black-and-white blur.

Dr. Ekunno pointed to a little white dot, then turned the volume up on the computer speaker.

Whomp whomp whomp whomp whomp.

"You see and hear? It's the baby's heartbeat!" he said.

"You hear it, Nette Pooh?" Mama was smiling from ear to ear.

"Yep, Mama! Listen how fast it's beating!"

"Very, very healthy, Lezley." Dr. Ekunno cleaned off my belly and patted me on the shoulder.

Mama left out the office with him, and I stared at the ceiling for a few extra minutes. My first baby's heartbeat. I just wished Mike was there, but he was in school.

I was four months and happy when Mike went with me to get the ultrasound that told us what the baby's sex was. Dr. Ekunno squeezed the warm gel on my belly and pressed the ultrasound wand against my skin like he had done before.

"Ahhhh! Ohhhh! Aha!" Dr. Ekunno was so animated.

Mike and me kept looking at each other.

"What is it? What is it?" I said, biting my lip.

"It is a boy!"

I looked at Mike and gave him a half smile. He smiled back.

Hearing the baby's heartbeat was one thing, but seeing that there was a person in my belly, coming from both of us, and that he was not only going to be a father, but he'd have his first son. I'm sure Mike was excited but probably scared. I was.

• • • •

"C'mon, Nette Pooh," Mama said, shaking me awake. "We goin' fishin'."

I grew up going fishing. My granny loved to fish, and so did my mama and all my aunts and uncles, but I wasn't trying to have Mama wake me up on a Saturday, as sleepy as I was and as big as I was, to go. But Mama helped me get out of bed. The sun was shining and it was a perfect spring day. I was glad I had shed my winter clothes, because my belly needed to breathe, and big T-shirts and stretch pants was about all I was fitting into these days.

Mama had the radio on, tapping her long fingers on the steering wheel to the music. She had packed up the car with all our fishing gear and even had some sandwiches and chips in a bag. It was early and hardly any cars were on the highway, so we'd be at the lake at the park in no time. I was glad, because I had to pee.

By the time I waddled out the park bathroom, Mama had our lawn chairs set up.

"Get you a worm in that box, Nette Pooh." Mama already had her fishing line in the water.

Her little boom box was playing classic R&B. I cast my line out, sat down in my chair, and let out a long sigh. Fishing teaches you patience, and that's what I needed. I had been anxious, but for the first time in this whole pregnancy, I felt relaxed. Putting that worm on the hook, casting that line, and sitting there, sometimes all day, just waiting to catch one fish. It was the one thing I could do where I could think clear and be at peace. We didn't talk about nothing serious; matter of fact, we didn't do much talking at all. I jumped when I felt a slight kick from the baby, then rubbed my belly. Mama and me both busted out laughing. Then she turned the music up and we enjoyed the rest of the afternoon.

· · · ·

Mike and me tried to go to the Lamaze class Dr. Ekunno had set up. There were mostly older couples there, like in they twenties and married. I felt out of place and awkward, being that I was so young. Mike was acting all funny, like he didn't want to come, but I made him. He kept checking the time. They instructed us to spread our mats out and sit on the floor. He sat behind me. Today, we were going to learn how to push when the baby was ready to come out.

The exercise was just about to start and I took one breath in and don't you know, Mike had started snoring.

"Wake up, boy!" I shouted.

"Huh? What you mean?" he snapped.

"C'mon, I'm ready to go. I can't believe you embarrassed me like this!" I quickly gathered my stuff and rushed out with him running behind me.

I was looking forward to us having that as something we did together for the baby. But it didn't really work out.

• • • •

My belly was sticking way out, and I was struggling to get down the hallways at school. Ladue had allowed me go to school all the way up to my ninth month if I wanted to. The school even gave me an elevator key so I wouldn't have to take the steps. We had another month before summer break, but I wasn't going to make it. By the beginning of May 1996, I couldn't take the bus ride or sitting in class no more. I was miserable.

The school made it official that they'd be sending a teacher to my house. I was so happy I wouldn't fall behind. A woman ran a program for pregnant girls through the school. I swear them white people had so many resources out there, stuff that a pregnant black girl going to public school in the city would never know about. I was excited that she was going to start coming right away; that way I wouldn't miss homework or my finals.

I opened the door and a petite Middle Eastern woman was standing there.

"Good morning! You must be Lezley. I'm Miss Hajid." She had a friendly smile and immediately extended her hand.

I was getting that nervous feeling again. I couldn't believe this woman was coming to me, looking out for my best interest, *showing* interest, driving all the way to my house. Right away we sat down at the table and got to work.

For the next couple of weeks I took advantage of the homeschool program. Miss Hajid helped me understand what I needed to do to be a good parent and how to take good care of my baby, but she also kept me from falling behind with my schoolwork. I liked my one-on-one homeschooling way better than going to classes. We had finished our lesson plan for the day, and she was straightening up her papers.

"Oh, Miss Hajid, you think you could come over here and tutor me even after my baby boy comes?" I asked, winking and pulling out an ultrasound photo, waving it in the air.

"Wow! That's amazing." She threw her arms around me and gave me the best hug she could give me with my big old belly in the way. "Lezley, having a baby is a gift, a blessing," she said, giving me a comforting look.

"I definitely know my baby is a gift, Miss Hajid. But I'm sixteen and gonna be somebody's mama, and I ain't married, and even though I'm determined to finish high school it's scary," I said, looking away.

"Listen, sure you're facing some obstacles, but look at you: you are tough and strong, and you aren't giving up. That's what makes me so proud of you. And you're gonna get the diploma!"

"Yeah, I'm gonna do it?" I asked, feeling hopeful.

"I have something for you and the baby," she said, pulling out a portable Sony Walkman CD player.

"Huh? What do this have to do with my baby?"

"Just trust me," she said, handing me the headphones.

I slipped them over my ears, she pressed play, and "Itsy Bitsy Spider" came on.

"I ain't heard that since I was a li'l bitty kid."

"It brings back memories, doesn't it? I want you to put those headphones on your belly and play music to your baby. And here," she said, handing me a stack of children's books. "I want you to read to your baby while he's still in there, and when he gets here."

I nodded, taking in every word she said.

"Lezley, you are going to be a good mom," she said, giving me a wink before packing up her bag.

"You think so? 'Cause, I think you can tell, having a baby wasn't really something I had planned," I said, looking down at the floor. "I'm a li'l scared, I guess."

"No, you didn't," she said. "But you can do it. Motherhood isn't easy for anybody, at any age. The important thing is that you don't give up on yourself or your baby."

It was her last day; I had taken my finals and was now just focusing on being a mother. As I watched her walk away, her words stuck with me. It was like she had given me hope. Yeah, I was sixteen, about to bring a new life into this world. His daddy was claiming him and all, but when it came down to it, deep down I knew it was going to be me and my baby boy against this world. All eyes were on me, and even if I made some more mistakes, I was determined to be a responsible mother.

• • • •

"Ahh, Lezley, so good to see you." Dr. Ekunno was his usual cheerful self. Me, on the other hand, I was nine months pregnant, miserable, and ready to pop.

"Just breeeeeathe, Lezley," he said, putting my feet in the stirrups. I was uncomfortable but tried to focus on a speck of discolored paint that was on the ceiling as I laid on the exam table not sure what he was about to do. Dr. Ekunno slipped his fingers inside me for an exam. "Ahh, ha, ohh-kay," he said, giving me a wide smile.

I frowned. Here I was, uncomfortable as hell, and this man was smiling like he just found a hundred dollars.

"Come here, look." He turned to my mama with a wrinkled forehead and nodded. "She is goin' to have this baby too-night. You see, Mother, her mucus plug is about to come out!"

"Oooh, that's nasty. I don't wanna see that," Mama said, frowning.

He pulled his fingers out, quickly removing the rubber glove, and gave me that smile again. I was scared, but when I looked over at my mama, she gave me one of those baby-everything's-going-to-be-fine looks that only a mama can give. It shocked me, because my mama isn't the warm and fuzzy type. I could tell she was just as excited and nervous for her baby girl and soon-to-be-here grandbaby as I was.

When we called my granny to tell her what the doctor said, she ordered Mama to bring me over right away. As soon as we walked in the door she made me sit down at the table. "You gonna eat some spaghetti, Nette Pooh, because wit that baby comin', once you get to that hospital, they ain't gon' let you eat." She put a heaping plate of spaghetti in front of me, and I dug in. Not long after that, at about 9:30 that night, I wasn't hurting, but I knew something different was going on inside my belly. I was feeling cramps coming on. Sure enough, I was starting labor and ready to go to the hospital.

As the nurse prepped my epidural, and I sat hunched over on the edge of the bed, I was glad I had eaten that spaghetti. Granny was right. It wasn't no telling when I'd eat again. They had already informed me that I could have ice chips.

Mike, my mama, my sister, my daddy, and some of my cousins were all there, but it was like all I could focus on were thoughts of my baby boy I'd soon be meeting. The long needle for the epidural gave me a slight pinch, then it was over. I had finally reached ten centimeters. The nurse prepped me for delivery.

At 10:00 p.m. Dr. Ekunno was in place at the bottom of the bed, and my legs were in the stirrups. The nurse instructed me to sit up and grab the back of my legs.

"Okaaaay, Lezley, you are ready to push! Push, Lezley, push!"

I started trying to do situps.

"What are you doing?" she asked, stopping me.

"I'm pushin'!" I said, panting like I had just done a full gym workout.

"Baby, that's not how you're supposed to do it," the nurse said, shaking her head. She began to instruct me in the right way to help the baby along.

"Lezley, just bear down like you're having a bowel movement," the nurse instructed.

"But that sound nasty," I said, moaned, curling up my top lip. Just then I got another contraction and screamed out.

"Bear down! I promise it's what the baby needs to get out," Dr. Ekunno said in a calm tone. "Now, Lezley, you are doing great, but as soon as you get another contraction, push like you just did." He nodded to his nurse to keep coaching me while he went to check on another patient.

For forty-five minutes me and that nurse went back and forth. Then all of a sudden a pain shot through me that had me hollering for dear life.

"It's comiiiiiiiin'! Ooooooh!" I closed my eyes as tight as I could, yelled out, and pushed at the same time, probably busting everybody in the room's eardrums.

Suddenly, I heard a tiny cry. It was my baby.

"Let me see! Give him to me." Tears were pouring down my face while they sewed me up. My baby had torn me up coming out, and I was going to have to heal from all the stitches for a while, but right now I wasn't feeling any pain, just joy and happiness.

Mike rushed over to me. We were anxious to see and touch our baby, but the nurse wanted to clean him up first. Since I was in pain from the stitches my cousin held him first and I watched her feed him a bottle. Then she brought him to me.

"Look at our baby," I said, looking up at Mike. "He so beautiful, even with his cone head."

"My li'l man is perfect. Wow." Mike couldn't believe his eyes.

May 20, 1996, Michael Orlandus Darrion Brown made his debut. I felt like we had our own little family. We had created another person, and it was blowing both our minds.

He was the most beautiful thing I had ever seen, so small. Mike Mike was perfect to me. I cried when the nurse finally handed him to me. I was amazed by the fact that I had created this person inside me. I just wanted to hold him forever and never put him down. I looked over at Mike, and as hard as he be acting, I saw a softness in his eyes tonight. The kind that only a man seeing his baby for the first time can have. He had his daddy's first and last name, but like I promised Brittanie, if I had a boy I'd name him after my brother, Bernard. Orlandus is Bernard's middle name. And Darrion, well, I just liked the way that name sounded. He had his *own* name and his *own* identity and, within it, a little piece of everybody that loved him. Since I loved nicknames, I'd call him Mike Mike.

CHAPTER NINE

BEAUTIFUL SURPRISE

The day I brought Mike Mike home from the hospital, it was a scorcher. Mama was so excited about her firstborn grandchild. Her latest piece of car was a little Chevy Chevette that we called the Silver Bullet. It was a straight-up bucket, and the air conditioner would only push out warm air.

As we pulled off from the hospital, in between smiling back at Mike Mike and checking him out through the rearview mirror, Mama reminded me that we had a stop to make before we went home. As long as I didn't have to move around much, I didn't care, and Mike Mike was sound asleep in his car seat. I slumped against the seat beside him, still exhausted and sore and swollen from my stitches.

I was miserable and burning up in her backseat, and rolled down the window to at least catch a hot breeze.

"Uh-uh, Nette Pooh, put that blanket over that baby's head 'fore he catch a cold," Mama ordered.

I don't know about how white mamas are, because I haven't ever had one, but I can tell you my mama used a lot of the same old-fashioned remedies on us that her mother brought up from the South. Her mama taught her those same superstitions and that's how I learned them. So, mama didn't care if it was 200 degrees, this baby was going to have a hat on his head so he didn't get no cold.

First stop was my Granny's. She, like Mr. and Mrs. Brown, didn't come to the hospital to see Mike Mike we took him to her. Mr. and Mrs. Brown weren't at the hospital to see Mike Mike be born either. They were excited, but being older, too, they had old-fashioned ways like Granny. Mr. Brown worked a lot and probably was on the road driving his truck or something. Mrs. Brown, like my Granny, felt like all those people didn't need to be at the hospital. She would meet her new grandson soon enough. But the difference with Granny was that you always took a new baby to see Granny at her house as soon as the baby was born. It was a family tradition. Next to your baby getting baptized, it was like getting an official blessing and proper welcome to the family.

When we got to Granny's everybody was there to greet Mike Mike just like when I gave birth—my Auntie Bobbie, some of my other aunties, and a few of my cousins, and Granny was standing with a smile in the middle of all of them. I thought my family was going to be really disappointed in me, but when my Auntie Bobbie, picked up Mike Mike, and held him gently in her arms, she looked in his eyes, and said, "You better not keep my niece up all night 'cause she gotta go to school," I was nearly brought to tears by her powerful words.

My family knew I was trying and they weren't mad at me.

"Look at this baby," Granny's eyes lit up. She didn't hold him long. I guess she felt like she was going to be spending enough time with him as he grew up. I was young and she knew I was going to be depending on family to help me get though this. "Go on an' get this baby home, Nette," she said, but not before giving me some of her sage advice.

"Now look, don't you be sittin' on no hard surfaces, or washin' yo hair, takin' a shower, or goin' outside for a while. You gots ta heal from this baby and neitha one a ya'll cain't be gettin' sick." She sent me on my way, and I didn't question what she said. I just knew I'd better follow her instructions.

Next stop was going to my daddy's house, where we had been staying temporarily since right before I went in the hospital. The house was big, but a lot of people stayed there. No place I really wanted to have a newborn, but we didn't have a choice. It was uncomfortable when I realized that I'd be sleeping on the couch with my baby. I needed a room with a door, but the door to my temporary room was the front door.

Mama was waiting for a new place to be ready for us to move in. In the meantime, at least we had a clean, decent place to be. So, as soon as I put Mike Mike's baby bag down, I was already counting down the minutes till we left. But I would make due. It would even be kind of fun being with my other side of my family, plus mama was there.

My daddy and auntie lived together in U-City, short for University City. This was another township within St. Louis County. U-City was interesting, because it stretched from St. Louis City limits to as far as the border of the small town of Olivette that spilled over into parts of Ladue. This street was nice, but it wasn't hardly close to Ladue.

Funny thing about a place like U-City. It was pretty much black where daddy's house was, and got more and more integrated the further out you drove. Then it had Jewish pockets, and big mansion-sized homes. But then you could cross over the main road, Olive Street Road, and it be small cracker jack looking houses in lower income pockets, mixed with renters and owners. I was young and only knew about my world, though, and to me this was still close to the city.

I wasn't going to complain about going back to Daddy's to Mama, because this was where we had to be right now. Mama was doing the best she could. It was just that bringing a new baby home you want peace and quiet and your own space, and I wasn't going to have that.

When we arrived on Jullian, my daddy's brother, Uncle Edwin, greeted us.

"Chile, bring that baby on up in here!" he shrieked.

Uncle Edwin was a gay man. He was tall, dark brown–skinned, and slim, and he could party hard. He loved music and to dance around the house. He was so into playing his music loud that in the living room he had these big floor-to-ceiling racks that looked like cages, and he had large, tall speakers inside, and he had hooked up an elaborate sound system. Uncle Edwin had money like that.

He was a truck driver. He always had a lot of cash in his pockets and a brand-spanking-new car when he came off the road from driving a job. He was like Santa Claus at Christmastime, and he would always buy a big old tree. His top priority was taking care of my auntie and her children.

Outside of Daddy, Uncle Edwin, my auntie, and a handful of other relatives there was also now my mama, me, Brittanie, and Mike Mike. The house had an upstairs, a middle floor, and a livable basement that had two extra bedrooms. So folks were all over the place.

I made myself comfortable on the couch and put Mike Mike in a fresh soft newborn onesie. He was so beautiful, and I never wanted to let him go.

"Look at Mama's sweet baby boy," I whispered, kissing him softly on his forehead. He cooed, and that made me tear up. I was still amazed that he had come out of me.

"I'm gonna keep you right here with me and protect you forever." I kissed him again and then inhaled his skin deeply. I laid him on my chest, and we both fell off to sleep. And that's how we slept for the next several nights.

• • • •

It had just turned a week that we were staying at Daddy's. One afternoon, Mama was fed up with something Daddy did. Brittanie and me were on the front porch sitting. I was rocking and playing with Mike Mike.

I heard Mama get loud. All of a sudden Mama bolted out the front door. "We outta here, Nette Pooh and Brittanie! Y'all get your stuff. We got someplace to go!"

That's all I needed to hear. I was moving fast, with Mike Mike in my arms, and Brittanie helped me gather all our stuff. The timing was perfect, because Mama had just got word from the electric and phone companies that we had lights and a phone at our new house.

"And I'm taking my meat, nigga!" Mama shouted at Daddy.

Mama took the empty trash bag out the trash can and went to the freezer and scooped out all the meat she had bought.

We shuffled out of there and never looked back at Jullian Street.

We putted off down Olive Street Road in the Silver Bullet. I looked over at Mama, and as mad as she was at my daddy, she kind of gave me a half smile, with our bag full of meat like we had just pulled off a major bank heist. Mama had a look of confidence on her face. And I was cool because I didn't have to sleep on the couch anymore.

I was glad to have Mike Mike home for real. Mama had surprised me and put all my things in place as part of my big welcome home with the baby, and had even displayed some of Mike Mike's toys and baby decorations. I laid him in an old wicker bassinet and sighed, as I looked around at all the toys, clothes, and other baby needs he had been blessed with. Mike Mike even had two of everything, from strollers to car seats to bassinets to high chairs. My family and the Browns spoiled him rotten.

My daddy came by a few days later to give me money. Him and Mama made up. That's how they did. Sounds kind of dysfunctional but I was kind of glad they were cool again.

I was extremely overprotective of Mike Mike. He was just a newborn, and it wasn't like he could get up and crawl or walk nowhere. I'd just sit and watch him in that bassinet, checking stuff like his breathing every few minutes. I worried about if he'd choke on a soft toy. My imagination was going wild. I guess because he was my first. It was setting into my brain that this was such a big responsibility for me to be so young. I was terrified of SIDS, and the thought of Mike Mike suffocating in a crib was enough for me to decide that what better way for my new prince to sleep than in a bassinet. I put his bassinet in the living room and started sleeping on the couch, so I could be as close to him as possible.

• • • •

It was summer; school was out, and all I could think about was Mike Mike. St. Louis temperatures could easily get up to the high 90s, and it was known to feel in the triple digits when that humidity set in. I didn't care how hot it was or about the fact that he was just days old. He was going to be dressed to the nines every day. Mike Mike was my new personal alarm clock, and we had a routine. I'd give him a bottle before bed, and that boy could sleep through a storm.

By 8:00 a.m., sometimes 7:00, I was up feeding him his morning bottle, washing him down, and dressing him. Mike Mike had so many clothes I could put him in a new outfit every day and not repeat it for a month. Then I'd finish by gently brushing over his little fine, curly hair. He was perfect, and I didn't want him to ever get dirty. I'd place him in his swing and watch him go back and forth for what seemed like hours.

One day I went out to get the mail and placed him in his bassinet. I was still healing from my stitches and moving slow. I was out on the porch when the wind slammed the door shut, and the lock turned. Oh, Lord, what was I going to do? I was home alone with Mike Mike and locked out in shorts, a T-shirt, and some flip-flops. My heart started beating fast. My baby was inside and wasn't nobody around. I panicked, running from one side of the porch to the other. The front door was so heavy that I couldn't kick the door, and I didn't have a phone to call a locksmith. The house was only one story, but the front windows were all locked. I saw that the only window open was a small window up high.

I kicked off my flip-flops like lightning and began to climb up our brick house, grabbing onto any brick that was sticking out the side of the house. With each move, I felt a pain in my lower belly. Then I'd scrape my leg. Beads of sweat were forming on my head, and by the time I reached the open window, the sweat was dripping in my eyes.

I grabbed hold of the windowsill, took a big breath, and, with all my strength, hoisted myself up. I let out a scream that would've woke up a deaf person. I crawled into the house, scraped and bloody. I was breathing so hard I felt dizzy. It didn't matter, as long as I had Mike Mike in my arms, safe and sound. After that happened, I understood the power of the bond between a mother and her child. I would have climbed a mountain or walked through fire to get to my baby. Wasn't anything ever going to keep me from him.

CHAPTER TEN

SCHOOLYARD STOMPDOWN

The summer was over, and as anxious as I was to get back in the school mix and to start my junior year, I was so attached to Mike Mike, part of me didn't want to leave him. I handed him to my mama.

"I'll see you later," I said stepping onto the bus. Me and Mama never said "goodbye." That was just our thing, because we never wanted things to be final. My friends were all smiling, but I felt like I was about to cry.

"Go on, Nette Pooh, Mike Mike gon' be right here waitin' for you when you get back."

I looked out the window until I couldn't see him anymore.

• • • •

Miss Hajid, who had homeschooled me, invited me to bring Mike Mike to school. She wanted to include him in her lesson plan talking about stages of a baby's development. Everybody was whispering and oohing and aahing as I walked through the halls with my baby. He was six months by now, showing his personality, giggling and smiling. I was proud to show him off.

At home with Mama, I was noticing she was starting to be on edge with me. Times were hard with a new mouth in the house. Meanwhile, me and Mike weren't getting along, because I didn't see him doing anything. He had dropped out of school, and he didn't have a job. He wasn't motivated. I had to depend on his parents. They were taking care of his responsibilities. Me and him weren't even acting like a couple. He wasn't affectionate towards me, and I wasn't interested anyway. Mike was coming over, and then we'd drive the baby to his parents' house, but we weren't connected like two people in a relationship were supposed to be. Thank God his mama and daddy were picking up the slack on his end, buying things for Mike Mike. I didn't like that Mike wasn't in school anymore. I wanted to graduate now more than ever.

"You gonna have to get a job and take care of yo' own baby. I gotta go back to work," Mama told me.

Outside of the time I was gone to school, I was doing my best to handle my responsibility, but when Mama said that, my heart sped up and my brain started racing. "What you mean you cain't take care of him, Mama? I am takin' care of my baby! You gettin' my check for him too!"

So each day my bus ride got shorter and shorter in my head because I spent that time worried about what I was going to do. At school I was totally distracted, thinking about what Mama was saying to me at home.

There were a lot of different beefs brewing at school now too. Some days I'd come to school and didn't feel like talking in the mornings. I may not warm up to people until after lunch. I might have had a long night. Some of these girls weren't trying to understand that.

It was mainly the same crew of chicks that was pointing at my belly when I was pregnant in class. Now they looking and pointing and whispering stuff like, "Humph, who got her baby while she at school?" Each day I just played it off, tried to stay focused on class and getting through the day, but my anger was bubbling up.

Walking in the house and seeing Mike Mike instantly made me forget about the drama at school. I felt guilty too, because I had to leave him and I know he missed me. My focus was on him once I got home.

One evening, I put my backpack down and started playing with Mike Mike on the floor. "Well, what you gonna do?" Mama snapped, starting in on me.

"Well, Mama, I've decided to go live with Mike and his parents. He's partially responsible for Mike Mike and maybe his parents could help out more, so I can continue going to school."

"You not gonna be over there sleeping with a man!" She angrily snapped back.

"That wasn't my intention. I'm trying to help you and help myself at the same time, mama! I'mma I thought I was doing the right thing by making Mike help me with our responsibility."

Mama jumped up in my face. I was scared she was gonna give me a whupping, but instead she punched me in my mouth.

Blam!

Standing there in disbelief, shaking my head back and forth. I felt my face swelling up.

"Mama! Why you'd hit me? Why? Why? Everything you just told me to do, I'm doing it, Mama. And I'm still wrong?" I was screaming at the top of my lungs.

Mama grabbed me and we started tussling. I didn't want to hit her back; I was trying to keep her off me. I broke free and ran as fast as I could to Granny's house. I wanted to see if she could talk to Mama. I thought I was giving my mother what she needed.

I didn't even think about the fact that it was dark and I was a girl out this late alone.

By the time I got around to Granny's, Mama had already called her and as far as they were concerned whatever your mama said, this is what you do. I opened my mouth to explain, but Granny cut me off. "Nette Pooh, don't you ever raise yo' hand to yo' mama!" Granny reeled back and smacked me in the face.

"Why did you hit me?" I asked, stumbling backward.

"What the hell goin' on, Nette Pooh? What you doin' to Granny?" Bernard demanded.

"Get out my face, Bernard. Granny just smacked me for no reason!" I shouted. "I'm outta here!"

"You ain't goin' nowhere," he said, grabbing me, yanking me by the arm.

I broke free and Bernard pushed me. Then I punched him, and we screamed and yelled and hit each other back and forth.

"I'm tired, Nette Pooh, just go!"

I stormed out the door. Snot was coming out my nose, mixed with my sweat and tears. I didn't see a light on at Nina's house, but I saw that Mr. Rhodes, Rhonda's granddaddy, was home. I frantically banged on the door, and when he opened the door his eyes went wide when he saw me trembling and crying. He let me in to use the phone, and within a few minutes, Big Mike was out front to pick me up in his new car, a Buick Regal.

I stayed at Mr. and Mrs. Brown's house that night.

I went back to Mama's the next day. I had to; she had Mike Mike. I took out of school for a week so that I could think and get a solid plan together, and temporarily went to the Browns' house to sleep. That time helped me to make a decision and that was to move out of my mama's house at sixteen.

• • • •

"Now, y'all cain't sleep in the same room," Mrs. Brown said, going over the rules of the house. Mr. Brown fixed me up a room outside Big Mike's in the basement. And Mrs. Brown had a plan for Mike Mike while I went to school.

Mrs. Brown had a friend who could help out with the babysitting during the day. Big Mike drove me to the bus stop in the morning, and Mrs. Brown dropped Mike Mike off at Miss Frazier's while she went to work.

A couple weeks went by, and the new system was working. I could do what I needed to at school and my baby was taken care of. One day, I got out of school early and was able to pick Mike Mike up myself. Miss Frazier seemed like a nice lady when she opened the door to let me in. I saw Mike Mike on the floor playing and ran straight to him.

His face had dried milk and snot on it. I curled up my lip. That morning I had put him in a brand-new Nike outfit with the shoes to match, and the knees of the pants were filthy.

"Miss Frazier, um, how Mike Mike get all this dirt on him?" I asked, frowning up my forehead.

"Now, Nette, you know a baby gonna get dirty. He'll be fine," she said, smiling.

I scratched at the dirt and it flaked off. Then I noticed his hands were sticky and dirt was under his nails. I grabbed a baby wipe and started scrubbing him. He was just babbling and cooing, and that made me forget about the dirt. "Hey, Mike Mike! Mommy missed you." I kissed his cheek and let out a big laugh.

• • • •

We were living together as a little family. I was just quietly wishing Mike'd put some effort into what he wanted his future to be. But I couldn't worry too much about him. I had to take care of my own business at school; I was just starting the second semester of junior year. If I could just get through the next five months, then it would be summer again and I'd be officially a senior. But it was like the harder I tried to make things work at school, the more they didn't. The gossips were getting to me.

Wigs were in style, so I started rocking them to school. I had curly ones, straight ones, and ponytails. I'd switch them up, thinking I was cute. One morning I was in the girls' bathroom before classes, fixing my wig. April ran into the bathroom and said, "Lezley, stuff is jumpin' off out here and some girls is talkin' 'bout you!" I knew exactly who she was referring to, and enough was enough. I snatched my wig off with the quickness and stuffed it into my backpack.

A fight had already popped off across the other side of the student lounge. Looking at the small crowd that had gathered was charging me up. Then it was like a ripple effect.

Suddenly, I looked over to my left and a boy had a textbook in his hand up in the air. He swung his arm down in full force, smacking my friend Phyllis in the face with the book. Just like a cartoon, a knot the size of a small orange swelled up on her head within seconds. Fire shot through me. April and me gave each other a look, nodding in agreement. That dude's girlfriend was standing near us. My adrenaline was on wild-out mode, and I took one swing at the girlfriend and April took another. We had jumped her and she was down on the ground.

People were running and screaming. Somebody rushed Phyllis off to the nurse's office.

April and me took off running, headed straight to the nurse's office to check on Phyllis. We made it there, and Phyllis was inside, but the nurse refused to let us in. April, being as scrappy and fearless as she was, balled up her bare fist and punched it through the window in the door. Shards of glass flew everywhere, and pieces of glass cut her hand and hit the nurse in the face. The nurse unlocked the door. "Do you see what you did to me?" she shouted.

Suddenly, a male teacher grabbed me.

"You are in big trouble! I'm taking you to the office and you are suspended!"

"Man, you ain't 'bout to do shit! Fuck you!" My chest was heaving, and I jerked away.

Right then, it was as if everything all around was moving in slow motion. People were running wild like it was Armageddon. Through the chaos, I could hear sirens, and I froze.

The police rushed in like they were SWAT, something I'd only seen on the news or in the movies. I was terrified when I felt one of the officers yank my arm hard. I looked around, and all of us were tattered, dusty, dirty, bleeding, and black. The police had rounded up every student they could see who had been fighting. We were kids and scared to death, and once a police officer's warning came over the loudspeaker, nobody was going to be bold enough to make a move.

There could have been some white kids fighting, but they weren't with us. I know the white people at Horton Watkins had never seen nothing like this before. It drew the line between blacks and whites. You could see the disgusted expressions from the faculty, and the fear in the faces of the same white girls who I used to laugh with or study for tests with. This was bad. Real bad. The police chained us together, and carted all our black asses off to jail.

The police made us all sit on a long, cold, metal bench at the station. "You'll sit here until your parents get here," an officer announced. I bet these white cops hadn't ever seen this many black faces in one place.

I was one of the last ones to be picked up. It felt like days, but it was more like several hours. The next morning Mama and me sat across from the principal and vice principal. My head was down. I was ashamed that I had disappointed Mama. All those mornings getting up at 4:00 and 5:00 a.m. so I could get a good education. I felt like I blew it. She just sat there in her Hilton kitchen uniform, with a straight face as they read off the list of what I had done.

"Lezley, you do realize that you cursed at the shop teacher, don't you?" The vice principal was talking down to me in his nasally voice.

I couldn't quiet my attitude. "Yes," I said, and pursed my lips and folded my arms across my chest. I felt like I was justified because the teacher had put his hands on me.

"Well, if you don't apologize, you are etching your suspension in stone, young lady." He let out a long sigh, and then looked at the principal.

"I'm not apologizing."

I felt bad about what had happened, and I knew it wasn't right to curse at the teacher. I was dead wrong, but I was too stubborn and proud and mad about the girls and the fight, but going to jail wasn't going to get me anywhere. I was digging a deeper hole for myself.

After a few minutes of silence, they gave me my punishment: three months suspension. I could feel the steam coming off Mama's body. It was like my insides collapsed, but I was still trying to put up a tough-girl front on the outside.

• • • •

I had plenty of time to spend with Mike Mike now. That was the only good thing about being kicked out of school, that and how it gave me some time to smooth things over with Mama. Mike Mike and me were still living at the Browns', but we had started spending the night at Mama's more.

My three month suspension gave me time to really focus on the small things in his development. I'd put Mike Mike on his tummy so he could learn how to crawl. It was amazing to see him go from moving around like a little fish out of water to scooting on the floor on his booty. The school had given me the chance to keep up with my studies, even while

I was suspended. I had three months of homework assignments to work on but since I wasn't turning in the work like a regular student, I didn't know whether or not I was falling behind.

The first morning back to school I looked in the bathroom mirror and made myself a promise: "I'm not going back on no dumb shit. I'm going back to graduate."

I stepped off the bus and into the school with a new attitude, but it was harder to get in the groove knowing my baby was at home. He was almost one and was developing fast. I felt like I was missing out on important time with him. It was hard to focus in class. Plus, different people who were involved in the fight came back too. The pot was being stirred again. I tried to close my eyes and remember the promise I had made to myself: *I'm not going back on no dumb shit. I'm going back to graduate.* But it was harder than I thought.

The school was big, but I would see the girls I had fought with at lunchtime and I tried to ignore and avoid them. But they'd go lie to the office and say I was giving them dirty, threatening looks. It was like they knew I was at my breaking point, and every dirty look wore me down a little more. I felt like no one understood what I was going through, and it was like I was in quicksand and I could see the path out, but I couldn't move my feet forward. I was ready to give up.

• • • •

One day when I was picking up Mike Mike something brown on the back of his shirt caught my eye. When I picked him up, the brown stain smelled. I pulled his pants down and took his diaper off. My breathing got heavy and I shouted, "Who's really watching my baby?"

"What's wrong, Nette?" she asked.

"What's wrong is my baby got caked-up doo-doo up his back, which means you ain't cleanin' him properly!" I was snatching up his belongings, throwing them in his bag as quick as I could. Mike Mike started to cry.

"Wait, hold on, Nette. Babies get dirty. Mike Mike fine," she begged.

"Naw, he ain't fine and ain't gonna be fine over here," I said, putting him down, pushing past her to get to the rest of his stuff. "It's OK, Mike Mike. Don't cry, baby." I picked him up again and patted his back to calm him down. "Look, he ain't gonna be comin' here no more!" I wrapped him up and stormed out.

I went back to asking Mama to watch Mike Mike after that. I tried even spending the night at her house more so that Mike Mike would be there already when it was time for me to go to school. One morning Mike Mike and me woke up to her shouting at me.

"I ain't gonna be able to keep Mike Mike, Nette!"

"What? You mean today?" I asked, wiping the sleep out my eyes.

"Yeah, this ain't gonna work!" Mama shouted again.

She stormed out the room like I had done something to her. Mike Mike was startled and started to whimper. I tried to rock him back to sleep as I wondered what the hell I was going to do now.

I stopped going to school for a week to figure it out. I had heard the saying "the third time's a charm" before, but for me my third time was hopeless. When I went back to school for what would be my final attempt, Mama decided to keep Mike Mike for me. But I couldn't make it work. I dropped out of school to find a full-time job.

CHAPTER ELEVEN

IT TAKES A VILLAGE

"Mama come quick! Look at Mike Mike!" I shouted excitedly. Mama rushed into the living room. The two of us practically held our breath watching Mike Mike try to lift up his feet. He'd wobble and we'd scurry to catch him before he fell, but he'd psyche us out and wouldn't fall. Mama and me were cracking up. I couldn't believe that he was ten months and counting, growing like a weed. I scooped him up in my arms and nuzzled my nose in his little chubby belly, then kissed his forehead before giving his thigh a playful squeeze.

Mike Mike and his daddy had the same birthmark, shaped the same way, in the same place. Mrs. Brown told me Mr. Brown did too, said it was the shape of a ham. I just thought it was the cutest thing on Mike Mike. Squeezing him right there, hearing his squeaky, loud, joyful laugh, cheered me up. There isn't anything like seeing a baby be happy.

Mike Mike was developing a sense of humor and had turned into a little jokester too. I started seeing him tease and fool us even back at my mama's house. He'd take the binky out and hide it in a hole behind my mama's bedroom door. We couldn't figure out where it was and we'd be looking all over for it, then Mike Mike would suddenly come out of Mama's room with it in his mouth and fall out laughing.

I had a lot on my mind, but Mama wasn't really the communicating type, and I knew she was enjoying us being there. Mike Mike had given her a reason to smile again and she was cheesing hard today. While she played with him, I sat down at her kitchen table and started reflecting on what I wanted to do with my life.

Hanging out with Mama today was making me miss being in the same house with her and Brittanie. It was cool living over at the Browns', but there were a lot of things that were starting to bother me about me and Mike's relationship. Me and Mike wasn't getting along because I didn't see him doing anything. He had dropped out of school, but didn't have a job. I wasn't working and was anxious about finding a job. I needed to get an income flowing in. We depended on Mike's parents, and I felt like we weren't on the same page about trying to better ourselves for our baby.

• • • •

Mr. Brown was crazy about some Mike Mike, too, and that boy was stuck to him like glue. Big Mike and me would be in the basement asleep, and Mike Mike's little footsteps would wake me up. Lately, I'd come upstairs and find Mr. Brown and Mike Mike in the kitchen like two old men hanging out. That is what mornings were like.

"What y'all doin' up here? You need me to help, Mr. Brown?"

"Naw, Nette, I got this. Me and Mike Mike is just fine," he'd say in a cheerful tone, busying himself in the kitchen while Mike Mike fed himself out of a big old jar of baby food.

One morning, I was headed back downstairs and Mrs. Brown stopped me.

"Nette Pooh, why don't you go on and go out with Michael today if you want to. Don't worry, I got the baby," Mrs. Brown said. She could see that Big Mike was hanging out a lot. He had a car and was gone all the time.

"Naw, that's OK, Mrs. Brown." I rolled my eyes and went back to folding clothes and looking through want ads in the basement.

• • • •

Fuck! I stared down at the two pink lines looking back at me. I was taking the pill. Damn, I must've messed up somewhere. I let out a long exhale. The last thing I was going to do was have another baby by Mike right now. He was already showing me he wasn't responsible. And I definitely wasn't going to tell my mama I was pregnant again. But I could trust Mrs. Brown, after all she was already doing Mike's part.

"You sure you wanna do this?" she asked softly.

"Naw, I'm not sure but I feel like this is what I gotta do. I can't have another baby right now. But I'm still scared." I mumbled. I was as sure as my name, but I was scared.

We stood at the clinic desk. I tapped my foot nervously.

"Do you have your ID, ma'am?" the nurse asked Mrs. Brown. But, Mrs. Brown wasn't my guardian and the nurse denied the abortion.

I paced the floor of my mama's kitchen. Nina was trying to calm me down. "Girl, it's gonna be OK. Look, I heard you ain't even gotta have your mama with you to get it done over in Illinois."

My eyes lit up. "You for real?"

"Yeah, girl, I heard that too. We gonna go with you. It's gonna be all right." Nina's friend Toya said.

The next day was Valentine's Day. Nina and Toya drove me to Granite City, Illinois.

They held my hands. I was squeezing so tightly my fingers went numb. My heart raced. *It's too soon to have another baby*, I thought, nervously shifting in my seat.

"Miss McSpadden?" A nurse peeking out of the door leading to the surgical area called out. My heart suddenly stopped, and I slowly rose.

As the nurse walked me back, my eyes welled up with tears. I looked back at my girls one last time. I didn't want to go through with the abortion, but I wasn't ready for no other baby. I was still trying to learn how to be a mama with Mike Mike. I felt bad as the anesthesia took me under. Then just like that, as if nothing had ever happened, I opened my eyes. I thought I was dreaming and shot up.

"Lay down, Lezley. You're not ready to get up." The nurse rushed over, trying to calm me down.

I felt a knot in my gut. The room started spinning and my feet felt like they were filled with water. My mouth was dry, but I began to salivate, and suddenly it was as if everything I had eaten over the past week bub-bled up and shot out of my mouth, splattering on the floor and all over the nurse.

"Nette, get your ass up and come on 'cause laying here you didn't gonna feel no better," Nina said.

She was right; it *didn't* get any better. I just felt fucked up and vacant inside.

God forgive me, but I just couldn't afford any more kids.

• • • •

By the time Mike Mike was getting close to one year old, I decided that regardless of what Big Mike was doing or not doing for himself, I was de-termined to get an income so that I could take care of Mike Mike and me. I didn't want to live at the Brown's forever. So every morning I got up and left the house on a mission to find me a job. Mike Mike was my reminder I had somebody who needed me and I couldn't mess up out there.

I didn't have a car at first so Nina helped me out a lot.

Honk! Honk!

She was outside in the driveway laying on her horn. I swung Mike Mike onto my hip.

"We comin'!" I yelled, peeking out the front door.

Nina and me hit the streets, on a job hunt. Nina always had a car, usu-ally a rental. She fucked with dudes with money. You know what they say about them kind of dudes, sometimes they call them D-boys, they have the money, the good credit, and that was like a ticket out of the hood.

She pulled in front of an office building. I gave Mike Mike a kiss on the forehead before dashing out the car. Within a few minutes I was back.

"What happened, Nette?" Nina asked, giving me back Mike Mike.

"I got the application, but I dunno, girl, you gotta have a high school diploma or your GED. I ain't going to get discouraged, though," I said, looking Mike Mike in his eyes. Just then I got a call from my girl April. Her boyfriend worked at the airport and said they had an opening.

In no time, I landed a job at the St. Louis Lambert airport working for

IPS, the airport's passenger transportation department. The pay wasn't so great, but I met a lot of interesting people and celebrities who came to town, and made good tips. Plus, I like that I had to wear a uniform. That made me feel important as I was transporting passengers in wheelchairs to and from, but I was still on the hunt. I was excited because Mike Mike was going to be turning one and it looked like I was going to be able to start saving a little money to get a car at least.

Over the next several months I hustled at the airport and eventually quit when I landed a job at a nursing home where my cousins Key Key and Tonya worked. It gave me an opportunity to check into a possible career in health care that could open up some big doors. The job Key Key and Tonya hooked me up with was good money and flexible hours. I was doing janitorial work, mopping floors and doing patients' laundry. We had to wear nursing scrubs even though we weren't working directly with the patients. I felt proud wearing them scrubs. To me it was the best way to show the world I could do something and amount to something. You would never know if I was scrubbing toilets or taking temperatures.

CHAPTER TWELVE

HE LOVES ME NOT

How does that saying go? "Mama's baby, daddy's maybe"? Yeah, that's how I was feeling. Mike Mike was about to turn one, and he was full of energy and a character. Sometimes I'd just turn on the radio and Mike Mike would get to dancing to the beat, doing a squat in place and smiling. My baby loved music early in life. I suddenly started to feel sad and then kind of angry, because there was so much to see as Mike Mike was growing, but Big Mike wasn't around. That was a shame too 'cause we were in the same household. One day, Big Mike wasn't around and I got tired of just being in the damn basement. I was missing my friends and itching to kick it.

"Girl, I'm comin' to get you and we goin' to the park!" Nina sounded hyped over the phone.

"The park? You mean the park on West Florissant?" I asked.

Fairground Park was one of the biggest parks in St. Louis, next to Forest Park, and it was in the heart of North St. Louis. It's funny, black people didn't used to even be allowed there, but now that the North Side is mainly black we have taken it over. I always had fun there growing up, especially every May for the Annie Malone May Day Parade. That's one of the biggest events in North St. Louis, a parade to support the old Annie Malone Children's home, an all black orphanage. People would be packed on the streets for miles, to see their favorite local dance troupes and the bands marching would be throwing down. You'd be out there looking cute, hanging with your family, and seeing all your friends. But I had no idea it would be jumping like that on just a regular Sunday.

My hair was already done, I had lost some weight after Mike Mike (even though Big Mike had called me fat on more than a few occasions), and I was feeling cute for the first time in a long time. I jumped into a blue jean minidress with the quickness.

Nina and some friends rolled up, and I kissed Mike Mike bye and thanked Mrs. Brown. Then I jumped in the backseat and we were gone. I was excited to see what all the hype was about.

The park was straight-up popping as we inched along, hanging out the windows. I saw crowds of people having a good time. Music was blasting, fancy cars lined the street and they were driven by guys with nice jewelry, wearing Girbaud jeans. I thought to myself, *Damn this is how people do it in the park? Shoot, I might be coming to the park a little more often.* This was a whole new world to me, and I got plenty of attention that day. I had never seen so many black people in one place. Everybody was just chilling, getting along. Nobody was fighting today. The police was just casually coasting up and down. I saw a couple black cops do a slow roll past us, and they gave a whassup nod to the guys standing near us. Today was a good day.

I got back to Mike Mike and returned to being a mommy for the night. When Big Mike came home, I wasn't even mad because I was too busy laughing at Mike Mike, making funny noises. Plus, that day out in the park had got me to thinking more and more about how big the rest of the world was.

• • • •

It was finally Mike Mike's first birthday. I was more excited than anybody; we had made it to one year. He was a baby and didn't know what was really going on. He just knew I was making a big fuss over him. I had gotten Mike Mike all dressed in a fresh Nike outfit, with new little Nike sneakers to match, and his hair was too funny. He hadn't had his first haircut yet, so he was sporting his own version of a mohawk. I was his proud mama, looking cute myself. I had a new hairstyle, blond on the top and long in the back. I called it my Dolly Parton hair. Nina came over to pick me up, but then this boy started crying and having a fit. I did not want him to get snot on his clothes or fall out on the floor and get dirty. I was so done with how he was acting, I was about to cancel his party. Nina just shook her head and laughed at me.

"Naw, girl we gotta got through with it. You gotta have a party for his first birthday!"

We had all Mike Mike's favorite Mickey Mouse characters on party hats, plates, napkins, the works. You would've thought I bought out the party store. Family and friends all met up at Showbiz Pizza and by the time we got there Mike Mike was laughing and ready to play. Showbiz was known for their stage and the life-sized stuffed animal band that played. A big old gorilla was the drummer. As soon as the stage lights came on Mike Mike's eyes lit up, and the band was jamming. Mike Mike was dancing and having the time of his life. I sat back and smiled.

It was after his big party, but Mike Mike was finally getting his one-year-old haircut. He was my big boy. Not just figuratively but literally. Mike Mike was stocky and solid, and my hip and back would be hurting if I carried him too long. A boy's first haircut is a big moment—one that, if you got a daddy and you know him, he should be with you for. Big Mike had said he was going to cut Mike Mike's hair, but he never seemed to get around to it. His little 'fro was growing so much it looked like a soft cotton ball. I wasn't going to keep waiting on Big Mike, and Bernard was on the spot with his clippers.

Me, Mama, and Brittanie were anxiously waiting for Bernard to get everything ready in the kitchen. He pulled a chair in the middle of the floor and put a stack of phone books on the seat. Mike Mike was moving like a wiggly worm.

"Boy, if you don't stop movin' around . . ." I ordered.

"No, Mama!" That was Mike Mike's new favorite thing to say, and it was driving me crazy.

"C'mon, Nette Pooh, hand him to me!" Bernard said, in between laughing.

He sat Mike Mike down and draped a big towel around his shoulders, like the real barbershop.

Bernard switched those clippers on, and Mama and me held our breath. Brittanie was like Mike Mike's own personal cheerleader, giving up fist pumps and dancing around. Then just as Bernard was about to touch down with the blade, Mike Mike wiggled free and jumped down on his feet.

"I tired!" Mike Mike proclaimed, snatching off the towel, letting out a big yawn.

We all busted out laughing, couldn't help it. We were able to convince him to get back in the chair, and Bernard moved fast, before Mike Mike quit again.

After that Mr. Brown found Mike Mike a regular barber, and he made going to the barbershop their Saturday ritual. I just wish it had been with his father and not his grandfather. But I saw that Mr. Brown was once again taking up the slack for Mike.

• • • •

It was Fourth of July, and my relationship with Big Mike took a turn that shamed me to my core. It was the first time, but not the last that Mike would put his hands on me.

I was so happy to be working, because I was able to get my hair done and buy an outfit for the holiday. I was looking too cute sporting a silky weave ponytail, a brand-new Nautica shorts set, my pom-pom tennis socks, and a fresh pair of K-Swiss. Mike had invited a bunch of his friends over for the Fourth. We were all outside, and him and his friends were shooting fireworks back and forth at each other.

"Don't get into a fireworks fight with your friends, Mike, and you see me and Mike Mike is sitting right out here on this porch," I said.

Then, one of his silly friends barely missed me and Mike Mike with a bottle rocket. I was done and got up and went into the kitchen.

A few minutes he came in and we exchanged words.

All of a sudden Mike got quiet and kicked me with all his might in my leg.

"Ouch! Did you just fuckin' kick me?" I winced, stumbled, then kicked him right back. His fist immediately barreled into my back. I punched him in return. Next thing you know, we were swinging at each other. He was way bigger than me, but I was trying to hold my own.

"Hey, y'all cut that out!" Mrs. Brown shouted.

He chilled after that. I stormed out the room, not really sure what had happened. I was stunned; he had never been physical with me before.

Not long after that, he came in the house one day and I was downstairs on his phone line, talking with some old friends from school. The other line clicked.

"Mike, you got a call," I said, handing him the phone. He walked out and walked back into the room, clicking back over to my conversation, but before he handed me the phone, he heard a guy's voice.

"Who the fuck is this?" he shouted into the phone. "You on the phone wit a nigga in my house, Nette?" He was so angry the veins bulged in his neck.

"Mike, stop trippin'! That's just my friend Deron and my girl KiKi. We were just kickin' it, catchin' . . ."

Before I could finish my sentence, his hands were around my neck. Mike yanked me by my neck and lifted me into the air and threw me across the room. I fell, then instantly jumped back up, confused and dazed.

"Mike, they was just my friends," I said weakly, between sobs.

He bent down and gently touched me on my arm. I jumped with fear. "I'm sorry, Nette, I ain't gon' do that no more. I just love you." He put his arms around me and held me close, but I started to see him differently.

• • • •

Mike Mike just kept thriving and growing and learning, and regardless of the emotional strain I had on me from Mike, I had to make sure my child didn't see what I knew in my heart was becoming an abusive pattern with

Big Mike. But I was definitely feeling restless like things were going to get worse before they were better.

• • • •

Money was tight for me, but I still wanted Mike Mike to have the best. So I got him started in preschool. I put him in a Christian private preschool in the nearby township of Florissant. But within a short period I withdrew him because it was too pricey at $180 every two weeks, and I didn't have any public assistance. I settled on a program that I had heard about at the YWCA in Pine Lawn.

I was coming up on three years at the Browns. Mike Mike was in a stable preschool and I was ready to go back home to my mama's house for good. She had been living around the corner from Mr. and Mrs. Brown, on Edmond Street. I didn't tell Big Mike I wanted to break up, but I let my actions speak for me by leaving.

CHAPTER THIRTEEN

BROKEN PROMISES

I was driving a peach Pontiac Grand Am by now. It was used but it was mine with no car payments, and sometimes I'd put Mike Mike in and and we'd just roll out go to the zoo, go to the park, or go visit Granny. We would just leave Pine Lawn. Other times I'd get him dressed, because putting him in cute little outfits was my favorite thing to do, and we'd just walk around in the neighborhood.

The best part of being on Edmond was that he could be with my mama and Brittanie all the time now, and Mike Mike had a lot of space to play. He started really showing that he had a love for animals when I got him his first dog. It looked like the Taco Bell Chihuahua dog. We named him Spike, but Mike Mike couldn't say that so he called him Pike.

One day, I found myself looking all over the house for Mike Mike. Brittanie and Mama were in a tizzy too.

"You think Mike Mike got out the house, Mama?" I asked, opening up the front door.

"Naw, that boy might be hiding under the bed," she said, walking off to check her bedroom.

"Shhhh! Come back, Mama," Brittanie said, turning down the television, motioning for us to all be still and listen.

I could hear the faint sound of Spike yapping and Mike Mike's little hearty laugh.

"It's coming from my bedroom," Brittanie whispered.

We tiptoed over to the bedroom door, and on "three" my mama

opened it. We thought we was 'bout to surprise Mike Mike, but instead we was the ones being surprised.

"Gun-gun!" Mike Mike shouted with glee. "Look, Pike!"

Mike Mike had gotten hold of the baby powder and thrown it all over the room. It looked like a small blizzard had hit. The room was white. The dog was white. Mike Mike was white.

We couldn't help but bust out laughing. We laughed so hard we couldn't even talk.

. . . .

I was going to the Browns' with Mike Mike almost daily. But Big Mike and me were a ticking bomb. There was still a powerful connection between us—there was an attraction there, and Mike Mike had bonded us together, like it or not, but I was ready to move on.

I had brought Mike Mike over to visit and me and Mike got into it. I just wanted to leave, but he had it in his mind that he was going to force me to stay. I broke free from his grip and ran out of Mrs. Brown's house and jumped in my car, quickly starting the engine. Mike was hot on my heels. Before I could shift the car in reverse. Mike was pounding his hand on the driver's window.

"Let me in! Get out the car, Nette!"

"No, Mike! Move, get back!"

He got so angry he slammed his fist against the windshield. I screamed, closed my eyes. When I reopened them the windshield look like a giant spider web.

I was pissed. My hard earned money bought this car. Suddenly, I didn't have a drop of fear in me.

"Really, Mike!" I shouted.

"Well, I ain't try to do it, Nette!"

I was furious. I put the car in reverse and peeled out of his driveway. I priced getting a new windshield, but Mike didn't have any money. I didn't have any money. So I just drove around like that, until I could save up enough to get a new one.

Then just as I was one foot out the door I found myself staring down at two pink lines again.

I had a new job at the Venture department store. I was so happy to be working. I was in charge of the cotton candy counter. As I watched the pink sugary confection whirl inside the large metal bin and swirl around and around from tiny sugar beads into a fluffy mound of pink cotton, thoughts about what to do with another baby went around and around in my head.

I handed a fresh cone of pink fluffiness to a little girl and smiled.

I was nineteen now, and I didn't want to go through an abortion again. But I didn't hardly have my shit together to take care of Mike Mike, and making cotton candy wasn't going to feed two kids. Plus, this was going to keep me tied to Big Mike.

I walked into the house and dropped my bag of baby goodies from my doctor's appointment on the table. "Mama, look at what they gave me today at the doctor's office."

"You pregnant?" Mama was happy. I was surprised. I was feeling panicked and confused.

"Mama, I really don't wanna have another baby with Mike. Will you help me get an abortion?" I asked.

"No, Nette Pooh, you know we don't do stuff like that." Her answer caught me off guard. But I guess, now I was a little older.

"Nette, it'll be all right. Plus, Mike Mike need somebody to play with," Mama said calmly.

• • • •

As I drove home from Venture that night on my way to pick up Mike Mike I drove past Mike's cousin's house. I slowed and did a double take when I saw Mike backing out the driveway with a girl in the passenger seat.

Heat surged through my body. Here I was the mother of his child, pregnant with another one of his babies, busting my ass going to work, trying to do right by him, and he had some heifer in his car. I gunned the gas pedal and started chasing his car. I was a speed demon racing over hills squinting through the busted window trying to keep up with Mike's car. Within minutes police sirens were going off. I was kicking myself that I had chased Mike and was probably going to get a fat-ass speeding ticket. Turns out they didn't pull me over for speeding at all. They got me for my busted window. Then, when they realized I didn't have insurance they had me trail them to the station, park the car, and call a ride.

I was at the jail, mad at myself for even getting in this situation. As the black female clerk was processing me, I just couldn't help but vent.

"Why is it that I'm tryin' to do right by this man, and he just keep doin' wrong? I got a son by him and a baby on the way. It just ain't right, and when I saw him with that girl in his car, somethin' just came over me, and that's why I was chasin' him."

"Hell no!" She shook her head back and forth. "You know what? My sister had an episode just like you did. Right here it says they stopped you for obstruction of view." she said, leaning over and whispering. "Look, I'mma let you go, and I'll tell you right now, if they stop you again, I'mma tell my supervisor I don't know how you got out. But I suggest you go home, park that car, and take care of your business!" On that note she gave me a wink, and I was free to go.

• • • •

I was five months and just wanted to get through the rest of this pregnancy as calm as possible, and I was trying to keep the peace with Mike. Then he came over to my mama's to cut Mike Mike's hair. It was just me and Mike Mike at the house. I was in a don't-feel-like-puttin'-no-clothes-on-or-bein'-bothered mood. I had on one of my granny's housedresses. We always called 'em dusters.

Mike Mike was playing with his toys in the middle of the floor when Mike and me started to get into it. Mike started cursing at me and I wanted him out of the house. Until now I had shielded Mike Mike from our fights.

As our voices got louder and louder, Mike Mike stopped playing and said, "Mama, what's wrong?" His little eyes were starting to puddle up. "It too loud. I scared."

"Mike, you gots ta go. You want a fight, and I cain't give you one. You need to leave, we cain't be doin' this in front of this boy," I pleaded. "Mike Mike, go in the other room now!" I shouted.

Mike Mike ran, but only to the other side of the room.

"I ain't leavin'!" Mike came closer to me.

"Mama! Daddy! Mama!" Mike Mike had worked himself up to a full-blown cry.

"Naw, fuck this!" Mike shouted, pushing me hard into the entertainment center. The television started to fall, but Mike caught it.

"Watch out my mama!" Mike Mike screamed, covering his eyes.

I stood up and tried to walk to the door.

"Get out, Mike!" He pushed me with all his might, and I flew into the wall. I froze in fear. Even he was stunned by what he had done. I tried to stand up, but I couldn't. My arm just clung to my body.

"Aw shit, my arm! My arm!" Tears burst from my eyes and I was screaming in pain.

Mike Mike ran over to me, his face frowned up. The more I cried, the harder he cried. Mike freaked out, darting from side to side. For the first time I saw that fear had gotten to him. He knew it was bad and he called 9-1-1, just before taking off running like the wind with the phone.

The baby was OK, and my arm was put in a cast. My mama and daddy had gone around to the Browns' to tell them but I didn't even bother going. Mike eventually did his regular thing and told me how sorry he was.

• • • •

At nineteen, I gave birth to a beautiful baby girl. I made good on my promise that Brittanie could name her. Déja was born April 22, 1999.

I only got a few minutes with Déja before the nurses took her away to the hospital nursery. It was so hard, because I wanted to hold her and feed her, but she had jaundice, so I had to watch Déja in the bassinet under them bili lights. When they brought Déja in the next morning, I was sitting in the window. They gently handed her to me. The nurses wanted her to get some natural sunlight. She was so tiny and delicate, and I must've stared at her all day, while I let the sun's rays bathed her skin. When they first handed her to me, I was overwhelmed with love.

I couldn't wait for Mike Mike to meet his baby sister, and the day I brought her home to my mama's house, he was jumping all around. He was almost three but was already making sure his baby sister was OK. I sat her baby seat down and turned away, and in a split second he had scooped her up and took off down the hallway with her in his arms like a football.

"Boy, get back here!" I shouted, running after him. I caught him, quickly scooping Déja from his arms.

"Mike Mike you scared me half to death!" I scolded, ready to tear his butt up.

"But, Mama, I love her," he said, looking up at me with the sweetest eyes.

That was the first indication of how protective Mike Mike was going to be of his baby sister. From the time he was a toddler, he loved Déja, and he never stopped doting over her.

• • • •

My feelings weren't there for Big Mike anymore, and it wasn't working with our first baby and I knew a second baby wasn't going to fix what was broke. I wanted out, but at this point I didn't even know *how* I'd get out. I thought finally getting my own apartment when Déja was almost one would help let me do that.

Who was I fooling? Mrs. Brown said she was helping to make Big Mike independent when she asked me if he could move in with me and the kids. I didn't want him to, but she promised to help me pay my bills in exchange, and Lord knows I needed the money. We made a plan that when I went to work, Mike would watch the kids. Day after day, Mike's friends and cousins were at my house kicking it.

One day when I got home from my second job, I walked into the apartment. The television was blasting, the sink was full of dishes, clothes were on the floor—it looked like a tornado had touched down.

"Mama!" Mike Mike ran toward me. Déja was walking right behind him.

"My babies!" I wrapped my arms around them and closed my eyes tightly, inhaling real deep. Then it was like fire shot through my veins.

"Mike!" I shouted, storming into the bedroom. "Mike, why these babies still in they pajamas?" I demanded. He was so engrossed in his video game, he didn't even look up. "Mike! You hear me?"

"Nette, I ain't got no time to hear yo' shit. Stop naggin' me and get out my face," he said, standing up, pushing past me and walking out the front door.

In that instant, it was like I was finally unthawing from a deep freeze. It was time to stop banging my head up against a brick wall. I had enough. I wasn't willing to let Mrs. Brown pay Mike's way anymore. He had to go.

• • • •

It was the day before my birthday, December 18, and I didn't need to turn another year older living this lie and pretending things were OK with Mike. I was glad he had started moving out. I dreaded that he was coming by tonight to get more of this things. I was in a festive mood, trying to get ready for my big party the next night. My cousin, Nina, and me were going to put up decorations and cook. We were just hanging out, listening to music, having some drinks. Mike Mike was playing in the living room and I was holding Déja.

Big Mike showed up like a dark cloud. When he walked into the apartment his face tightened when he saw Nina and my cousin. He never liked them.

"I'm finna get the rest of my shit," Mike said. He had some words for my cousin and Nina and then he turned to me, "And I'm tired of you!" His veins were bulging out of his neck. My cousin and Nina just tried to stay cool, but things were heating up fast. I stood up and handed Déja to

Nina. I didn't want my babies hearing all this cussing and hollering and screaming.

"Hold up!" I was tired of hearing it and I wanted Mike to get the hell out.

We began shouting back and forth and I got so angry that he was here, I swung my fist at him. Mike grabbed me and we got into a tussle. Nina immediately scrambled to get Mike Mike and held both my kids close. My cousin grabbed my phone.

"You gotta leave, Mike," I screamed. He was towering over me like a big concrete building, but I felt ten feet tall. I wasn't going to let him intimidate me.

"Shut the fuck up, Nette Pooh!" He warned.

"Naw, Mike, this shit is over. Get out! I don't want Mike Mike and Déja seein' this!"

He dragged me to the bedroom.

The next thing I knew he reached into the top of the closet and pulled out a double-barreled shotgun.

"What the fuck you sayin' now!" he said training the gun on me. My eyes went wide. I didn't even know he owned a gun.

"Mike, what you doin'?" I screamed, and we began to wrestle. I knew if I was going to make it out that room, I had to fight. Mike Mike and Déja's faces flashed before my eyes as Big Mike slammed me down on the bed and shoved the barrel of the shotgun against my throat. He started to choke me with it. I was gasping for breath. I could hear my babies screaming in the background. Tears flowed down my face. *God, please don't let my kids see this. God, don't let this man kill me,* I thought.

I wriggled free and ran out into the living room. Nina and my cousin were holding my babies and Nina was trying to get the phone to call the police. She was shaking like a leaf.

"Get out! Get out, and get my kids outta here!" Nina tried to grab a blanket to cover Déja, and ran out the house with the phone to her ear and my baby in her arms. I tried to cover Mike Mike's eyes, and together we ran out. Mike was in the room still. I could hear glass breaking. We hid in a corner of the building. The sirens were blaring, getting closer and closer.

"It's gonna be OK," I whispered, trying to keep them calm and stop their tears. Mike ran out, jumped in his car, and I heard his tires burn rubber outta there.

"Mama, you OK?" Mike Mike asked, patting me on my arm.

"I'm OK, Mike Mike," I said, cupping his little face in my hands. "And everything is OK now. Mommy love you." I just held him tightly and prayed this would all go away like a bad dream.

The police came, and as they took a report, I thought about what I was doing. I saw what this whole night had done to our two kids. But did I really want them to see their daddy get locked up? No. So I decided not press charges.

• • • •

Nina moved in to be a babysitter so I could keep going to work. It was the best of both worlds. I could go to work, but then when I came home I was having fun. She cooked and cleaned, and helped me with the kids. She really had my back. We were having fun, and I was enjoying my apartment. But my finances were still tight.

By the time I was twenty-two I was eligible for my own welfare.

"Do you know you've had six jobs in one year, Miss McSpadden?" the nerdy white social worker asked me in a flat tone.

"Yeah, you 'bout right," I snapped, feeling like all my flaws were on display. What did I want to do with my life? I had to figure out a plan for myself. I couldn't just keep going from job to job. I had my food stamps but didn't have a paycheck. Until I could get a good job, I had to get some money coming in to pay for food, clothes, and day care. I had to get some independence with my own place, too.

• • • •

Sitting in the welfare office was humiliating. I never wanted to be there. But I had to put my pride aside, because my kids had to eat. As kids, we joked and called lean food days "Friday moments." In other words, you got sugar, but no Kool Aid; peanut butter, but no jelly; bread, but no bologna. But I couldn't just keep making rice and potatoes stretch. I needed help with groceries. I had seen my mama on welfare, and I didn't like it. To me, public assistance was like losing, and I didn't want to lose anymore. I took the assistance that day but promised myself to keep it at a minimum. I wanted to get off welfare as fast as I had got on.

When I got home that night, I collapsed on the couch and held Déja and Mike Mike close to me. I was tired but I wanted to read to them and tuck them into bed. After they fell asleep, I told myself that tomorrow would be better.

• • • •

I had a stroke of luck. Brittanie had started doing work in the dietary department of another nursing home called Delmar Gardens. They had a job opening actually working with patients. This was my shot. Back when I was doing janitorial work at the nursing home, I noticed how the patients were being treated. I didn't like it. I knew I could be good working with older people. I could definitely treat them kinder than the way I saw some of these nursing assistants and even nurses treating they patients. I didn't have any experience. But there was one thing I was never short on and that was nerve. I decided to just go for it.

I remember I was terrified walking up in Delmar Gardens when they called me in for an interview. The job would have me working with the patients, and the chance to actually get my Certified Nursing Assistant certificate. Getting a CNA would open even more doors for me.

"Lord, please help me get this job," I silently prayed to myself.

There were four other girls in the waiting area. I smoothed down my blouse and skirt, shifted in my seat, and was hoping I didn't start sweating. In the interview room two white women were sitting behind a table.

"Close the door, Lezley," the plump blond one said with a half smile. I had a dry lump in my throat. I sat down and smoothed my blouse again.

"We weren't gonna give you the job, based on your application," the dark-haired one who was kind of scrawny said, pausing, then flipping through her notepad. I stopped breathing at that point.

"But, errum. . ." My eyes got wide as she cleared her throat and drank a sip of water. "We were very impressed with your presentation. You are very professional, and your attire says you came here to get this job. Congratulations, Lezley!"

I almost fainted and lay right on that table in front of them white women. Not only did they give me a try without the experience, but also I was able to get in a four-month CNA course. It was on!

I worked at the nursing home and then took class once a week, *and* got paid to go. There were lots of other black women in the class who were older, and I was learning a lot from them, too. We'd bring fish-fry lunches, and I even put a weave in a coworker's hair. When I went in front of the state board, I passed the test and got a fifty-cent raise and a title change.

The biggest lesson I had to learn when it came to health care was to how to keep my emotions in check. I was proud that I was the kind of person who spoke my mind, but my mouth would also get me in trouble, and it lived up to its reputation for sure the day me and another CNA had an argument. I didn't like how she was taking care of one of the patients, and we broke the rules and argued in front of the patient. I got fired on the spot.

I was back to square one.

• • • •

One night Nina and me were going out. I was ready to kick it at the haunted house down on the riverfront. I dropped the kids off at Mrs. Brown's house. When I made it back to Nina's car, I let out a breath.

"Whew, girl, I was so glad Mike's ass wasn't there," I said.

"Girl, that nigga crazy. I don't know how you deal with it!"

We pulled off and turned the music up loud. We had just gotten a block away from the Browns' when I saw Mike running toward the car.

"Damn, Nina, there he go, fuck!"

"I gotta stop; ain't no other way for us to go," she said, worried.

She slowed down at the corner stop sign, and before I could lock my door, Mike ran up to the car and ripped my door open.

"Get yo' ass out the car, Nette!" he shouted, reaching toward me with his big hands.

"Hold up, Mike!" I started swinging. "Why you doin' this?" I screamed. I kicked and punched as hard as I could, but I wasn't a match for his strength.

Just then he swooped down with his right arm and pulled my wig off. All I could hear was Nina's screams. "Mike, let Nette go, please!" She was crying, too.

"So now you just gon' be out like some ho?" Mike said, punching me.

I was blocking my face, praying that he would stop hitting me. Suddenly, he did stop and pushed me down in the street. Nina helped me up. My hair was all over my head, and my head was throbbing from him pulling my hair, but I had managed to protect my face.

"You feel like a man now, Mike? You got yo' shit off now?" I was so angry and hurt that I was spitting as I shouted.

"Fuck you, Nette!" he said, brushing his clothes down and walking away.

Nina wiped my face off. I was busted up with bruises, but I put myself back together.

That was the last time Mike hit me. I was determined he wasn't going to stop my flow. I wasn't married or on anybody's lockdown. I was young and free and working on getting me in order.

PART TWO

CHAPTER FOURTEEN

FOOD ON THE TABLE

My days were filled with running around trying to get everything done—paying bills, cleaning the house, working at F&G Foods, shuttling the kids to school, to Mrs. Brown's, and to Mama's. There wasn't even time to breathe. But, busy as I was, I could feel myself smiling more, and the kids seemed happy. But men have a way of coming around, just when a woman has found calm waters.

I would see Andre around the Walnut Park area. Walnut Park was in North City near where we lived on Mimika and Emma. Everybody knew him and gave him respect, and in the hood that made you "the Man."

Andre's hood props were mainly because in the streets he was a small-time dealer, the local bud man. He was a couple years younger than me, and if I was out in the streets with friends, he'd try to holler, but I was like, "Boy, please." I didn't think anything of it until one day while I was at work I looked out the door and saw a brand-new, spotless, white Regal pull up and park. It was Andre.

"What you doing here, Andre?" I asked, giving him a skeptical look.

"Lezley, that's my son!" Rita called out from the back. Andre was grinning so hard his face could have broke.

"Lezley, my son really like you," she said, pulling me to the side. "Now, I told him he can't handle you. You got two kids and you ain't got no time to play no games."

I fanned him and Rita off and wasn't thinking about no Andre, but then he started showing up, waiting on me to get off work, or he'd bring me something to eat. The more we talked, the more I started liking him.

Andre started making me feel important. My flaws didn't bother him. Andre showed me attention. He treated me like a lady.

But I was still trying to tighten my life up so I was taking it really slow. Besides, I wanted to really know the man before I got involved again. I need someone who could love me enough and love my kids as well.

I didn't renew my lease on my apartment because I couldn't afford it by myself. So me and the kids moved back home to Mama's on Edmond.

When Andre brought Déja a battery powered car for her second birthday, Mike was standing across the street with some friends. He just watched us.

Three days later, Mike came driving down the street with a friend. He saw me sitting in the car with Andre and he threw a bottle at his car, shattering one of Andre's windows. Andre got so mad, he burned rubber down the block trying to get back to his house. I tried to calm him down, but there was no getting through to him. Next thing I knew he was out of the car and had jumped in his other car and left me behind.

When I got back to my mama's house I found out that Mike and Andre had had a run in and Andre had used his gun. Luckily nobody got shot. At that point, I couldn't communicate with Mike anymore, and I had to put Andre on ice. I was distraught. I had to decide if I was going to end my relationship with Andre or not.

Mike was still living with his parents. I hated being so close to where he was, but it meant the kids still got a lot of time with the Browns and we were close to Pine Lawn Elementary where Mike Mike was going to go that fall.

It was a big moment for me to drop Mike Mike off at Kindergarten on his first day. I wanted the teacher to know how special he was to me.

Taking Mike Mike to school and kissing him goodbye was one of my favorite parts of the day, that and getting him ready.

I was a young mama and I loved dressing him up, especially when he went to school. Mike Mike had always been a husky kid, short and chunky, and making sure his clothes had a good fit was challenging at times. Mrs. Brown would cut, hem, sew, nip, and tuck, and we would get him right. His hair was always in a fresh low cut.

Before I knew it, he was in second grade. I had a meeting with his teacher who was concerned that Mike Mike was facing some challenges.

"Miss McSpadden, we think Michael has ADHD, attention deficit hyperactivity disorder. He is having difficulty concentrating." She was very matter-of-fact. "They have medicines for this type of thing."

I cocked my head to the side, trying to process what she had just said to me. "Hold up, ma'am. Are you saying something is wrong with my son?"

"It's a learning disorder," she said.

"What do you mean learning disorder? He learns perfectly fine at home. He plays video games, puts puzzles together, and he recites things back to me." I swallowed hard to keep from being emotional. I don't know what kid his age is going to pay attention the whole time.

"Well, Miss McSpadden, it's just an observation. The school can help if you decide to get further evaluation."

"Thank you for your observation, ma'am, but with all due respect, I observe him every day. We don't need any medicine." I grabbed my purse. "We are going to be all right, I'll take my son to his doctor to get a proper evalutation," I said politely and strutted out that room.

I was smart enough to know that a whole bunch of medicine can't be good for anybody, let alone a kid.

I took him to the doctors anyway, just to be safe. They immediately gave him a prescription of Aderall. Mama gave him the medicine once in his food and it had Mike Mike walking around like a Zombie. I told her never to give it to him again. I even told the school that. Nothing was wrong with my son.

• • • •

Mrs. Brown got Mike Mike a bike. It was so exciting to see him learn to pedal and balance, and suddenly he was off. I was worried about him riding through the neighborhood. I warned him and Mrs. Brown about him riding off her street. Pine Lawn might not be the projects, but it was rough over there, known for gangs. I wanted an adult to have him in sight. I didn't want him riding around the corner on Crescent or Lorraine. These kids were capable of taking his bike, and I didn't want him to get hurt.

Sure enough, not long after he got the bike, I was in the car with Andre when his phone rang.

I could hear Mike Mike talking fast, "Andre, some boy knocked me off my bike and took it!"

His words were choppy, he was crying so hard. I was anxious, trying to get the phone from Andre. He waved me off.

"Hold up, Mike Mike. Calm down," Andre said.

"What happened?" I couldn't hear Mike Mike's voice no more. "Uh-huh, OK. I'm on my way."

I was a nervous wreck and Andre wouldn't tell me anything. He just pressed his foot on the gas to get us to Pine Lawn faster.

"Mike Mike, who got your bike?" I demanded when we got there.

"I don't know, Mama," he said, looking down.

"Yes, you do, damn it!" I was getting revved up.

"Hold on, Lezley. He a boy; I know where he coming from. Don't worry, Mike Mike. You wait here."

Andre told Mike Mike to get in the car. Within minutes they spotted the kid sitting on Mike Mike's bike. Andre grabbed the kid by his collar and made him give Mike Mike's bike back. Andre didn't hurt the kid, but he put some fear in him.

Andre could be so attentive and caring and giving. But on the flipside he was becoming more and more controlling. He would snap on me when we'd be talking, and the next thing you know we were arguing and cursing each other out. But when he was taking care of my baby, I was happy.

When they pushed the bike up the walkway Mike Mike was so excited it was as if Superman had come to his rescue.

Mike Mike was always my child who didn't ask for much and whenever somebody did something for him, he was grateful. He was bigger than most of the kids in his class and that made him a little self-conscious. He wouldn't even take his shirt off when he went swimming. At the same time, everyone at school seemed to like Mike Mike. We got through ADHD evaluations. I just kept pushing him to be the best he could be. I was a single mother, but I always let my presence be known at his school. So if the teachers could give him a little extra help in reading or writing, that's what I made sure happened. I was determined to make the school see how special he was.

We hit a bump when he had a scuffle with two boys who double-teamed him at school in a fight. I freaked out when the principal called. I raced through the front door of Pine Lawn Elementary and burst into the principal's office. I spotted a kid who was wearing French braids and one of his braids had been pulled loose. Another kid was sitting nearby and his shirt was half outta his pants. I was afraid to see my child with a black eye, a busted lip, or worse. But when I found him sitting at a desk in a small area off the principal's office perfectly fine, I was confused.

Mike Mike was quietly eating his lunch just like nothing had happened.

"Hi, Mama!" He said totally unbothered.

Ms. Baker, the principal, was a petite, skinny white lady. She looked kind of nervous when she saw me coming because she knew I didn't play when it came to Mike Mike or Déja. I was always up at his school—picking him up, going to parent-teacher conferences, or making sure he got that little bit of extra help in reading and writing.

"Ms. Baker, this isn't how my son's been taught. He doesn't act like this!" I pleaded.

She asked me to calm down, then explained that the three boys had gotten into it at lunch. As punishment she had each of them write an essay on nonviolence. Mike Mike chose to write about Martin Luther King Jr. and she wanted to highlight him at the Board of Education. She thought it would be inspiring for all the kids to hear Mike Mike's words.

I was speechless and filled with pride. I knew that it wasn't a good thing that he had had the fight with the boys. But that he had written something that even the principal was proud of took my breath away.

On the day of the assembly, Mike Mike stood in front of a microphone and bravely read his essay out loud. Mike Mike had his family there cheering him on. When he finished reading, they gave him a big gold sticker.

"Mama! Look they gave me a gold sheriff's badge," he bragged.

"Mike Mike that's not a badge, it's a gold star and it means you're officially smart."

My heart felt so big. I was crying as I told him how proud I was of him and hugged him hard.

Sometimes, with all three of us running around so much, I worried that he didn't know how proud I was of him and what a help he always was to me.

With Mike Mike and Déja both in school now. It was getting harder to juggle getting them back and forth and keeping a job that had reasonable hours. But I had started working at the Abbey Nursing Home. Miss Vivian was my charge nurse and supervisor, and it was a lifesaver when she told me I could bring my kids there after school. My coworkers were cool too, but I was still nervous about bringing the kids to work.

The first afternoon I did it, I took one of my breaks just before they got out and went to pick them up. Andre would come get them after they did their homework and take them to my mama's house.

Before we went inside, I explained the rules one last time. "Now y'all know you at Mama's job. This is how I pay the bills and keep food on the table and clothes on y'all's backs. So y'all gotta be quiet and mind your manners. Mike Mike, remember you the oldest, so I'm dependin' on you."

"Yes, Mama," Mike Mike nodded and grabbed Déja 's hand.

"Déja, make sure you listen to your brother," I said, turning to her.

"Okay, Mama," she said, gripping Mike Mike's hand tightly.

I put them in an empty room and gave one last warning. "Mike Mike, what you gonna do?"

"I'mma sit here and wait on Mama 'cause she gonna be back here soon!" he proudly repeated. I couldn't help but smile.

Sure enough, it being an unfamiliar place, those little rug rats got out of that room and started looking for me. One of my coworkers caught them wandering and ran and got me. Mike Mike was leading Déja around;

she followed his every move. I had to chuckle at how cute they were.

We had got on a good routine at my job. I'd see a couple clients, then check on them.

"Mama, Déja in here scared," he said, laughing.

"Stop!" Déja would swat him and poke her lip out.

"Mama, Déja scared of the old people because they be slobbin' and some of 'em got their tongues hangin' out," he laughed, sticking his tongue out his mouth.

"Mike Mike stop that!" I didn't want anybody to see him, but I was struggling to hold my laugh in.

CHAPTER FIFTEEN

GHETTO ROSE

Me and Andre were far from perfect, but he always made up for any problems by taking care of me when it came to money. He even got me a car. I saw that this was his way of having control, but I put up with his attitude and behavior.

Andre was getting bigger in the streets and so was his ego. We got an apartment together, but within a matter of weeks he was showing me signs that felt like a man cheating. He didn't come home for two weekends in a row. Mama was impressed with Andre. So when I told her I was going to put him out she tried to convince me not to do it.

"Nette, this man payin' all the bills, and takin' care of you. You need to be with him."

"Mama, I got a job. I can pay my own bills!"

I didn't care. When he finally got back in, I put him out. He tried to explain that him being gone was part of his lifestyle. He was a D-Boy, and sometimes they just had to be out all night to make money. Some women can handle it. Some can't. I was definitely beginning to wonder which one I was. I knew he had to hustle, but I also wanted him home with me. Even though the question of whether or not I really wanted to be with a man in the streets like that was in the back of my mind, I decided to stick it out, and stay with him.

• • • •

That good news for our family was that Mama was about to welcome another grandbaby. Brittanie was pregnant with her first child, a girl.

The night she went into labor, she came and frantically woke me up. I was half-asleep on the couch in Mama's TV room and I could hear Brittanie talking to Mama. Then, she came in and held up her hand, "Mama said this looked like a chicken bone."

"Girl, that's your mucus plug."

Neither one of us believed her until her water broke just as the ambulance arrived. I dropped the kids off at Mrs. Brown's on the way to the hospital. Mama stayed in the waiting room with Déja, and I was in the room with Brittanie.

I didn't know what was wrong with me, I had to rest every time Brittanie got done pushing, but I was right there with her. I never left her side. She gave a final push and out came a beautiful baby girl. I looked out the window and smiled. It was January 19, 2004, and the first snow of the new year was falling. Now it was my turn to name a child. I had the perfect one for her, too.

I held her in my arms, before anyone, Brittanie or my mama, and looked into her tiny eyes, then I handed Brittanie li'l miss. Lakiah Deayra. We decided to call her Kiah for short.

• • • •

Andre always said he wanted me to have his baby. Here we were six years later and two lines were staring back at me again.

Sitting across from Andre I said, "I got some news. Well, I'm pregnant."

"Wow, you gonna have my baby? That's the bomb! I'mma be a daddy!" Andre was practically jumping around with excitement.

A smile spread across my face. This was something that we both wanted. When you with a man and you get pregnant and you know that you both want the same thing it's a good feeling. I was happy he was in this with me. Me and Brittanie both lived with Mama, where I'd stay through most of my third pregnancy. Mike Mike fell in love with Kiah right away. He sat on the couch and very tenderly held the newest member of our family. For such a chunky, big kid he was always very gentle.

My pregnancy was moving along and Andre went with me to find out what I was having. I walked out of the doctor's office to where Nina was sitting with Andre.

"I'm having a boy," I said, holding up the ultrasound.

"Look at this picture!" She jumped up, holding up a magazine ad with a Chinese baby pictured on it. "Andre said this how ya'll baby 'gon look!" She said cracking up. Then me and him busted out laughing too.

"My son gonna be a junior, too!" Andre just couldn't stop starring at the ultrasound picture.

Then one morning, several months later, I was getting Déja ready for school. Mike Mike had stayed over with the Brown's the night before.

"Mama you peed on yourself," she said, tapping me on the back.

"No I didn't, Déja," I said, looking down, confused by the puddle of water I was standing in.

I knew something was wrong. I called Mr. Brown to come and get Déja and take her to school. By the time I reached the hospital with Brittanie and Nina, I was in labor. Andre got there just in time. The baby's heart rate was racing, and his blood pressure was elevated. I was terrified. The doctor gave me an emergency C-Section.

Andre was right there and his chest was all poked out. He was the proud new father of Andre Jr. Delivered September 21, 2004. He weighed five pounds eight ounces, and because of his low birth weight he couldn't suck his bottle very well. So, I had to massage his jaws when I fed him to encourage him to keep sucking. Once he'd get all his milk down I'd say, "That's my moo moo!" So the name Moo Moo just stuck. Andre's phone had been buzzing like crazy from the time he got to the hospital. So, he ended up leaving a little while after the baby was born. It rubbed me the wrong way, but I was too busy looking into my new baby boy's face, amazed that he had made it here after such a big scare.

• • • •

Meanwhile, my living situation was erratic, and I was running from pillar to post, but there were bigger things at play.

Big Mike called to let me know that Mr. Brown had been sick, but no one knew it was as bad as it was. He had had a bad cough in recent months, and Big Mike told me that his dad had gone to the hospital on Monday.

On Thursday when the phone rang, I was hoping Mike had good news, but the long pause on the phone when I answered was the news I dreaded. Mike's voice was empty and weak.

"Nette, he died."

"Aw, man, do you want me to come up to the hospital?"

"Yeah, please."

That might have been one of the very few times I heard Mike break down. He was hurt, weak, and lost. I needed to just get there to see Mr. Brown.

Andre flipped out and didn't understand that this wasn't about consoling Big Mike. This was about supporting the family. All of me and Mike's bullcrap had to be thrown out. We had children together. Mr. Brown had been like a father to me. But more than that, he had a special relationship with Mike Mike. Déja was seven and telling her would be much easier than Mike Mike, who was ten now. He was maturing and I worried he'd have more questions than I had answers for. I had to tell him that the man who'd been his hero was gone.

I sat down next to Mike Mike and Déja on the couch. I was shaking, trying to keep my emotions together. I wouldn't be no good to them if I was all broke up.

"Grandaddy got sick and passed away." I spoke slowly and took a breath in between my words.

"He died, Mama?" Mike Mike frowned, then lowered his head. His tears started to flow. Just seeing him cry broke me. My eyes filled with tears.

"He loved you more than anything, Mike Mike." My voice was shaky now.

"You think he in heaven?"

"I know he in heaven."

Mike Mike was still my baby, and I held him in my arms and let him cry. His best friend was gone forever.

At the hospital, the lights were stark and everything was just cold-looking when I walked down the long hallway to Mr. Brown's room.

He was still lying in the hospital bed, but he didn't look peaceful. There were still tubes coming out of his body, and the room was too quiet. They had put tape on his eyes to keep them shut. I stood there for a minute with Mike, and when he walked out, I touched Mr. Brown's hand. I closed my eyes and prayed, asking God to receive him into heaven. Then I looked at Mr. Brown and thanked him for being like a father to me. He was a peaceful, kind man. I kissed his forehead and said my final good-bye.

Mrs. Brown and her pastor, Pastor Larry, were in the hall. I hugged her tight. Mike's new girlfriend was sitting nearby. I nodded to acknowledge her. As everyone was getting ready to leave, Mike pulled me to the side.

"Nette Pooh, I just need to ride wit you for a minute."

I was a little leery but said OK. I could tell he just needed to be around family right then, and no matter what, that's what I had become.

When we got in the car, the thought of Andre popped into my head. I know how niggas be thinking and acting, and I wasn't trying to have him or nobody else spot me with Mike.

"Okay, I gotta ride over on Acme and pick up Nina," I said, starting the car and driving off.

I picked Nina up and our other girl Toya, and as we were walking out Nina's house, lo and behold, here come Andre driving down the street. He pulled over when he saw my car and walked over, only to find Mike.

He tapped his gun on the window.

"Andre!" I called out in a panic.

"Hold up, Andre! Let me explain!" Mike pleaded from inside the car.

"Naw, nigga, I don't wanna talk!"

"Andre!" I said, running down the front steps and ducking between two nearby cars.

"Oh, what, you tryin' to save this nigga?"

"No I was just givin' him a ride from the hospital. It ain't like it look, Andre," I pleaded.

The anger was pouring off him, but he put the gun back in his pants and jumped back in his truck.

"C'mon, y'all, let's go!" I called out to Nina and Toya.

We jumped in the car and were off. I was sweating and shaking. I just wanted to get Mike to his mama's.

As we coasted down Natural Bridge Road, one of the main North Side thruways that took you from the city to the county, the car was quiet and I was starting to calm down.

"Nette, stop at Mac Liquor for a minute," Mike said.

"For real, Mike?" I peeked at Nina through the rearview mirror. She nodded as if it was OK. "I really need to get back to the kids," I said.

"C'mon, Nette. I need a drink to take the edge off."

Parked in the liquor store lot, something just didn't feel right. Next thing I saw was Andre's truck riding by, down Natural Bridge. Thank God he kept goin'. My heart began to race faster and faster. Mike was taking his sweet time getting back to the car. I barely let him get in and close the door before I started up the engine. Before I could shift the car into reverse, a green Chevy Cavalier pulled up, coming to an abrupt stop. It was Andre in a different car.

Mike jumped out and took off running. Andre was pacing the parking lot like a madman. My stitches hurt and I could barely move. I was struggling, trying to get out the car to calm him down.

"Andre, wait, it's not what you think," I pleaded from the car. In an awkward move, I hit the gearshift, sending the car into reverse, and me and Nina hit a light pole.

The police had swarmed the scene within seconds. Andre jumped back in his car, threw it in drive, and sped off. Flashing lights were everywhere.

I was in tears, with my face buried in my hands as the police began to question us about what had happened. Nina was hyped up and running off at the mouth, just like she was some kind of ghetto news reporter. "OK, see, Officer, that was old baby daddy took off runnin', and then that was the new baby daddy that just skidded off!" Nina was talking a mile a minute.

The police took our statement, then let us go, especially since nobody got hurt. I think they realized right away that this truly was a hot ghetto mess. I was embarrassed. Thankfully Andre did leave, or they might have caught him riding dirty. That's all I needed was for him to get busted with some drugs and locked up.

• • • •

I went to Mr. Brown's funeral. Moo Moo was eight weeks old, and Mike Mike and Déja needed to be with their daddy and grandmother.

Mike Mike and Déja sat close to me at the funeral. My son, especially, was taking it all in, quiet, looking at everyone's reaction, listening to what people were saying. When the pastor was reading scriptures, Mike Mike was paying attention, taking it all in. He looked composed even as his tears flowed. When he wiped them, he patted me on the hand like he was consoling me. Seeing and understanding death for the first time is real big. He was handling it like his granddaddy's little soldier.

Mike Mike and Déja rode to the cemetery in the limo with Mrs. Brown. I rode with Big Mike in his cousin's car.

Mike pulled close and leaned into my ear. "Nette, let's get married." He was trying to give me his best sensitive thug look.

At that moment I just wanted to push him out the car. There was a time I would've cried tears of joy if Mike had asked me to marry him, but not now.

CHAPTER SIXTEEN

GROWING PAINS

Late one night, I was flipping through channels and found myself watching the movie *Boyz n the Hood* again. It got to me. I thought about how hard it had been for Mama to raise us. I understood why she'd sent Bernard to live with Granny and Aunt Bobbie. Thinking about my life I was scared. I wondered, *Will I always be a single parent strugglin' in the hood?*

I had two sons now. Mike Mike was getting older, and it was dangerous out there. Mike Mike wasn't a thug. He wasn't a street dude. He wasn't a hood kid running around. You weren't going to see him walking down the street bouncing a ball on the way to the corner store. No, that wasn't my son. Then coming back, getting on his bike and hitting a couple corners, causing chaos with no roughnecks. No, that wasn't my son! I was doing my best raising him with the help of his grandparents.

I had just finished a catering job for work and my phone rang. It was Mike Mike.

"Hey, Mike Mike. Whassup, baby?"

There was a long strange pause, then in a muffled voice he said, "Mama, I'm hungry. I don't like what Granny cooked."

"I'm on my way, baby."

I hung up with an uneasy feeling. Ten minutes later I was running up Mrs. Brown's front steps and banged on the door. It felt like it was taking forever for somebody to open the door. Before Mrs. Brown could invite me in good, I was looking around her and saw Mike Mike sitting on the couch. He was crying, holding his face. I ran to him, kneeling, taking his face in my hands to check him out. His eyes were swollen and black-and-blue, his lip was busted, he had a knot the size of a small egg on his head, and his cheek had been scraped.

"What the hell happened? Mike Mike, what happened?" My voice was rising, my eyes darting between Mrs. Brown and Mike Mike. I stood up, ran into the kitchen, and got some ice, wrapped it in a paper towel, and gently put it on Mike Mike's head.

"Well, see Nette," Mrs. Brown stammered. "I didn't wanna call you."

"Call me? This is my son, Mrs. Brown. If something happen to him, I need to know before anybody else do!" I said, taking his hand and placing it on the makeshift ice pack. I started pacing the floor, demanding answers. "Mike Mike, what happened?"

Mike Mike had been at the park two blocks down the street from the Browns' house. The park where his bike had been stolen years before, the park that was still off-limits. I didn't even like calling it a park, because it didn't have swings or slides or a trail. It was like a deserted lot on the side of a barbershop with leftover playground parts.

Mike Mike was big for his age, had been since he was young, and this one boy was always trying to coerce Mike Mike into being in his gang. There were other kids in the neighborhood who followed this dude around with their chests poked out, trying to bully any kid they thought was new to the neighborhood or who wasn't from around there.

The boy had tried to fight Mike Mike, and Mike Mike didn't want to fight him. He pulled a gun out on Mike Mike and hit him in the face.

I dropped my head, collapsing in a nearby chair.

"Mike Mike I tell you what I don't want you to do, and you do it anyway and then this happens," I said shaking my head.

Here I was thinking that having my kids here was making life better for them. But seeing Mike Mike beat up and scared like this was proof that it wasn't. I just wanted to provide for them, but my progress wasn't happening fast enough. There isn't anything worse than a mother feeling like she can't do for her kids the way she wants to. I was mad at myself, feeling like I was losing my power as a mother.

I made sure he ate a good dinner, kissed him good-bye, and told him I loved him. As I was driving back home, I started to cry. The movie hit me all over again. I felt like I couldn't even be there for my oldest son like I wanted and needed to because I couldn't get out of my own damn way with my issues.

• • • •

I had Mike Mike and Déja settled at Mrs. Brown's, and I was working at St. Louis Parking, a public parking lot. Andre's mama, Rita, had gotten that job for me. Moo Moo was about eleven months old when I got the news that my uncle Carl's son got shot and killed over on Goodfellow Boulevard, and the family was all gathering on Acme Street that day to have a memorial for him.

Afterwards, I went back to Andre's apartment. I hadn't stayed there the night before, but was spending the nights there regularly. But, Andre made a rule that I couldn't leave anything behind when I left. I was constantly carting around not just my stuff, but Moo Moo's too. Andre's younger brother, Beanie, was there with him. I sat Moo Moo down and tried to chitchat with Beanie and not deal with my suspicions that Andre had been with another woman. But when I walked into the bedroom, Andre started going off, yelling at me, accusing me of not making up the bed.

He was standing by the bed and the doorway was next to him. When I tried to walk past him, he grabbed me and started punching me in my face. He was much taller and bigger than me. He had me held at arm's length, by my hair. He began punching me in my face again and again.

God just don't let me die. I don't want to leave here like this.

My nose burst open and blood gushed out. Maybe I deserved this. I was gurgling and choking on it, and blood came out my mouth. It was splattered on the walls all over me, him, everywhere. He suddenly stopped and walked away. I stumbled to the bathroom to look at myself. I had two black eyes, welts across my neck and face, my lip was double the size. He fucked me up. He had never put his hands on me like that. I could hear Moo Moo faintly crying in the other room.

Andre locked me in the room for several hours. He came in and out to clean up the blood and was still talking to me real bad.

"See what the fuck you did? See what the fuck you made me do?"

It had become my fault. I was quiet. I feared that if I said anything he'd just do it again.

He left after a while and came back and demanded I started gathering my belongings. Then he dropped me off at Mama Lady's house. Nina was sitting in her mama's kitchen. I didn't want to make eye contact with anyone. So I went to Mama Lady's bedroom and sat down. When she came in I told her what happened. She was an understanding woman. She wasn't telling me to leave him, but she made it clear that I didn't need to be around Andre with no baby or my other kids. She was shocked too, because she took a liking to Andre.

By the next day the word had spread to my family. After all, my granny did live across the street. But I tried to avoid her because I didn't want her to see what this man had done to me. I didn't want to go outside, where folks were coming by to see what had happened to me. I wore sunglasses and put a weave in my hair to help cover up the cuts and bruises, and to hide the patches of my scalp where my hair had been pulled out.

My mother rushed over, and I turned away.

"Why won't you look at me, Nette Pooh?"

I turned and met her eyes.

"What the fuck! That mothafucka is going to jail, Nette! He cain't get away with this." The next day Andre came back to Mama Lady's house to bring Moo Moo some shoes. When he got there, there was a crowd of my friends and family waiting for him.

"Why the fuck you do that to my cousin? Bitch, we'll fuck you up," one of them shouted.

Andre hopped back in his car and started talking shit and backing up at the same time. He skidded off.

My father showed up next, and he took me to the St. Charles Police Department.

After the beating, my family swooped in and took care of me. Brittanie moved into her first apartment, a cute two-bedroom in the Normandy Villas complex, and Moo Moo and me stayed with her for a while. It was summertime, so I didn't have to worry about getting Mike Mike and Déja to school. They just stayed at my mama's, while I hid myself for several days. I didn't want them to see me looking like that.

The state picked my domestic violence case up, and it went all the way to them assembling a grand jury. Now I had to deal with answering a lot of questions about Andre and his life and business. I was suddenly kicking myself for opening this nasty can of worms. I didn't want my kids to ever know what Andre had done to me, or what a fool they mama had been.

Once my eyes healed and the bruises went away, what I felt was shame and fear. But to tell the truth, I was less scared of Andre than I was of what would happen if he went to prison. I was on the fence each time I had to go in for questioning.

Then I just stopped going to the meetings with the grand jury. I still had his child and I was worried about him being taken to prison. What if I had to bring Moo Moo to see him there? I just wanted to get on with my life.

Unfortunately, the State picked up the charges and still arrested him. I hadn't spoken with or seen Andre in several months, and I was happy to be free from his controlling ways. Out of sight wasn't totally out of mind, but I was working on that, too.

Money was an issue more than ever. I went on food stamps. I didn't have a car anymore. I couldn't afford a new one. But, I did eventually find a small place to rent in the University City area, not far from where we'd stayed with Daddy when Mike Mike was born. Kingsland Avenue was a nice residential block. Along with working and my Section 8 housing subsidy, I was able to pay the rent and bills.

One afternoon, I fired up the grill. Brittanie was expecting her second child. I had a little extra, and I wanted to make her favorite, steak. It was her one craving during her whole pregnancy. Kiah and Moo Moo were toddlers and having a ball playing with Mike Mike and Déja. We had the music going and between the kids' laughter and the smell of charcoal and steak I couldn't remember being happier.

It took a year before I let Andre see me again. However, Mama Lady had been helping me take care of Moo Moo during that time, and she orchestrated Andre visiting him at her house. I wouldn't even take him to Rita's place. One day I came over and Andre was still there. My heart fell into my stomach.

He spoke to me. I spoke back then walked on past him. Like there was nothing between us.

I got a notification that my application was approved on a small three-bedroom house in a quiet neighborhood called Berkley, where the houses had small yards, and they were ranch style mostly, with uniform siding.

Things were looking up. I was twenty-six years old and finally felt like I was growing up. It was our first house that we'd be living in as a family. I even found a job that I liked a lot. I was working at Straub's Supermarket, a gourmet grocery store, working in the deli department. I always loved making people happy with food, and now I was going to get paid doing it at a place where I might have a real future.

CHAPTER SEVENTEEN

STRONGER WITH EACH TEAR

That June Mike Mike graduated from Pine Lawn Elementary. When he graduated from kindergarten I cried—my baby was growing up and moving on up—but this was different, this was a big achievement. He'd be going to middle school in the fall.

I was excited to see his accomplishments on paper when I got home from work that evening. He had awards for perfect attendance, and was even recognized as an outstanding student and for completing the sixth grade. He was so proud to show me everything. I was disappointed that I couldn't be here to cheer him on, but he understood that I had to work.

The other good news was that Brittanie was moving in for a while with her kids. Her son, MJ, had arrived, and she wasn't working so she kept the kids when I was at work. It was feeling like a normal household, especially when Mike Mike and Déja would argue about washing the dishes. But I got the biggest kick out of seeing my influence on Mike Mike in the kitchen. I had never given him a formal cooking lesson. I guess he just watched me and my mama a lot—unlike me, he didn't run his mouth when he was in the kitchen, he paid attention.

The kids were still in the Normandy school district. Mike Mike had left Déja at the elementary school and went on to junior high. On weekends when they were home, Mike Mike would make what became his famous Saturday morning breakfast spread—pancakes, eggs with cheese, sausage, and bacon. His bacon was the bomb! But you could only eat it once a week because he deep-fried it. I used to be telling him that was way too much grease, but that was his specialty. Then after that we might spend the day playing cards. His favorite game was Black Duce.

By that next fall, Mike Mike had gotten in the swing of being in junior high. He had learned how to read his schedule, and to get his bus on time. Meanwhile, Déja had found her independence without her big brother at school with her. I had to bust my butt to keep up with the bills, and that meant working a couple of jobs and being gone from home a lot. I would leave before the kids got up some days and be back home and gone again by the time they got out of school. But I knew Mike Mike could handle it. He helped me in every way he could with the littler ones, even basic cooking and cleaning. I had to do a lot of parenting over the phone, too.

I worked evenings till closing, and I wouldn't get home sometimes until eleven o'clock at night. I would have Mike Mike drop a load of clothes in the wash, make sure the kids got a bath, and he would heat up or cook whatever I'd set out for dinner. I'd bark out orders over the phone like a drill sergeant. "And don't let nobody in the house! And don't be outside when it get dark, and get y'all's homework done. " I had to put the fear of God in those kids.

I was Mama and Daddy, but I didn't want to be. When a boy is between eleven and thirteen, he's starting to deal with his hormones and I was having to explain the birds and the bees, because Big Mike wasn't helping me out in that department. Déja being a girl, she had her mama to talk to, but Mike Mike needed and wanted his father. I wanted to put off talks about sex for as long as I could.

• • • •

I got a call on Valentine's Day 2007 that shook me. It was Andre. I didn't say anything for a long time. I had, for a minute, lost the power of speech. He started explaining how he knew he had done wrong by me in the past but just wanted to prove to me that he still had my back and loved me.

He asked if he could take me out again. I know I should've said no, but his words were everything I had wanted to hear.

That night Andre showered me with jewelry and new clothes. He told me how sorry he was for beating me like he did. I was sucked in by his every word. This man was crying. Crying! Have you ever seen a grown man cry? I cried with him. We still had love.

When he asked me to stay the night, I did. He made love to me like he did back when we first started dating. Eight years ago. And it was like every bad, cruel, painful thing that had happened between us disappeared.

The next morning I tried on one of the outfits he had bought me. I hadn't had anything new to wear in a while, and it felt good to slip into some fresh clothes. Andre always had good taste. After that we started quietly seeing each other again. But I wasn't about to tell Mama, or anyone.

Old habits are hard to break, and Andre began slipping back into his old ways, and so did I. The pressure was mounting between us and he'd push me or slap me, and it felt like things would never be right between us and that too much damage had been done.

Having a man around had never made my life better, and I realized now that if my life was going to change it was up to me. And my kids—well, they never had any shortage of love. They had their mama, they had their grandparents, and sometimes they had their daddies. But the men I'd chosen weren't the male role models they needed, and that was becoming clearer to me now that Mike Mike was thirteen.

• • • •

I had been in denial about the possibility of being pregnant, but I couldn't put it off any longer. I looked at the stick.

Damn . . .

I slowly got in the passenger side of Andre's car and let out a long sigh. "So, um, I'm pregnant," I said looking straight ahead.

"For real?" He said, grabbing my hand. "Then I guess you just gonna be fat ridin' around in your Mitsubishi Galant."

"For real?" I perked up instantly.

Hearing that I was going to finally get the car that I had been waiting for for so long, changed my whole mood. Andre's smile and gifts could always make me happy.

I felt like cooking. I had seasoned up some pork steaks and put them in the skillet. Then I put some potatoes on to boil and started sautéing some fresh green beans. Within a few minutes the whole house smelled like I was preparing a holiday feast. The aroma of the simmering peppers and onions led Mike Mike right to the kitchen. He came in with his headphones on bobbing to a hip-hop baseline and sat down at the table.

"Mama, what you cookin?"

"A li'l somethin'-somethin'. Why, you hungry?"

"I'm always hungry for your food, Mama," he laughed.

I thought it was a good time to break the news to him that I had just found out I was pregnant. I had had Moo Moo five years ago, and I admit, I thought I was done. I don't want to call it a mistake because I knew I was going to love this baby as much as I loved the three before, but it certainly wasn't planned.

"How you feel about being big brother again?" I asked raising my eyebrow.

He didn't say anything for a while. Then he looked down and said, "Mama, please don't have this baby. I don't want you to have another baby."

"Mike Mike, why you sayin' this?"

"'Cause Mama, you havin' a hard enough time takin' care of us."

His words knocked the wind outta my lungs for a moment. Looking in his eyes, I saw his fear and I put his larger hands in each of mine, clutching them tightly. I wanted to reassure him that we were going to be all right.

He was about to be fourteen and my soldier, but he was still my little boy.

"Mike Mike don't say that. Listen, for real, nobody wanted me to have you, 'cause I was so young, but that was my choice to bring you here. So that's why I'll forever do right by you, Déja, Moo Moo, and now this new baby I'm expecting," I said touching his face.

I knew right away that he wasn't trying to be mean or hurt my feelings. Mike Mike was a kid and he had seen me struggle, and he didn't want to see me in a bad way any more.

"I'm just sayin', Mama," he said, lowering his eyes.

"You know, Mike Mike, at five years old, we knew two things about you. You liked animals and video games," I said getting him to crack a smile. "That meant you was carin' and inquisitive. Boy, I swear you had every game system from Super Nintendo to GameCube . . ."

He burst into laughter.

"Right, that was your thing. I remember when Uncle Bernard tried to get you into sports, but you wasn't havin' that. You liked playin' outside, but your butt didn't like to practice." I gave him a playful shove.

"Sports just ain't really my thing, Mama."

"Mike Mike, when Auntie Brittanie and our cousin Raquel would take you out to the park or the mall, and y'all would have to do walkin', you'd be like, 'Auntie, I'mma tell my mama on you for makin' me walk!' Then you'd just quit and Auntie Brittanie would have to put you on her back and carry you home from the bus stop to stop you from cryin'!" We both cracked up.

"Mama, you makin' that up!"

"No, I ain't, but I'd rather you learn them computers than run with a football anyway!" I gave him a big hug. "Look," I said, taking a long pause. "I hear what you sayin' about me and this baby, and I ain't gonna have no more babies after this. But you gotta trust me that we always gon' be alright. I promise."

I gave him another hug and sent him on his way. I know he was worried because of all he'd seen me endure. But, I needed him to know that his mama got this.

• • • •

It's a good thing, too, because Andre wouldn't come to the hospital. He even demanded that I not give the baby his last name. Strangely, the pain of childbirth was the last step I needed to break ties with him. I named my new princess Jazmine, Jazzy for short.

The streets got a lotta ears, and they always report back to me. Turns out Andre was having another baby at the same time with somebody else. He didn't want anybody to know about his second child with me.

He ended up showing up at my house when Jazzy was a few months old to apologize for not being there for her. I guess him handing me a stack of money was supposed to make it all OK? This was the same money that was supposed to be for that Mitsubishi Galant. Humph, I gladly took it and was happy to see him leave.

Watching his car pull away, I suddenly realized that what I always thought was love between me and Andre wasn't love at all. In fact, I had never had anybody around me growing up who could show me what real love was. I'd seen a man hurt a woman physically and emotionally plenty of times, but never show pure kindness. I wanted to know and feel what Mary J. Blige was singing about. Maybe one day I'll see it, touch it, and have it. But for now, I was turning the page to a new chapter in my life.

CHAPTER EIGHTEEN

BOYS TO MEN

When I had a lot on my mind, preparing food was always my escape, and catering orders for Straub's would keep me busy for the next six hours. I was busy slicing meat when I felt a nudge from my coworker, who was pointing toward a slim-built brown-skinned brother who was standing near the front case. She and three other coworkers were acting like they hadn't ever seen a man before. I curled my lip up, thinking, *Oh hell naw.* He might have looked nice in the face, but the brother had two ponytails.

They were acting so silly, but nobody else had the courage to ask if he was a new hire.

"You finna work here?" I asked. He looked at me as if he didn't know I was talking to him. "Yeah, I'm talking to you. Are you finna work here?" He nodded yes and smiled.

"Y'all hear that?" I announced to my female coworkers. "OK, thank you, sir. They wanted to know," I smarted and went on taking care of the customers I had lined up.

He started just coming around whatever area I worked in after that. I might be cutting up cheese or slicing meat, and lo and behold here this man come. Outside of the ponytails, he was cool, and he could dress under his smock, but him following me around the store was borderline creepy.

"How you doin' today?" he asked, flashing his big smile.

"Fine," I said flatly.

I shook my head, thinking to myself, *I don't know why he be talkin' to me.* One day I came in on my day off to get my check. I was going over something with another coworker and felt the weight of his eyes. I stopped my conversation abruptly, whipped around, and jokingly lit into him, catching him off guard.

"Uh, why are you starin' at me?"

He laughed, and I shook my head, grabbed my check, and left. But there was something about that moment that got me. He caught my sense of humor, and nobody had really done that before.

The next day I came back to work, and we properly introduced ourselves. His name was Louis, and he asked me for my phone number. I told him I had to think about it. Next thing you know, a female coworker rushed up to me as I was headed out for my lunch break.

"Did he ask you for your number? 'Cause he asked me for my number, and he asked another girl, too" my nosy coworker said.

"Really, he did?" I shrugged my shoulders and walked off. The last thing I was interested in doing was getting in the workplace gossip mill.

Louis would always come around when I was having lunch outside and sit at my table. That day he came up and asked me, "Lezley, you never gave me your number. Why?"

"Well, my coworker over there said you asked for her and another worker's numbers."

"No, I asked the lady over there you pointed to if she wanted something to drink. I only did that 'cause it was hot outside."

I knew he liked me when he asked me to walk back inside with him. Next thing I knew, he was motioning for the nosy coworker to come over.

"Louis, you best not ask that lady what she said," I whispered.

Louis didn't hesitate. "Can I talk to you for a second?"

She nodded her head. "Um, did you think I meant somethin' when I asked to buy you a soda?"

"Well, yeah," she said, suddenly feeling unsure.

"No, we work together. I thought you might be thirsty 'cause it was hot outside."

Louis had settled any hesitation I had right then and there.

We started going out a bit, and I had decided that I wasn't going to have a bunch of expectations this time.

Louis impressed me. Not with money, a car, or the respect he got on street, but because he was a hard worker, he even had his barbering license and cut hair on the side for extra money. He was an honest guy and a brother trying to *earn* his way out of here. I hadn't ever seen those qualities in a guy I dated.

I heard a song the other day by Kirk Franklin. The lyrics were saying that God won't ever put more on you than you can bear. But I was suddenly questioning just how true that was. At the start of this year, I told myself that 2011 was going to be the bomb. I had been dating Louis for several months, and I had finally brought real closure to my relationship with Andre. Instead, I had been just four months into the year when 2011 actually *dropped* a bomb on me. My Granny died April 6, 2011. She was eighty-four years old. It might sound a little fucked up or selfish, but I wanted God to tell me why.

Mike Mike was fifteen, Déja was twelve, Moo Moo was seven, and Jazzy was two. I had gone through a period where I wasn't going around Granny too much, sometimes months at a time, and I would be right across the street at Mama Lady's house a lot of those times. I knew I wasn't living right, moving from place to place, and dealing with men who I had had my children with, wasn't treating me right, or being there for our babies. I didn't want to see her like that, 'cause I knew if she asked me anything I wasn't going to be able to lie. So, it was best to stay away. I was just starting to come around her more, and now it was too late.

Granny was the glue to our family. Sitting in the church listening to the eulogy, I had a revelation. This woman had made something out of herself, coming from Mississippi with not a lot of education, then making a life here in St. Louis and raising eight kids. Even with all the mistakes I've made, I suddenly saw that if Granny could do it, so could I. I began to cry. There was so much that I didn't get to say to her in the end, but now I had to show her how thankful I was to have her for these thirty-one years. I had to show her that I could do better and that proof was gonna be in her great grandbabies being successful, and healthy, and me making sure they always know what a great woman she was.

• • • •

My phone rang as I was heading out to work. It was Andre's mother, Rita. I was rushing but didn't want to blow her off. I answered, and there was a long pause.

"Lezley, have you talked to Andre?" Rita's voice was faint on the other end.

"No, I haven't talked to him this mornin'. The last time was 10:30 last night. He brought my Moo Moo home. But he was supposed to come back and get Moo Moo this mornin' for school, and he never showed up."

As soon as we hung up, I texted him: YOUR MOM IS TRYIN' TO GET IN TOUCH WITH U. U NEED TO CALL HER.

I got no response.

I went to work. Nothing was really on my mind, but I just felt strange. I got back home after picking all four of my kids up from school. I had even seasoned up some meat and had some tacos cooking on the stove. The smell of the onions and cumin was filling up the house. And, one by one they made their way to the kitchen. I fixed each of them a plate and the kids tore those tacos up.

I slipped off to my room for a quick nap. I was getting some good sleep in, too, until my phone rang. I turned over, checked the time, and it was 5:00 p.m.

The caller ID read RITA.

I wasn't in the mood for a lot of chitchatting today. I was also hoping she wouldn't ask me if the kids could come over. I let the phone ring a few times, then answered.

"Hello," I said.

"Hello?" It wasn't Rita's voice on the other end.

I sat up abruptly. I didn't recognize the woman's voice.

"Um, you know . . ."

"You know what?" My leg was shaking like crazy.

"They found a body overnight."

"And?"

"Well, you know, we had been lookin' for Andre . . ."

"And?" I was getting more agitated.

"The police had been lookin' for Andre, and they said it was him . . ." her voice trailed off.

I didn't even bother to hear the rest. My brain exploded. I threw the phone across the room. I jumped up and ran out of my room and through the house. My eyes were wide, I was pale, and I was screaming like a madwoman. The kids were stunned. Nobody moved, nobody said anything. I burst out the front door, running down the driveway and into the street. I ran back into the house, hysterical. Mike Mike handed me the phone again.

Andre was dead.

I sat semiconscious, staring out the front window, puffing on a cigarette. When his cause of death was described to me I was told they didn't shoot or stab him, but that he was bludgeoned to death with dumbbells and some other heavy object. My stomach was queasy just thinking about what they had done to him. His bloody body was tossed in the back of his own truck and driven to a nearby creek, then dumped in the water. After that the killers used his cell phones, credit cards, and went joyriding in his truck.

Nobody would tell the police anything. Word on the street was that it was some guys from the same Walnut Park area that he was from. They were supposed to be his homeboys. He loved the hood, but the hood had just proved that it don't love nobody.

At his funeral I found out Andre had eight kids. I was heated. I was ready to flip out up in this funeral home, but I knew I couldn't. I felt deceived.

I started to cry. Andre and I had eleven years and two kids. The more I thought about each of those eleven years, the harder I cried. I was crying for the pain I had endured with him. I was crying for his mama. I was crying for Moo Moo who was six years old, and had spent a lot of quality time with Andre. Andre took Moo Moo to school regularly, and Moo Moo even had a room at his house. Jazzy on the other hand was a baby. She would never really know her father.

• • • •

I was at Straub's scooping potato salad into a pint for a customer when I felt my phone vibrate. I saw that Mike Mike's school was calling and asked one of my coworkers to take over. I slipped into a back room at the store. The school nurse was on the other end, and I was terrified that she was calling to tell me that my son had been hurt. She explained that Mike Mike had come down with a bad headache. It was one of the busiest days at work, and I wanted to make sure that the boy wasn't trying to just get out of school.

The nurse gave him aspirin, but said his headache hadn't gone away and his blood pressure was running high. Something was seriously wrong. I took him to his pediatrician who wanted Mike Mike to see a cardiologist right away. When I heard that, everything in the room felt very far away and I was filled with a quiet panic.

Then I found out that his Medicaid didn't cover him to see a cardiologist. I yelled at the insurance people over the phone. I pleaded with the doctors to make an exception. In the end, Straub's allowed me to add him into my work insurance. So I quickly got him in to see a heart doctor at the St. Louis Children's Hospital where they could start monitoring him, but before we could go back for a follow-up, he had another episode at school again. I rushed him to the emergency room.

"Mama, am I gonna be OK?"

"Of course, baby. Don't be thinkin' nothing bad. We gonna find out what's wrong with you. I promise," I tried to hide my own terror. Mike Mike was a sophomore in high school, he was already towering over me, but in that moment all I could see was my little boy, and I could see he was afraid.

When we got to the hospital, they admitted him immediately to ICU. I was pacing and wringing my hands.

"Mama, what does all this mean?" Mike Mike asked looking at all the monitors they had him hooked up to.

"Mike Mike, they just wanna make sure your heart is OK, but don't talk. I want you to rest."

"Mama, you think they gonna find out what's wrong with me?"

"We gonna get through this, Mike Mike." I just held his hand until he drifted off to sleep.

When the doctor pulled me out of the room to explain what they were going to be looking for, I just couldn't hold it together any longer. I broke down crying.

Mike Mike was suffering from hypertension. He was overweight and his heart was working too hard.

After his hospital stay, they put him on meds, but Mike Mike would complain occasionally about chest pains and headaches. I knew that it was all about changing my son's lifestyle, his eating habits for one, and trying to get him to exercise. But it's tough getting a teenager to understand the seriousness of things sometimes.

"Mike Mike, what did you eat yesterday?" I probed.

I seasoned up some chicken cutlets and laid them on the grill outside.

"Mama, I didn't eat nothin' bad." I could hear it in his voice that he had probably eaten something fried or ordered a pizza at one of his grandmothers' houses.

"Mike Mike, you have to do what the doctors say. You are the one who's going to suffer, but it hurts me to see you in pain."

"Mama, don't worry. I'mma be fine," he winked.

I made his plate with the grilled chicken, broccoli, and rice, and he complained. Mike Mike was hardheaded, and didn't think his illness was all that important.

It wasn't until we found ourselves back in ICU and he was hooked up to more machines that he began to take the hypertension seriously. His vision was impaired and he was in bad shape. I just kept praying, "This too shall pass."

He wasn't a talkative kid, but I knew he not only felt bad physically, but that he was worried about what was happening to him. Seeing all the doctors and the nurses discussing their reports in front of him, and then discussing what test they were going to run next, shook him up. After several days in the hospital they released him, and Mike Mike immediately started eating fruits and vegetables and smaller portions, and even though he wasn't an athletic kid, walking to and from school was something that he started to really enjoy doing.

I bought him a portion plate so that he wouldn't overdo it, no matter how good the food was. I had to encourage him to do right even when I wasn't around. I needed my baby to take care of himself. I couldn't imagine losing my son to a heart attack or stroke. He was still just a kid. He had his whole life in front of him.

Mike Mike's hypertension made me pay attention more to his overall health.

So, when, on our way back to Mrs. Brown's house after he spent the evening having dinner and doing homework over at my house, he said, "Mama, I have to sit close to the board in class. Somethin' don't feel right," I took it seriously.

I knew his blood pressure was causing headaches but I wanted to be sure that there wasn't anything else wrong. So, getting his eyes checked was next.

Sure enough, he was nearsighted.

When we were sitting in the doctor's office, I had wanted to get him some nice frames so badly, but I couldn't afford them.

"You like these, Mike Mike?"

"Yeah, Mama, but these look cool," he said, flashing his smile as he picked up a pair of frames—they weren't designer or name-brand glasses, either, they were just the basic frames the insurance would cover. "I'mma wear my glasses. I don't care about no brand."

And he did wear him too—and he could see better and think better.

• • • •

On June 16, 2012, what would have been Granny's eighty-fifth birthday, I got the heart-stopping news that my big cousin, Tracey, who I had always looked up to lost her daughter, Kiera, to a serious illness. I was hurting for her; I couldn't imagine losing one of my babies. How do you pick up the pieces after that?

When it rains it pours. Just as we'd gotten through Kiera's passing and Mike Mike's health crisis, my landlord lost the house we were living in in Berkeley. Then we moved to Hoard Street and Mike Mike enrolled in Jennings High School and Déja enrolled in Jennings Junior High, Moo Moo was in elementary school, and Jazzy was in daycare. It was Mike Mike's job to walk Moo Moo to and from school. I was dealing with the fact that Mike Mike wasn't adjusting to Jennings High School well. He missed the friends he'd grown up with in the Normandy schools, he wasn't engaged at school, and he wasn't keeping up with his work.

But, Mike Mike missed his friends at Normandy and Déja wanted to be where her brother was, so I reluctantly agreed to let them both go back to school in the Normandy district and I would drive them back and forth all the time.

I was nervous about Mike Mike and Déja living over there in that neighborhood, though. Things had changed since I'd been there hanging out with their daddy. Pine Lawn wasn't ever a real safe place, and it had gotten worse. I mostly worried about Mike Mike's safety. He was a growing boy, and there were a lot of gangs popping up in that area. He was big for his age, and I didn't want the boys in the streets trying to test him. I was glad he was so into his video games and that he'd rather be in the house.

I was happy when Déja decided to come back home with me. She has always been my child who would change her mind like the weather. After just a short while she decided she missed her friends and the school and wanted to move back to Jennings.

Louis and me were getting closer and he moved in. I was excited because I'd finally have a responsible man in the house also helping share the financial load.

Around this time, my mama had moved into the Canfield Apartments just off West Florissant. It was a complex that ranged from low-income to working-class. Some were typical one- and two-bedroom apartments in two-story brick buildings, but Mama got one that was more like a small house with a basement in it.

Mike Mike would visit my mama a lot. Brittanie and Bernard had moved into a new place on Solway Street, which wasn't far from Mama.

• • • •

It was the end of the day, and I had just taken my clothes off and was about to take a hot shower when the phone rang.

"Mama, my toe hurtin' real bad. Can you come and take me to the doctor?" Mike Mike said in a muffled voice.

"Your toe? That same one you broke before?" I asked skeptically. Last year he had slipped in the kitchen and broken his toe while I was at work. He toughed it out so long I barely got him to the doctor that day. But I didn't think it was his toe tonight. Whenever he called me talking about "Granny ain't cook nothin'" or telling me some other lame story, something was really wrong. I jumped back into my clothes and rushed out of the house. Sometimes you just need to lay your eyes on your child to check things out for yourself.

Mike Mike came right out of Mrs. Brown's house when I pulled up. It was dark outside, and he hopped in the passenger seat and immediately looked down. I couldn't see his face, so I hit the light. Mike Mike had lumps and bruises all over his face.

"Oh my God, Mike Mike!" I gasped, gently turning his face toward mine. "What's wrong? Who did this to you, Mike Mike?"

"Mama, I had a fight with this dude from school the other day, and then the dude's brother and uncle came over and jumped on me." His voice was low and shaky. I knew he wanted to cry but was trying to show me he wasn't weak.

Tears welled up in my eyes.

Mike Mike began to slowly explain what had happened. "I had a fight with this dude at Normandy. I ain't wanna fight that dude. He just kept pushin' me." He sniffed again.

"I know, Mike Mike," I said, shaking my head, trying to keep from crying myself. He didn't like trouble, but it did always seem to find him. It's like people want to see what he can do for his size.

"I bet it was about a damn girl," I smacked. He nodded. "Did you hurt the dude, Mike Mike?" I asked, putting my hand over my mouth.

"I got the best of him, Mama," he said while struggling to hold his tears back. Then a single tear rolled down his face. "The dude's uncle and his older brother came over and jumped on me to get me back." He burst into tears.

My son was scared. I was scared too. I raised my fists and pounded them on the steering wheel. "Mike Mike, who is this boy? Who is his people? Where they live?" I shouted. I wasn't angry at him, but my emotions were taking over. I felt helpless.

"Well, Granny tried to run out an' help me . . ."

Mike Mike cleared his throat and explained how Mrs. Brown had gotten pushed to the ground in the scuffle. What kinda grown men would jump on a teenager and then rough up his grandmother? I had no words that I could get out. I dropped my head.

I got Mike Mike's wounds cleaned up and him settled, and made sure he got himself ready for bed. I walked outta Mrs. Brown's house—my heart was racing, my mind going a million miles an hour. I pulled over and burst into tears.

I didn't have no church where I could call my pastor to come pray for my son. But I knew one Bible verse, and now was as good a time as any to put it to work. I closed my eyes and quietly prayed to God.

The Lord is my Shepherd. I shall not want.

He maketh me to lie down in green pastures.

He leadeth me beside still waters . . .

I had gotten the news of another death in the family. My mother's brother, my uncle Carl got the news on May 10, 2013, that his son Terrell had been shot and killed in Sacramento, CA. Uncle Carl had already suffered the loss of another son to street violence in 2005. Terrell's murder scared me more than ever, with Mike Mike being a young black man out here. I didn't want to think about anything happening to him.

I was now seriously questioning that whole notion that God don't give a person more than they can bear. As far as I was concerned, God had some explaining to do.

CHAPTER NINETEEN

MANCHILD WITH PROMISE

September 2013 was the start of Mike Mike's senior year.

"Boy, what is you doin'? What is all this on my table?" I had walked into the kitchen and found Mike Mike at the table with all these computer pieces spread out.

"Mama, don't touch nothin'. I'mma clean it up in a minute. I'm fixin' somethin' on my game."

He was in deep concentration. I lit a cigarette and leaned against the wall. I was watching my child do something I'd never seen before. I thought he was going to leave permanent grooves in his forehead he was concentrating so hard. He sat semi-hunched over. His eyeglasses had slid down on his nose.

Mike Mike looked like a doctor performing brain surgery, placing one tiny computer piece after another tiny piece inside other larger computer chip pieces. Then he pushed green wires into tiny holes in a plastic box. I was getting a headache just watching. It was like one big electronic brain that he had just put back together. Mike Mike placed the last computer piece in place and then stretched his back and smiled, pride beaming out of him.

"Mike Mike, look what you did!"

"I ain't know you was still in here, Mama," he said, a little embarrassed.

"You fixed that whole computer, Mike Mike?" I was amazed.

"Yeah, Mama," he said matter-of-factly.

"My baby is a genius!"

"Aw, that was just a li'l somethin'-somethin'," he blushed.

"Boy, you really are good at this."

"Yeah, you think so, Mama?" he asked, flashing me that grin of his that grabbed my heart every time, no matter that he'd been using it on me since he was an itty-bitty boy.

"I know so! You my brainiac," I said, leaning in to kiss him on the cheek.

Mike Mike had always been into his video games, but he was using his brain in a different, bigger way now. I just wanted him to be around more people like him so he could learn and grow.

I was headed in late to work one morning after a doctor's appointment and decided to drop off some clothes for Mike Mike at Mrs. Brown's.

I dashed up her front steps and rang the doorbell. When the door opened, it was Mike Mike standing in front of me.

"What the hell you doin' here?"

"Um, well, I wasn't feelin' good, so I wasn't gonna go, and then . . ." He was stumbling and stuttering all over the place.

"No, you bullshitin' me! You take yo' ass to school!" I said, pushing my way into the house. "Do your granny know you here?"

"I don't know. No," he said, rolling his eyes.

"Naw, Mike Mike. Look, you cain't just decide you don't wanna go to school. You don't have a choice. You s'posed to be graduatin' this year!"

Mike Mike looked away. This wasn't too long after we'd had a big fight about him getting failing grades. I was furious but tried to keep my cool.

"Mike Mike, is somethin' wrong at school? You know what? You gonna come home with me and ride that bus up to Lucas and Hunt Boulevard, or I'll drop you off on my way to Straub's."

"I don't know if I'mma graduate. Miss White said I ain't got the credits."

"Oh, I'mma get to the bottom of this. I'm callin' whoever this Miss White is now!"

My brain was in overdrive. I was trying to map out a plan in my head. I didn't care if we had to get up at 5:00 in the morning, I was going to just have to do it to get Déja, Moo Moo, Jazzy, and Mike Mike to school, then myself to work.

I couldn't dial the number to the school fast enough. I fired up a cig-arette. Mike Mike was giving me attitude, but I didn't care. My leg was shaking like crazy. I took puff after puff in between barking orders into the phone for the school secretary to get me to a lady named Miss White. On second thought, I hung up. In person would be better. I called out sick.

I sat in front of Miss White and looked her up and down.

"Well, Miss McSpadden, we didn't even know you existed," she said, slightly sarcastic, peering over her reading glasses. She leaned back in her chair and adjusted her suit jacket, which was a little too tight. It turned out Big Mike, who registered Mike Mike for school since he lived in dis-trict, didn't put me down as an emergency contact. So while he and his girlfriend had been receiving calls from the school, I'd been in the dark.

"First, of all, I'm Mike Mike's mother, and I've always existed. Just 'cause a father registers a child don't mean the mama ain't nowhere around. I'm here to tell you that starting today, his mama is taking charge! I want to know what does my son need and how do we help him?"

I just wanted him to get his diploma. At this point his biggest chal-lenge was getting through the schoolwork.

I developed a relationship with Miss White after that day, and she was doing a weekly check-in with me about Mike Mike's progress and what he needed to do. We were all determined to get him into that cap and gown. But when it was all said and done, I needed Mike Mike to step up. One day she called me while I was at work to tell me he wasn't turn-ing in homework on time.

"If Mike Mike isn't doing what he needs to be doing, then damn right, you better call me!" I was in between preparing a catering order and wrapping a customer's sandwich in the back with the phone cradled between my ear and shoulder.

After that call, Mike Mike was at my house doing homework before I drove him back to Mrs. Brown's house. He threw his pencil down and pushed away from the table.

"Mike Mike, what's wrong?" I asked, putting my hand on his shoulder.

I knew he was frustrated and wished I could've helped him more with the work.

"Is the work stressin' you?"

He nodded.

"And, Mama, that teacher don't like me."

"No, Mike Mike, *she* don't need a diploma. It has everything to do with completin' what *you* s'posed to."

I had to make him understand so he didn't do like I had done for so many years of my life. I had been blaming other people for what I needed to be doing.

"Look, Mike Mike, just like you write your rhymes, you can write these essays. I'm bein' hard on you now because you gotta do this work to get where you need to go. I want you to be better than me, and to do more than me and yo' daddy. I might not have finished high school myself, but you my firstborn, and I know you can do what I didn't." Mike Mike was quiet. He was a boy growing up, and it was hard getting him to listen sometimes, but I know he heard me loud and clear that night.

I pulled to a stop in front of Mrs. Brown's house and turned to him. "Mike Mike, you have to do what you're supposed to do, not what you want to do and say that's good enough you've done it. You are not an adult, and you're not a boss. You gonna have to take orders from somebody. People are always gonna be tellin' you or askin' you things until you learn how to do those things and you become a boss of your own. So get your shit together so you can be on the tellin'-and-askin' end instead of the other way around."

He kissed me good-bye, gave me a hug, and got out the car.

It was a hard period, but we made it through the first semester, and 2014 was starting. I just had to keep pushing him. Mike Mike and me went back and forth so much I wanted to scream, but just when I was feeling like there was nothing else to do, something clicked. I finally broke through to him and he started working harder. Normandy High School got him linked up with the PAL Center. It was a special program that would help him get his diploma that was set up within the school. PAL stood for Positive Alternative to Learning. I felt like everyone was rooting for my baby. I thought about that African Proverb: It takes a village to raise a child. That always meant so much to me when Mike Mike was born, because my family and the Brown's helped me so much because I was so young when I had him. But now it had new meaning. Mike Mike's village had opened up to the staff and administrators at the school, too. I had all the support I needed.

Years back, when Mike Mike was evaluated by the school as having ADHD, I said that my son just learned differently. He had a visual and creative mind. So when I sat down with the administration and they created an Individualized Education Program, or IEP, for Mike Mike. It was set up to spell out his learning needs, and what the school would provide to help him and how his progress would be tracked. So to come this far after he had overcome so many obstacles, I knew we was going to be alright

He was so determined to finish school that he went to both sessions of special classes, from 8:00 to 11:00 a.m., and then again from 11:00 a.m. to 1:00 p.m.

"I'mma get this done, Mama!" he promised.

I knew he wanted it not just for me but for himself.

Slowly but surely things were getting on track, but I was still holding on to my fear that he wouldn't get all the schoolwork done, so I took him to Job Corps so I could show him options for life after high school.

When we arrived, we were greeted by an instructor who was our tour guide for the afternoon. He was a middle-aged, balding black man who looked tired and worn-out, like he didn't want to be there. Even the suit he was wearing slouched.

Mike Mike had a cautious look on his face as we passed other young guys his age who didn't seem like they was doing much more than chilling up in there. Nobody seemed too motivated. We were trailing behind the instructor, so I asked him what was wrong.

"Mama, this place got a lotta rules. It's like a bootcamp. I ain't feelin' livin' up in here either."

"Look Mike Mike you ain't gotta do nothin' that don't feel right. You haven't gotten put outta school. You ain't twenty-five with a record. You aren't out of options. You got choices."

Mike Mike was quiet for the rest of the tour, and by the time we heard one of the last student's testimonials, he pulled me to the side again, "Mama, I realize I don't wanna just go to Job Corps. I'd rather work hard at school and get my diploma."

At that moment I saw a fire in his eye.

"Mike Mike, I'm proud of you for saying that, 'cause here, sure you can take up a trade, but with a high school diploma you can go anywhere, even to college."

On the ride back home, I was filled with emotion. Mike Mike still had a long way to go to get that paper, but I knew he was going to do it. My baby had patience, resilience, and determination.

• • • •

It was a big month of joy. Mike Mike's birthday was coming and we were getting closer to him getting his diploma, too. I thought I was excited, but Louis was just as hyped pressing me to find out what Mike Mike wanted to do for the big one-eight.

Lately, we were stronger than ever. It had been almost four years. I always said I wanted a man who was my equal and I had finally found that in Louis. When Louis and me first started dating, it was just a few weeks in when he turned to me with a playful, boyish grin, and said, "You know if we still together three years from now, we gonna get married."

I didn't think anything about what Louis was saying. I never thought seriously about marriage. But now my kids were getting older, and life was good. I was ready to make him make good on his promise. I was dressed and waiting in the living room for him to get home from work. Louis walked in with his work clothes on and I decided to call his bluff right there on the spot.

"So are we gonna get married today?" I said smacking my lips.

"Yeah, you ready?" he said, taking my challenge.

"Okay but I ain't waiting for you to get changed and dressed."

"So I'm rollin' like this?" He flashed me that same boyish grin from years ago.

Next thing I know we were standing in front of the judge at the county city hall. We didn't have rings or anything, but Louis professed his love and we made it official. We didn't even have a photographer. An Asian couple who had just gotten married videotaped us and we took a selfie. It wasn't the way I used to dream about, with the big fancy dress, bridesmaids, flower girls, and a big old diamond ring, but it was real. I had a man who wanted me just as I was. This was real love, and I didn't have to search, or wonder any more. It was official and we may have done it a little backwards for some people, but it was just right for me. We were excited to start planning for the big wedding and were going to have all the kids in it.

• • • •

May 20, 2014, was Mike Mike's eighteenth birthday. Every birthday was a big birthday, but as I started having more kids, we started picking out special ages to do parties.

Mike Mike and Déja both being teenagers was definitely breaking the bank, but you only get these times once. I wanted to make sure I could make as many of their birthdays as memorable as I could.

For Déja's fifteenth we surprised her. Brittanie drove Moo Moo, Jazzy, and her kids to pick up Déja. I was already at Skate King skating rink with Mike Mike, their cousins, and a few of Déja's friends. Each person was standing on the corner with a sign that had a letter on it. Together they spelled out HAPPY BIRTHDAY, DÉJA. Mike Mike was standing next to his cousin Li'l Don. The two of them was straight clowning, dancing, and being goofy as Brittanie pulled up with Déja.

Déja was all smiles. She was especially happy that her big brother was there. Mike Mike was known not to skate, but me and Brittanie were determined to get him out there today.

"C'mon, Mike Mike, get out here with us!"

"No, I ain't skatin'!"

But I'm the mama, and mamas always win. I convinced him to put on some skates. He was about seven feet on them, and his tall butt couldn't stand up on them for nothing. Mike Mike's knees were wobbling, and we hadn't even made it to the rink floor yet. Brittanie had Mike Mike on one side, and I had him on the other.

"Okay, Mike Mike, we gonna lift you up. Put your foot forward on the break," I said.

"One, two, three!" Brittanie counted.

We tried to pull him up, but Mike Mike was too busy trying to hold his pants up. His feet were just slipping and sliding, moving back and forth in the skates. We was trying not to laugh, but it was hard, and the more we snickered, the madder he got.

Déja was coasting along with her friends, moving along to the music.

"Man, naw, I ain't finna do this!" he said with a frown.

He had finally gotten up but was leaning on the wall.

"Mike Mike, c'mon, lean your foot forward" I said, trying to control my urge to laugh.

"C'mon, one, two, three!" Brittanie cheered.

Then, just like a cartoon, his legs got to moving like scissors and that boy landed flat on his butt.

"Ouch! Boy, you done hit my toe!" I shouted.

"I ain't gettin' up! Take these skates off me. I cain't pull my pants up!"

"Mike Mike, how you gonna pull your pants up and you cain't stand up on your feet?" Brittanie teased.

But Mike Mike wasn't playing anymore. Brittanie took one foot, I took the other, and we got those skates off him as fast as we could, but we fell out laughing while we did it, because here he was bigger and taller than us and pouting like he was five.

"I told y'all I don't skate, uh-uh!" Mike Mike said, standing up. He quickly pulled his pants up and was back to being cool again.

For his eighteenth birthday, Mike Mike didn't have to worry about roller skates, just having a good time Mike Mike style. He had gone from kiddie parties with cake and ice cream and party hats to deciding that for his menu for his sixteenth birthday on out, he wanted me to serve his favorite food: grilled barbecue chicken breast. Having family around was a must too.

Mike Mike sat down in Louis's makeshift barber chair, a stool he put in the middle of the kitchen floor. Mike Mike's teen years brought a lot of phases with his hair. One minute he wanted to grow an Afro, the next he wanted a low fade, then he'd go back to a longer 'fro style, but never braids. He always joked about how curly and shiny Louis's hair was and called him Ginuwine, after the R&B singer. Today, Mike Mike was going for a mohawk.

"Hey, Ginuwine!" he joked. "Can you hook me up?"

"I got you, Mike Mike." Louis laughed, shaking a plastic barber cape out, then snapping it around Mike Mike's neck. Louis turned on the clippers, and Mike Mike lowered his head for Louis to go to work.

"You good, Mike Mike? 'Cause today's a big day. Eighteen, man," Louis said, guiding the clippers over Mike Mike's head.

"Yeah, I'm cool. I'm tryin' to figure some things out too," Mike Mike replied.

"Well, you know it's all about makin' the right choices. Everything you do from here on out is a life choice. No more go to the principal office if somethin' go wrong," Louis said, turning the clippers off.

"I know. I'mma have more responsibilities when I get outta school," Mike Mike said, looking at him.

"That's why you gotta be prepared out here, especially as a black man. I'm proud of you for not ever gettin' in no gang or even havin' a baby young," Louis said.

"Naw, Louis, I wanna be ready for havin' kids and stuff. Let me ask you this, Louis. How long would it take for me to go to school to be a computer programmer? I'm thinkin' 'bout doin' somethin' like that."

"I'm not sure. Maybe a year or two. They gotta lotta programs out here," Louis said, stepping back to check out his work.

"Yeah, I'm thinking about that place Vatterott."

Then he proceeded to hit Louis with a flurry of questions, from "How long was it for you to get your barber license?" to "How much money can you make doin' that?"

When Louis finished, Mike Mike checked the cut out and gave a nod of approval.

"Stay focused, Mike Mike."

"I'm listenin', Louis. That's what I'm tryin' to do."

"And this gonna be your summer to just expand your mind, feel me?"

"That's whassup," Mike Mike said, standing up, giving Louis a pound. Mike Mike turned to walk out the kitchen, but Louis stopped him.

"Listen, one more thing, Mike Mike," Louis said, clearing his throat. "Even though I'm with your mother now, you still the man of the house. I'm gonna always be here for you even when you think I'm not." Mike Mike and Louis hugged each other. Louis was just a friend like that to Mike Mike. He never tried to be his daddy. Seeing them together made me feel like I had done something right.

The birthday barbecue was in full swing in my mama's backyard. I had granted Mike Mike's wish for tonight's party to just be about him and the fellas. I put some ice on the sodas and beers that was in the cooler on the patio and made my way back in the house, because no females were invited tonight, especially his mama.

He might've been trying to do some things like get a little drink like teenagers be sneaking. I wasn't tripping like I did when he was seventeen. I knew he was protected with Louis and Bernard being there. Plus, he was right at my mama's house if he did get a little tipsy. I was loosening up, because he was eighteen, he was responsible, and I trusted him. We had made it through the storms of life and we were here, baby. Eighteen! Louis was on the grill, and Mike Mike, Bernard, his cousin Maurice, Mike Mike's friend Anthony, Louis's son, Li'l Louis, and Louis's homeboy, Shannon, and my half-brother, Leslie, were all sitting around the table.

I spent the party in and out of the house refreshing the cooler with ice, picking up plates and trash, and putting out new food and more chicken.

I finally decided to take a breather. I stood at the patio door taking it all in. I couldn't believe Mike Mike was eighteen. He still had some maturing and growing to do, but he was on his way. I looked over at Louis, and smiled to myself. I was so happy that Mike Mike and Louis had connected and was cool from the jump. Also, I had to pinch myself sometimes that I didn't have a bunch of drama in my life, even with a man around. We had our ups and downs like most couples, but Louis wasn't abusive. To him, a real man didn't put their hands on a woman. Plus, me and this man could cook in the same space. We just had good chemistry like that. We both enjoyed cooking and making sure people enjoyed themselves when they were eating. The kitchen was normally my territory, where I found peace, but I didn't mind letting Louis invade every now and then. I guess this was proof enough that God had a plan when we got together. I giggled to myself and even felt myself blushing a little bit. It's funny, I guess you never know how love is going to come to you when it finally does.

Just as the night was ending, I heard some thunder in the sky. Mike Mike was making his way back inside with a stack of paper plates.

"Mama, move wit yo' short self, shorty! You just so little, that's why don't nobody believe you my mama! Move, get outta my way," he teased, sliding me out the way when the rain started coming down.

"You had a good time, Mike Mike?"

"Most definitely, Mama!" he said, bending down to kiss me on the cheek.

"After you graduate, I want you to enjoy your summer of freedom, 'cause you earned it," I said, handing him a card and some money.

"Thanks, Mama."

He kissed me again.

"Me and Maurice gonna go downstairs and hit the studio. I made some new beats!" Mike Mike smiled and looked back at me one last time before disappearing into the basement, where he'd set up a makeshift studio in Mama's laundry room.

I finished cleaning up and headed downstairs to say good-bye to Mike Mike. The beat coming from his computer had me bopping my head. I crept down the steps. Mike Mike had his computer on Mama's dryer and was punching buttons on the keyboard like he was in a state-of-the-art studio. Maurice was across from him in his headphones, silently practicing a rhyme from a notepad.

Mike Mike suddenly broke out, spitting a rhyme. I looked at my baby and I could see all his passion and promise. These eighteen years had been hard, but he'd come through; we'd come through. He was gonna be fine.

• • • •

While I was working at the counter, I got a call from Miss White. A little part of me always started sweating when her number popped up on my phone, but this morning she was calling to say Mike Mike was graduating with the alternative graduates in the summer class. When I hung up I was shaking all over. Tears began to fall from my eyes. I got chills up my spine and stood up and shouted, "Thank you, God!"

I turned down Mrs. Brown's street and started honking my horn like crazy when I spotted Mike Mike up ahead. I had held the news in all day. I jumped out of the car and ran to him.

He knew that I knew the good news and let loose the biggest smile I'd ever seen on his face.

"Mike Mike, you did it!" I said throwing my arms around him.

I wanted to pick him up and spin him around, but my baby was too big. Instead he swung me around.

"I'm really gonna graduate." In one way, he was saying it like he almost didn't believe it. At the same time, there was a confidence that I saw in his eye that I hadn't seen before.

"Everything's gonna be good now. We been through a lot, but you over this hump and you gonna be able to graduate and make a good life for yourself."

We stood on her porch and hugged for a long time.

• • • •

It was a month before the actual completion of the program, and I walked around with a smile on my face every day. Nothing was going to bring me down, and I had become a regular crybaby. I even cried tears of joy when I ordered him a cap and gown, and the school took pictures. I was at work floating on cloud nine, showing his picture to any of my coworkers who would listen.

"Yeah, Miss B," I said to one of my older coworkers. "The proof is in the picture!" I bragged.

The week the program ended for Mike Mike, my cell rang. The screen read MS. WHITE. I quickly answered.

"We are going to have a small ceremony today. I really want to give you the diploma," she said.

"No, no, he earned it. I have to work. I cain't get off till 2:30, but he'll be there!"

Big Mike took Mike Mike up to the school but didn't stay for the graduation. Mike Mike's cap and gown was at my mama's, so they gave him one to wear, but it was too small. He wore it proudly, though.

I drove like a bat out of hell, blasting my music, singing along with the radio. I was trying to make it to Mike Mike before he left the school. I pulled up, and everyone was gone. I had missed it. My heart sank a little, but the news was too good to sit around wallowing.

I decided to drive the route he usually walked. I turned down St. Louis Avenue and spotted him up ahead in his stonewashed jeans, white T-shirt, and red baseball cap.

"Mike Mike!" I shouted out the window.

He stopped, turned around, and made a slow jog to the car. We were both smiling and speechless. I immediately saw the large brown envelope in his hand. He had on his eyeglasses and looked so studious.

Mike Mike held up the envelope.

"Get in the car, Mike Mike. Let me see it!"

He got in and pulled out his diploma.

"See, I told you, you could do it," I said, admiring it like it was a precious gem.

"Yeah, I know, Mama."

"So where you wanna go?" I was ready to celebrate.

"Naw, Mama, just take me to Gun Gun's. I'm finna go hang out with Brandon an' 'em."

I tried to cover my disappointment. "Aw, OK, it's cool. I just want you to have fun."

I wanted to go kick it, just me and him. I was gonna treat him to a big dinner, then scoop up Déja, Moo Moo, Jazzy, and Louis, and we all just have a big party. But Mike Mike was my simple kid. He didn't want all that fanfare.

We coasted along, headed to my mama's house. Mike Mike turned up the radio and was nodding his head to the music.

This was a summer of celebration. I decided to host the Fourth of July festivities at my house. Louis set the music up and had the grill going. That was his territory. I had all the eyes on the stove occupied. I was in my zone, going from seasoning up my baked beans to stirring my spaghetti to testing out my famous barbecue sauce. Louis navigated his way into our narrow kitchen and handed me a pan of ribs hot off the grill. I slid them into the oven next to a tray of chicken wings and breasts.

Brittanie, her boyfriend, and her two kids had just arrived. Bernard, Mama, and my daddy were sippin' on beers. I was lookin' out the kitchen window on to the driveway at Déja, Moo Moo, Jazzy, Louis's son, Li'l Louis, and Mike Mike. They were all shooting fireworks, laughing, having a good time. Nothing made me happier than the family together.

• • • •

It was hot, and the sky was clearer than it had been in a long time. I woke up thinking about my granny so I called my mama to ask if she wanted to go fishing.

Me, Louis, Moo Moo, and Jazzy pulled up in front of Mama's house, and my uncle Carl was already out front. Brittanie's car was parked in the driveway. Louis honked twice.

"C'mon, Uncle Carl! Get Mama, too. I ain't tryin' to be late to the lake," I said.

One by one the whole family filed out the house—Mama, Brittanie, and her seven-year-old son, MJ, and ten-year-old daughter, Kiah. Uncle Carl was bringing up the rear, when all of a sudden, out came Mike Mike trying to tie his shoe and keep moving at the same time.

"Mike Mike, you comin' too?" I was grinning ear to ear.

"Yeah, Mama," he said, leaning over to hug me. "I gotta show y'all how it's done!"

"Yay, Mike Mike!" Jazzy was jumping up and down.

Moo Moo was trying to be cool like his big brother and just flashed a grin as Mike Mike dapped him up.

Mike Mike lifted them both up and put them in the back part of the truck, where Kiah and MJ were huddled up. Brittanie, Mama, Uncle Carl, and Mike Mike all crammed in the backseat. I felt like driving and jumped behind the wheel, and we were off.

I turned up 95.5. "Funkin' for Jamaica" was on, and I was feeling good. All I was missing was Déja. She was going to miss out this time on our big family outing because she was getting her hair braided.

Today was like the good ol' days when our family was bigger and my granny was still living. I was getting a little full inside, coasting up Highway 270, just thinking about those times.

An hour later we had parked and set up our fishing lines in the water. Music was playing, and we kicked back in lawn chairs. I peeped Mike Mike again, remembering when I was at this lake pregnant with him. Even in this heat, it was peaceful and calming out here.

Even though Spanish Lake, Missouri, was only about thirty minutes from my mama's house in Ferguson, it felt like we were farther away, but we were actually right in Aunt Bobbie's neighborhood which was a quiet subdivision.

When it was time to break out the sandwiches, Mike Mike gave me that now-you-know-I'm-hungry-Mama look. "My baby can eat!" I said, handing him two.

"Mama! I ain't a baby no more."

"Look, I don't care if you just had a birthday and you think you all grown 'cause you eighteen. You still my baby!" I hugged and kissed him.

"C'mon, Mama, wit your short self," he said, chuckling.

After five hours, all the kids was sweaty and worn-out from running and jumping and fishing. All the grown people were exhausted too. Everybody had caught a fish but Mike Mike.

"Hey, y'all, let's roll!" I called out.

"Man, I ain't leavin' till I catch a fish," he announced, before stepping in a soft, muddy area of the grass. "Dang! My Chucks!" I knew he was going to be in a mood if we left now.

"OK, family! I know y'all ready to go, but we cain't leave till Mike Mike get him a fish," I announced. All the kids were moaning and groaning.

Me and Mama took turns moving him to different fishing spots along the lake. Then his line started to jerk.

"I think I got one, Mama!"

Everybody started jumping around, shouting, "Get it, Mike Mike! Get it! Get it!"

Mike Mike yanked that line out the water, tossing that mug up in the air, and held up his fish as proud as he could be.

"OK, Mama, we can gon' and go!"

CHAPTER TWENTY

ME AND GOD AGAINST
THE ODDS

On August 5, 2014 Mike Mike and Maurice were in the basement at my mama's making beats. Me, Brittanie, and Mama were upstairs when the boys decided to get some fresh air. The rain had just ended.

A few minutes later, Mike Mike started calling, "Mama! Gun Gun! Brittanie!" He was standing on Mama's back porch looking up to the sky. He was taking pictures with his phone. "C'mere, I got something to show y'all!"

"Mike Mike, what you doin'?" I asked, stepping outside.

He made us all gather around.

"You see these clouds?" he asked, pointing to a picture on his phone.

"Yeah, and what exactly are we lookin' at, Mike Mike?" Brittanie asked with a frown.

"I don't see nothin'," my mama said, squinting.

"Me neither, Mama," I added.

"Aw, man, I cain't believe y'all don't see that. It's God and the devil fightin' each other." Mike Mike leaned back and folded his arms across his chest.

Mike Mike looked at us like we were crazy. I knew Mike Mike smoked weed. I didn't approve of it, and he knew that and didn't do it around me. Maybe he was high, maybe not—either way he was wrestling with something bigger that night.

"I don't hardly see none of that," Mama said.

We waved him off and headed back into the house, but Brittanie said, "Mike Mike, maybe it's only meant for you to see it and not me too."

"No, just look at the picture, Brittanie!" he said, getting frustrated. To him, whatever he saw was clear as day.

The next day Mike Mike was still trying to show all of us that picture, but his phone just up and stopped working. It wasn't the battery. It just stopped. But something had taken over him. Something I hadn't ever seen or heard before. It was deep. I didn't know where it was coming from neither. It was all about God.

Mrs. Brown had church every Saturday in her living room with her pastor, Pastor Larry. Mike Mike and Déja had grown up being around those weekly gatherings. Me, I've never been a member of a church or gone to one regularly, but I've always believed in God. When I was growing up Granny's house was the centerpiece of religious holidays like Christmas and Easter. She'd prepare a feast, and Mama would dress us in our best dresses and hats. Even though Mama didn't take us to church, we always knew that God was who you prayed to and got your blessings from. So, I've always considered myself a Christian.

Like most kids, Mike Mike and Déja both were bored sitting through those Saturday church gatherings. He tried to skip them every chance he got. But as he got older, especially once he got into high school, he started to check them out more. I think he was finding his own way. He had made up his mind to build his own kind of relationship with God.

Mike Mike was on a mission to spread his message, and none of us were understanding it. He was clearly discovering his own connection to spirituality. He talked to Bernard, and Bernard being a deep thinker, he may have understood Mike Mike the most.

"Bernard, I been tryin' to get everybody to understand what I saw in the sky. It was real," Mike Mike said, sitting next to him in Mama's backyard.

"Yeah, man, I feel you. It's a lotta spirits and stuff out here in the universe," Bernard nodded. "But, Mike Mike, whatever relationship you got with God, that's yours you ain't gotta defend it if folks ain't feelin' what you sayin'."

"I'm saved, Bernard. See, look," Mike Mike held out his hands. "See I don't bite my nails no more 'cause I am not worried," he said pointing to Bernard's hands. "See you still bite yours 'cause you have demons attacking you. I don't know more," Mike Mike said, giving him one of those I-got-a-secret-but-you-don't-know-it looks.

Friday, August 8, 2014

Mama took ill. She was having chest pains and shortness of breath. Brittanie rushed her to the hospital. The doctors thought it was her heart, but it ended up being stress. They kept her overnight for observation. We were all relieved that she was going to be all right. I honestly think the stress had just built over the years, working hard and worrying about making ends meet. Plus, we all could probably cut back on smoking cigarettes like we do. I'm guilty, Mama, and so is Brittanie.

I was at Mama's with the kids, waiting for Brittanie to get back to the house. I needed to feed the kids and make sure she had something to eat when Brittanie got here. Plus, cooking was a good stress reliever for me. Chicken and noodles was hearty and healthy. I had two pots going, and as the water started to boil, and I dropped the noodles in one and the chicken breasts in the other, I started thinking about how relieved I was that nothing happened to Mama more seriously. I cut up my celery, carrots, and onions. Suddenly, as I thought about all that me and Mama had been through over the years, and how we had finally made it to see Mike Mike graduate, and Déja become a teenager, growing into a young lady, and Moo Moo and Jazzy both doing well in school, I was overwhelmed. I wasn't ready to lose my mama. We had come so far in our relationship, she had seen me get to a good place in life with a good man, and even though money was still tight, things were OK with me. The water boiled over and I wiped my face.

Times like this, watching Moo Moo, Jazzy, Déja, and Mike Mike tear them chicken and noodles up touched my heart. Just to think there was a time I couldn't have all my kids at one table at the same time. They always knew, no matter what, that Mama was gonna make something good to eat.

You would've thought some kind of alarm went off the way all them kids jumped up from the table when they were done. TV shows, social media, homework. They all went off to the bedroom, where they hung out. Mike Mike seemed like he was really on a mission, racing back to the basement where he was working on his computer.

Them kids was outta here.

Brittanie opened the front door, looking tired and worn-out. It was a sticky, hot night, and she still had her scrubs on from work. I knew she had to be hungry and made her a bowl.

Mike Mike came back upstairs from the basement with his laptop and went into the living room where Brittanie was. I busied myself cleaning up. A few minutes later she came into the kitchen, tears streaming down her face, and sat down at the table, but she didn't touch her food.

"What's wrong, Brittanie? Why you cryin'?" I asked, putting my hand on her shoulder.

"Mike Mike just said Mama not gonna make it," she sniffed, wiping her eyes. He had made his prediction so matter-of-factly.

"Why did you say that to Brittanie?" I called out to him.

By now he had packed up his computer and slung his backpack over his shoulder.

"Where you goin'?" I asked.

"To Vyron's," he snapped, heading out the door.

"Mike Mike! Come here!" I said, standing with my hands on my hips. He never turned around.

"Nette Pooh! Somethin' is goin' on with Mike Mike," Brittanie said.

"Nette Pooh, yesterday, Mike Mike told me something weird about his stepmother, Calvina, dyin'. Big Mike had told him that she was sick in the hospital, and Mike Mike told his dad that she wasn't gonna make it, then Big Mike got mad and hung up on him. When I asked him why he said that about her, he wasn't tryin' to take back what he said to his daddy, either," Brittanie told me.

"Brittanie, you know Mike Mike just probably goin' through some things. He gon' be all right."

"I'm tellin' you, Nette Pooh, somethin' done took over Mike Mike. Somethin' I ain't ever seen or heard before. I don't like all this stuff he sayin' about death."

"He'll be fine, Brittanie. Stop worryin'."

I got my good-night hugs in and left. I know when something's bothering Brittanie it's hard for her to let it go. I'm the same way. Her and Mike Mike always had a closeness. Sometimes he'd tell her something before me, and I was his own mama. I was sure when he was ready to talk, he'd call her.

• • • •

Mike Mike was definitely thinking a lot about life, and he was thinking about death too. He didn't seem scared about Gun Gun dying, or his stepmother. I don't know what Mike Mike had been reading or who he had been talking to, but he seemed like he had a lot on his mind. So he took it to social media.

In his final days, his Facebook posts, which I didn't see until much later, had a fervor and spirituality that I'd never heard from him before:

August 6, 2014, at 11:40 p.m.
We in a world full of hell and certain people that are chosen to move on to the next

August 6, 2014, at 11:41 p.m.
Dont hate each other love each other as if we were all a big family aint no tellin when u go need the next person just because you fucked up on yo behalf we better than that yall betta step up to the plate and make sum changes flat out

August 6, 2014, at 11:49 p.m.
Its not only one god everyone has their own god and it takes you to bring that god out of you

August 6, 2014, at 11:50 p.m.
Because the real you wants better for you and the people around you all
you have to do is forgive thats all and move on and better thingz will fall
in place slowly I promise

August 7, 2014, at 5:07 p.m.
Its funny how I was raised by church folks but neva read the bible but I
have a full understandin of the illuminati its not devil worshoping it's the
other way around

August 7, 2014, at 5:09 p.m.
I honestly believe that the person that is sacrificed has to be a love one in
order to test how you can deal with your stress

August 7, 2014, at 7:18 p.m.
Trynna heal and feed all my people we shall not fear no evil fuck the BS
be about you business and kill that fake shit with kindness we all will face
the truth sooner or later but for as of now u go either learn or fall off the
cliff left senseless after all you told me to mind my business while I was
trynna stick my hand n yo shit and pull you out of it

August 8, 2014, at 3:14 a.m.
I believe I found the answer to my question to why I feel like Im breathing in water my home boi sis told me she once heard before that god got
swallowed by a whale and was sent to deliever a message to some other
kingdom or something IDK

August 8, 2014, at 3:14 a.m.
Yall seeking for the truth help me bring it out

August 8, 2014, at 3:16 a.m.
The truth hurts like a mug fucka I swear but ill neva give up on you all

August 8, 2014, at 3:22 a.m.
I could use a hug right now FR

August 8, 2014, at 3:23 a.m.
The devil still after me as well but he hatin cause im back and im turning hell into a true fairy tale

PART THREE

CHAPTER TWENTY-ONE

WON'T BRING HIM BACK

When something bad happens—I mean really bad—you find yourself trying to put it all in some order, make it make sense. But when it's something so messed up, sometimes it's like a million pieces of a puzzle scattered out in front of you. How are you supposed to put that together?

August 9, 2014

Bernard was at Mama's house with his girlfriend, Kat. I had planned on going by there on my way home. Brittanie was on her way to get Mama something to eat at Subway.

When Brittanie drove past Mike Mike, she was on her way out of the Canfield Apartments complex, and he was headed back in, walking down Canfield Drive with a skinny short dude wearing dreads. She figured she'd just catch him back at Mama's.

Something was about to happen, but none of us knew it.

"I'm finna go to work, Mama," Bernard said, checking his watch. They left. Mama was there with MJ and Kiah. Déja had just called to check in.

"Gun Gun, you OK?" she asked.

"Yeah, I'm just waitin' on Brittanie to come back with my food," Mama said.

"OK, I'm home with Jazzy and Moo Moo. I'll see you later. Oh, tell Mike Mike to call me."

She hung up and just as Brittanie was coming back in the front door with the food, Kat came running, out of breath, her chest heaving. She could barely get her words out.

"They, they, they just shot Mike Mike!" she screamed.

"Who?"

The bag of sandwiches slipped from Brittanie's hands and landed with a thud on the floor.

"Oh my God! Oh my God!" Brittanie let out a moan.

Mama stood up slowly, thinking Kat must've made a mistake.

MJ and Kiah started screaming, talking over each other, "Mike Mike! Mike Mike got shot? Mama, what is happening?"

"Don't leave this house!" Mama ordered MJ and Kiah.

Brittanie burst out the screen door and took off running toward Canfield Drive, which was just off the short lane Mama lived on at the back of the complex. Mama was running behind her. The last thing she was worried about was her heart.

"Nette . . . Nette Pooh!" Brittanie's voice cracked, in and out of a high-pitched quiver, then they stopped. Between big gulping sounds, she got out eight words to me: "Nette Pooh, the police just shot Mike Mike."

I was paralyzed at first, and then a gust of wind shot through my body. I took off like lightning. All I could think was *Oh God, I gotta get to my son, make sure he all right.*

I burst into the front doors of Straub's, frantically shouting, "I need to get to my son! The police just shot my son! Get me to Ferguson, please!" I screamed before collapsing into my coworker Erica's arms.

• • • •

Mama was huffing and puffing by the time she reached where Brittanie was standing. Her mouth was moving like a fish that had been washed up on the riverbank. She couldn't breathe. When she saw Mike Mike's body laying out there in the street, she screamed.

"Can I hold him?" Mama begged the police. Of course they wouldn't let her. Mama stumbled back to the house.

Brittanie's phone rang. It was Déja. "What happened to Mike Mike?"

"Déja, I'mma call you back," Brittanie said.

"Tell me what happened?" Déja begged.

"The police shot Mike Mike, Déja," Brittanie said.

Déja started screaming into the phone, and then she hung up. She immediately got Moo Moo and Jazzy together, and they started walking to Mama's house.

By the time I jumped out of my coworker's car at the top of Canfield Drive, it was filled with people and police cars. I spotted Big Mike and we both started running.

They had covered Mike Mike's body by the time we got there, but Brittanie, Mama, Bernard, and Kat had seen him. I was going out of my mind begging for information, answers, something. But the cops told me nothing, no matter how loud I screamed, cursed, or punched the air.

Time kept ticking. One hour, two hours, three, then four, then four and a half. Covered or not covered, he was left out like old rotting garbage. Leaving somebody's child out there like the police did wasn't procedure, or protocol, or even human.

My baby's body, underneath a white sheet, motionless. The bullet had blown his red cap off and it was resting quietly several feet away.

Then time just stopped and so did my breath.

• • • •

They took Mike Mike's body away and didn't even allow me to give him a proper good-bye. Maybe I wouldn't have wanted to see him like he was, but I'm his mama. That should've been my choice. They said it was because this was an official police investigation. But how are the police going to investigate themselves?

Louis grabbed a piece of cardboard, scribbled words on it, and ran to the corner, holding up a sign that read FERGUSON POLICE JUST EXECUTED MY UNARMED SON.

I waited and waited, walked up and down the hot concrete, sweating till my hair fell limp and began to curl and kink up at the roots. Who had killed my baby? I was on a mission, and I needed his name. I wanted to know what he looked like. I wanted to look him right in the eye, and ask him why. Why had he, a police officer, just murdered my unarmed son. But all the cops were tight-lipped. They were protecting the killer, but who had been protecting my son?

I was dizzy under the sweltering heat. Brittanie was trying to be strong for me, but she kept breaking down into tears herself. At one point we was both walking around aimlessly trying to get answers.

"Nette Pooh, we need to find somebody . . ." Her words trailed off. Her face had a pained and confused expression on it. I saw a short, round officer and swiftly made my way to him. I was determined to get his attention. He sharply motioned for me to back up.

"Just settle down!" he ordered.

"Settle down?" I said, jumping up and down. I threw a plastic water bottle hard at the sidewalk. The water splattered on the pavement. "That muthafucka shot my baby, and you tellin' me to settle down? Kiss my ass. That's what you do!" I turned and walked away, but not before taking my hand and yanking a piece of the yellow crime-scene tape down.

• • • •

Me and Brittanie slowly moved toward the bloodstained pavement where Mike Mike's body had been left under the baking sun and stood in a daze, and I began shaking my head. "Why?" I called out. The police had left him out there like he wasn't nobody's. But I needed them and the rest of the world to know that Mike Mike did belong to somebody, a whole damn family, and he was mine before he was anybody else's.

A crowd of strangers gathered around, chanting, "Hands up! Don't shoot!"

A hand reached through the crowd and handed me a bouquet of roses. I pulled off each rose petal and dropped it on the pavement, covering what was now sacred ground to me.

More police cars rushed into the area. It was as if they were daring anybody to get out of hand. Helicopters swarmed overhead. News cameras were rolling, and some guy clicked photos of me. A TV reporter shoved a microphone in my face and asked, "What do you have to say about what happened to your son?"

"What I got to say is to the policeman who murdered my son," I said, looking directly into the camera. "You're not God! You don't get to decide when you get to take somebody from here!" I could feel a powerful force rising up in me. "You don't do a dog like that. You didn't have to shoot him eight times if he was doin' nothin' to you and you was tryin' to stop him!"

Each word I shouted made my body jerk forward. "You just shot all through my baby's body. This was wrong and coldhearted!"

"What are the police saying to you right now about what's happened to your son?" the woman reporter asked me.

"They haven't told me anything. They wouldn't even let me identify my son. The only way I knew it was my son was from people out here showing me his picture on the Internet!"

"He threw his hands up! He ain't have no gun. The boy threw his hands up, and the police just shot him," I heard a woman yell out from the crowd.

Louis was holding me from behind, but when we heard that, he slumped over my shoulders and started to wail in a low tone.

"You took my son away from me!" I wanted my words to rip through that officer. "You know how hard it was for me to get him to stay in school and graduate? You know how many black men graduate? Not many! Because you bring them down to this type of level where they feel like 'I don't have nothin' to live for anyway. They gon' try to take me out anyway.'"

All breath had escaped me. I felt myself getting limp, but Louis was right there holding me up on my feet.

A man stepped through the crowd and ushered us over to a prayer circle. Some were young, some old. There were arms stretched out to the sky and toward me.

"Lord, we just come here now, and we ask that you lift this family up, this mother and this father."

His words were firm, and I started to feel breath in my body again.

A woman reached out and placed her hand on my arm.

"We know that you are the answer to everything and every situation.

God, we ask that you help us to endure this situation," the man continued.

The crowd started growing larger and larger. I didn't know who was a preacher or just a caring supporter, but I welcomed everybody. I had never had this many people praying around me in my life, let alone for me and mine. Another man joined in with his spirit-filled message, raising his arms in the air. "You are the strength of our lives, and, Lord, we need you this hour. Strengthen us today. We ask that your will be done!"

I turned back into Louis's arms, and he rocked me back and forth.

I was begging the police for answers, but my words fell on deaf ears. The cop who killed my son had vanished into thin air.

My son was gone.

• • • •

That night, me and Louis, Mama, and Brittanie went up on West Florrisant to stand with the protestors for a peaceful candlelight vigil. But you could feel the tension building in the air. Young people were getting fired up as they shouted, "No justice, no peace!" The chanting got louder and angrier. "Hands up! Don't shoot!"

Suddenly, I heard the sound of breaking glass, and store alarms began to sound. We were rushed away from the scene into a nearby building with NAACP leaders. I watched black men and women, even kids as young as ten, running afraid. I saw people covering their faces with bandannas and T-shirts, running with everything in their hands from car rims to sneakers to boxes of hair extensions. Car tires skidded and burned rubber out of parking lots.

I was furious as I watched all this. These people were disrespecting the memory of Mike Mike, and none of this was going to do any good for my cause—seeking justice for my son. My legs felt weak, and I was light-headed. I just wanted to go home.

August 10, 2014

It had been twenty-four hours since Mike Mike was killed. I still didn't have no answers. I still didn't have a name of the cop. I was sitting on the edge of the bed, a cigarette hanging half off my lip, just looking into space, sweaty and cold at the same time. My heart was beating slow. I don't know what time I woke up or went to bed. The world was spinning one hundred miles an hour around me, but I was stuck on Canfield Drive.

I heard voices coming from the kitchen—Louis, Daddy, I don't know who else. I couldn't make out what anybody was saying. The kids were at Mama's. I needed to check on them and Mama and Brittanie, but I couldn't stop shaking long enough to actually get up and move about. I felt like if I did I'd break into a million pieces. I closed my eyes and the tears came again. This time harder. My whole body began to tremble.

Mike Mike's cell phone was broken, so I didn't speak to him the night before he was shot or that morning. But I didn't worry because he was with his grandmother. I was racking my brain trying to piece together everything we talked about in our last conversation.

"Mama, my phone broke; I need to get my phone fixed." I could tell he didn't want to ask me for no money. He hated to be a burden.

"I get paid next week, and I'll give it to you then," I said, busying myself, folding laundry.

"OK, Mama."

Mike Mike was never a kid who asked for much. I knew how much his phone meant to him.

"Mike Mike, look, I'mma get it fixed. Just use your laptop if you need to do that social media stuff," I said.

But it was too late now.

August 11, 2014

The next morning the television flickered. I saw the St. Louis County police chief, Jon Belmar, appear on the screen. I could only get a moan out to Louis, who was in the other room. He sat down next to me and grabbed my hand. My stomach began to churn.

"I cannot say at this time how many times the subject was struck by gunfire. It's hard to know if it was more than just a couple, but I don't think it was many more than that. The medical examiner is conducting a medical examination today to determine that, and please keep in mind it's going to take as long as six weeks."

He still refused to name the officer who had shot Mike Mike.

"They need to show the cop's face like they showing Mike Mike!" Louis said, shaking his head.

"They some cowards!" I screamed at the television.

I didn't want to see another second of the news. I stalked into the living room and sat down for what seemed like hours in a zombie state. I didn't even hear my husband let my coworker Miss B in. My face was swollen, and I had cried so much it hurt to even look up. She touched me on my shoulder. I turned toward her.

"I just came by to see if you needed anything, Lezley," she whispered softly.

I couldn't answer. She swallowed hard, not sure what to say next. "I'm not gonna stay, but we all prayin' for you. Your customers are, too. Um, Mrs. Hirschfield came by the store and wanted me to give you this." She pulled out an envelope and handed it to me.

I opened it slowly and pulled out a picture. It had a tiny note written on it. I couldn't believe it was a class picture of me in the fourth grade at Reed Elementary. I was trying to make sense of how Mrs. Hirschfield got this.

"That lady was real upset after seein' the news. She wanted us all to know that she really knew you. She even wanted everyone to know that your son couldn't have done nothin' wrong, because you were a good person, and you had to have raised a good son."

Just like I didn't notice Miss B coming in, it didn't register that she had left. I just held the picture, my hand trembling. Her son had been my elementary school classmate, and they remembered me from back then. From the moment I met her at Straub's, it always felt like I knew her from somewhere else. Now it all made sense.

"They gonna set up a fund for you at Straub's," Louis said softly.

I turned toward him and nodded, placing my hand over my mouth. I had been loyal to Straub's for all these years, but I never imagined that they'd do something like this for me.

Even as my community pulled together to support my family, last night's looting made it clear that things were becoming dangerously divided in St. Louis.

For the black people, Mike Mike getting shot was like an old scab being pulled off a wound filled with racism. Young people were mad about not having jobs, money, how the white police mainly be treating young black men—pulling them over, locking them up, beating them down. Older black people felt like it was time to raise their voices. Some white people just saw the shooting as the police doing their job and looked at the black people out there looting as animals. I was upset at the looting, too. Why would we tear up our own neighborhood? And I didn't want anybody doing nothing in Mike Mike's name if it wasn't about getting that cop convicted. At the same time, I been around a long time, and I know what it's like to be mad because you feel like you don't have any opportunities out there. I just didn't want any more violence. I didn't want anybody else to get hurt or killed.

My cousin Chevelle was rounding up lawyers. I didn't know at the time that Daddy had called Reverend Al Sharpton.

• • • •

"Nette, we gonna get the Trayvon Martin lawyers, Benjamin Crump and Daryl Parks. We gotta make sure you get the publicity you need, and they the new civil rights lawyers out here. What do you think?" Chevelle's voice was going in and out. I was only seeing parts of him. His long, slender fingers rubbing the top of his salt-and-pepper-speckled hair, the hem of his tailored slacks, and the leather laces of his Italian dress shoes made a quick clicking sound from him nervously tapping his foot.

I could hear Daddy's voice from the kitchen. "Yeah, my name is Leslie McSpadden, and my daughter's name is Lezley McSpadden too. She's the mother of Michael Brown. He laid in the street for four and a half hours. Yes, he was my grandson from Ferguson!" Daddy would raise and lower his voice each time he got frustrated from explaining.

It was all too much filling up my brain. I just wanted to escape. I crawled back into my bed. Random thoughts bounced inside my head. I closed my eyes, but all I saw was Mike Mike's face.

CHAPTER TWENTY-TWO

THREE SIDES TO EVERY STORY

There was a lot happening and Chevelle was trying to give me and Louis an update. The police investigation was ongoing and Dorian Johnson, the boy who had been with Mike Mike when he was shot, had surfaced. We kept hearing a loud sound in the air above.

"It can't be an airplane, it's too small," Chevelle said, looking out the front blinds.

Suddenly we heard thunderous shots go off and then we heard helicopters coming and we turned on the TV and we saw that some protesters had been teargassed and one of the protestors threw a smoke bomb back at the police.

I was shaking with fear. It was all happening too close to our house and my other babies.

Six days had passed since Mike Mike was killed. School openings were postponed until August 19. I was relieved. I just wanted to keep my kids in the house. I feared for their lives. I didn't want the media to harass them. I worried about them going back to school too soon. Would they be able to handle it? Would the kids ask them a lot of questions? How were the teachers going to treat them? Right now, I just wanted them with me.

"I don't want y'all goin' out the house or goin' to Granny's," I said, pacing the kitchen, puffing on a cigarette. "I don't want you nowhere near Canfield." Déja knew I was mainly talking to her.

Déja was sitting at the table scrolling through her phone, looking half interested.

"Why, Mama?" Jazzy asked in a soft voice, peeking around the kitchen entry.

" 'Cause Mike Mike ain't here no more," Moo Moo said, leaning against the refrigerator. He lowered his head, and tears began to fall down his chubby cheeks.

He reminded me so much of Mike Mike. Moo Moo was ten now, and he was laid-back like Mike Mike. He was chunky like Mike Mike was at his age. I didn't know if he was gonna get as tall as his brother, right now he was short. He wasn't going to get as tall as Mike Mike, but he was going to be a healthy, thick boy.

Jazzy, only being five, still had that baby thing. She teared up. "Mama, Mike Mike ain't have no weapon," Jazzy said, twisting her mouth as she began to cry.

I grabbed them both in a hug and held on for dear life. I turned and looked at Déja. Her and Mike Mike were tight. They weren't just brother and sister, they were best friends.

"Y'all, go on in your rooms for a while."

"Mama, we cain't stay in here forever!" Déja said. There was a quiver in her voice. She got up and tried to walk out of the room.

"Déja!"

I grabbed her, threw my arms around her, and just held her close. I rocked her in my arms, and we cried softly together.

The outside world had sucked me into a firestorm of confusion. I had to go to the store to get food and necessities, but now people had seen my face plastered on television. If I went in the grocery store or Walgreens or even the damn McDonald's, people were looking, pointing, asking me how I was doing.

The police were finally going to release the officer's name. I wanted to look the cop in his eyes so he couldn't escape the face of a mother in pain, so that he couldn't just run away from being held accountable. He couldn't just walk away like he had done when he shot my son in cold blood.

The lawyers had me on a whirlwind of interviews. I had never been on an airplane in my life, and now I had to fly to places like New York and

Atlanta, Los Angeles to Geneva Switzerland, and too many other cities to count. I had so many people telling me what to do, where to go, how to act, and what to say that I barely knew my name.

The lawyers insisted that me and Big Mike present a united front like two parents who had raised Mike Mike together. I was doing everything I wasn't *asked* but *told* to do.

I wasn't in any shape to speak to the media, and so I asked Chevelle to stand with me and speak on my behalf. Louis was right by my side every step of the way, which was a comforting reminder of how much this man had my back. He kept me strong enough to do what the lawyers said and appear in the media with Big Mike.

It was important to show that Mike Mike wasn't just some black boy in the hood that didn't have a daddy. No, he belonged to a family that loved him.

August 16, 2014

Governor Nixon issued a state of emergency for the Ferguson area and that they were imposing a curfew. "If we are going to achieve justice, we must first have and maintain peace," Nixon said. "This is a test. The eyes of the world are watching." I wasn't convinced that the police or the governor were really going to deliver justice, but I did feel like I was being watched.

I pulled all the blinds shut. I was starting to feel paranoid that folks knew where I lived. I was at home on the phone with Chevelle, holding my breath waiting for the police chief of Ferguson to release the name of the officer who had shot Mike Mike.

Ferguson Police Chief Thomas Jackson stood in front of the media and shuffled his papers. He was shifting and stuttering as he presented the timeline of how Mike Mike and the unnamed officer "interacted." My breathing quickened, my skin felt clammy. As the chief stammered, he turned redder and redder.

"Umm, anyway, so I'm here, umm, to talk about, uh, two things. Uh, first of all the name of the officer involved in the shooting, and then I've got a lot of Sunshine Requests for information I'm gonna be releasing information about a robbery that occurred on August ninth immediately preceding the, uh, altercation and shooting death of Michael Brown."

What the hell was this? I hadn't heard anything about a robbery. I was gripping the side of my chair with my other hand so tight my knuckles were turning white, as he went on and on about Missouri's law that says, "Records of public governmental bodies are open to the public." I was furious that the police were using this law now at their convenience.

"Um, it's important to note that I, uh, I have made contact with someone who is in contact with Officer Brown's family, um, to make them aware of this, uh, information being released."

I let out a loud sigh. "This is an insult! Listen to him hemmin' and hawin'. He just called my son Officer Brown!" I shouted at the TV.

I didn't want any of this to be real. This was a bad dream, and I needed somebody to wake me up. I needed Mike Mike to walk through the door and give me that playful smile so I could be like, "Boy, you play too much!"

"Um, uh, I'm sorry, the officer that was involved in the shooting of, um, uh, Michael Brown was Darren Wilson. He's been a police officer for six years, and he's had no disciplinary action taken against him. He was treated for injuries, which occurred on Saturday. Again, I won't be taking any questions at this time, but the packages will be passed out by my officers."

The police chief went on to spell out the officer's name and talk about the video they released. His name didn't tell me anything about him. That name could've belonged to a black or white man, but when I did finally see his picture, I saw evil. I saw a coward. He was this person who used his badge to his advantage. He wasn't protecting and serving anybody. I wanted to go to trial just to see the person who took my son from me in the flesh.

The police had a strategy. Their handouts to the press and the release of the Ferguson market video were conveniently released to the public. The police were crucifying my son. How was this just and fair? The police had drawn a line in the sand, making it clear that they'd protect their own by any means necessary. I knew right then and there I was about to be in the fight of my life.

But I believed that the truth would come to light.

• • • •

After the police chief's announcement and meeting with Governor Nixon, I had an intense urge to know what was real and what wasn't. "Chevelle, they said that's Mike Mike on the video," I said, taking quick puffs off my cigarette. "Mike Mike don't steal. You know that."

"I know. Have you seen the video? They're tryin' to smear his image, Nette!" he said, shaking his head.

"No. I don't want to. You know what they tryin' to do, and my son ain't here to tell the truth!" I felt my blood pressure surge. "What I want the police to show me is somethin' that can give me some type of understandin' as to why my son is dead. That's still my main question. Not the store, not the tape, but why my son was shot and killed!"

"We need to watch it, Nette." Chevelle pressed play on the computer, and when the video was finished, he began to pace, rubbing his temple.

We were racking our brains to figure out how we could let the public know that there had to be some kind of terrible misunderstanding. We had to set the record straight. That video doesn't show the whole story.

We didn't have any facts to go on, but there was one person who did know something and that was Dorian Johnson. I didn't know Dorian, although he had been on the news boasting about being Mike Mike's best friend. But if Mike Mike's mama didn't know you, and I knew all his friends, then you weren't no real friend. But I sure wanted to meet him now.

• • • •

I wasn't seeing too much of anything with a clear head, but what was getting harder and harder to deny was race. Seeing Canfield covered by a mostly white police force, and this white police chief passing out packets and tripping over his words, and the white police officer who had disappeared on paid leave after shooting my black, unarmed kid, it was impossible not to see this as a black-and-white issue.

There had now been several politicians either reaching out to me or speaking out in support of Mike Mike, from Missouri Congressman

William Clay Jr., to Missouri Senator Claire McCaskill. I appreciated it, but the main ones I should've been hearing from were the ones from Ferguson and St. Louis, and I hadn't heard a peep from them. But the governor did want to sit down with me. I didn't know what to think about that.

My attorneys, Ben Crump, Daryl Parks, and Anthony Gray, along with Adolphus Pruitt of the NAACP, set up a meeting at the downtown Drury Hotel for the governor to meet me. Former state representative Rodney Hubbard was there to give me his support too. I sat quietly next to Louis and Chevelle, wringing my hands in anticipation. Louis nudged me when the governor entered.

I could tell Governor Nixon was a tall man when I saw him on television, but seeing him in person, he was even larger.

"Let me give you a hug," he said, leaning down. Hugging him was like hugging a big tree with a suit on. "I wanna give you another one, and it's from the first lady." He leaned back in, stiff in his blue suit. He had no passion, no emotion.

Governor Nixon didn't seem sincere at all. It was like he was here because it was a good political move.

During the visit, I listened and cried a lot. Attorney Parks got some updated information and announced that Mike Mike had been shot in his head, that was what they called the "kill shot." That knocked the wind out of me. Nothing else that the governor talked about meant anything.

"Huh? Nobody told me that! Where?" I demanded.

Attorney Parks pointed to the top of his head.

I began to shake uncontrollably. I let out a bloodcurdling scream, and the room went blurry, then black. My breath was cut off like a hard fist being punched in my throat had stopped it.

The meeting was over.

August 17, 2014

So, if "the eyes of the world are watching," like Governor Nixon said then somebody ought to be able to tell me something about what happened at the Ferguson Market and the handful of mystery cigarillos my son supposedly stole, and what really happened on Canfield between that cop and my son? I wanted to go after the police hard for answers, but pushed that thought to the side, because I had just gotten slammed with the latest news that the private autopsy me and Big Mike had requested, found that Mike Mike had been shot at least six times, including four times in the right arm and twice in the head.

My head was now spinning in another direction. All of the shots were fired to the front of Mike Mike. What did all of this mean? It certainly didn't prove to me that Mike Mike was in the wrong, definitely not wrong to make it okay to fire over and over. My son was unarmed and had on flip flops. Whatever happened to officers using a stun gun? That officer unloaded his gun on a mission to kill, not arrest or ask questions. I spoke to the pathologist about how those bullets entered my son's body. He described that the bullets broke and shattered bones, and bounced around like pinballs in a game. I don't believe there was any way Mike Mike could have had any strength to charge that officer.

• • • •

I'd been driving myself crazy trying to pick apart what could have happened. So, I was anxious to finally meet the last person who was with Mike Mike and the one he had talked to last, Dorian Johnson. I was hoping he'd tell me everything that had happened, 'cause the whole Ferguson Market piece didn't fit into any puzzle for me. I had taken Mike Mike to the Ferguson Market regularly. It's one of the few stores near Mama's house. That and Sam's Market next door. Mike Mike would always go buy a green tea and some chips. I'd never taken him there and seen him buy cigarillos, though. That was a whole different store run for him.

Mike Mike knew I didn't like him smoking weed. I put my foot down about him smoking. So he'd never even think about buying a cigarillo in front of me. It just baffles the hell out of me, because the store workers knew my son. For years he had even gone there with my mama or Brittanie or my Uncle Carl. I had a lot of questions, but now I was going to finally get some answers.

• • • •

I walked into Mama's house with Chevelle and Louis. It was eerie today. Walking into the living room with all the pictures of her grandkids on the walls, in frames on the table. I brushed my hand over her black love seat that Mike Mike sat in all the time. Mike Mike's diploma was front and center on the table behind the love seat. I swallowed a dry lump in my throat. A large picture of Brittanie, Mama, and Mike Mike greeted me next. Tears began to roll down my cheeks. The coffee table had a big, framed picture of Mike Mike in his cap and gown. Mama was most proud of that one. I had to turn away. I wiped my face and walked into the kitchen and sat down with Mama at the table.

I was meeting Dorian Johnson for the first time today. My leg was shaking something fierce.

I opened the door to let Dorian in. He was thin, mousy. He was shaking too and in tears, and the first thing he said to me was, "I'm scared for my life. I don't know what to do and where to go. I think they gonna try to kill me."

I didn't have much sympathy. I know that's wrong. He was still some other mother's child. But the bitterness in me was bubbling up in my throat.

"If you knew my son and you were claiming to be a friend, why didn't you go right to his grandmother's house on Canfield when this happened and tell her what had just happened to her grandson? You kept runnin'. You already was some distance from Mike Mike. You was runnin' because you was wrong!" I said, bursting into tears. "You kept runnin' for three days. All we hearin' is that this person was with Mike Mike, but we don't know who he is. You ain't a friend; you don't know him for real!"

I calmed myself and tried to start over. "You were with my son; you could've told me everything. The police are down with the officer. They ain't gonna tell me the truth and tell me what really happened. Why did it take you three days to come talk to me?"

He couldn't answer. He was stumbling and stammering like the police chief. I just shut down and stared at him. Dorian hadn't told no type of truth. He hadn't told what was talked about before they went to the store—what was talked about while they were walking to the store, when they got in the store, when they left out the store. He didn't tell me none of that. Dorian Johnson was the last person with Mike Mike; the least he could do was tell me what happened. But Dorian hadn't told me any more than I knew before he got here. Meeting him was yet another disappointment on the already discouraging road I was traveling.

I'm of the mind that when you making up shit and don't want to tell the truth, it's usually because the truth involves yo' ass.

CHAPTER TWENTY-THREE

LET MY BABY GO

August 18, 2014

There was a war zone just blocks away. I barely found the energy to get out of bed or go past my front room. Ferguson police had everything from helicopters to armored vehicles, and they was locking up so many people, young or old, anyone who even looked like a threat.

President Obama spoke. I had been waiting for him to say something. The more it looked like Wilson might get away with it, the more I prayed that the president would do something, set something in action. I listened carefully as he took his place in front of the microphone.

"I've already tasked the Department of Justice and the FBI to independently investigate the death of Michael Brown. I made clear to the attorney general that we should do what is necessary to help determine exactly what happened and to see that justice is done. I know emotions are raw right now in Ferguson, and there are certainly passionate differences about what has happened. But let's remember that we're all part of one American family. We are united in common values and that includes the belief in equality under the law, respect for public order, and the right to peaceful public protests.

"Now is the time of healing. Now is the time for peace and calm on the streets of Ferguson . . ."

I didn't think much of what he said, because it wasn't much. The most encouraging thing he said was that Attorney General Eric Holder was going to come to Ferguson.

Me and Chevelle, and Louis had to meet the attorneys downtown at the Eagleton Courthouse to get debriefed by the FBI about the investigation. I sat in the lead agent's office with a blank expression on my face as he explained how over forty agents were going door to door looking for witnesses. Chevelle tried to explain that there are people coming up to us out on the streets daily saying they saw what happened. The agent assured us they were checking things out. I felt like they were just brushing us off. Just then, another agent peeked in and announced that Attorney General Holder was calling for me. My heart quickened. I was too nervous to talk to him by myself. I asked Chevelle and Louis to be with me. We were led to a private conference room. I sat motionless, my heart was pounding, I held my breath when he began to speak. His voice was warm and fatherly as he expressed his sympathy. He assured me that their investigation would be thorough. When he vowed his support to do everything in his power to bring justice to this case, my tears began to flow. I closed my eyes. I felt like the government was bringing in the big dogs for me. My prayers had been answered.

I just had to tie a knot in my faith and hang on a little longer, and hope Attorney General Eric Holder was going to open the door to justice.

• • • •

The county coroners were communicating with the lawyers because we ordered a special autopsy, and then the state had done their autopsy. His body went through a lot before the funeral home got him. It was all too much.

My baby had been gone for fifteen days. Mama and Louis and Brittanie and I had been trying to plan the funeral, but we didn't even know when we'd get his body back from the city.

But Austin Lane, the funeral director, had called to tell me to bring the clothes to the funeral home. How do you dress your son for his grave?

This morning, every time I got up out of bed, I had to get right back in it. I must have done that four or five times. Then I found myself wiping the same spot on the counter for minutes on end. I folded a basket of laundry. I was trying to do everything I could to delay leaving the house.

The men's department at Macy's felt like it was closing in on me, as I stood in front of a large table piled high with neat stacks of sweaters. I wasn't sure if I was going to throw up or pass out. My eyes were welling up again. I was jittery, and my hands wouldn't stop shaking.

"You gonna be all right to do this?" Louis asked, gently rubbing my back.

I was trying to keep it together because we were out in public. Several people had already passed by pointing and staring. The black people gave me smiles, asked for hugs, then whispered, "Keep your head up, sister!" The white people who recognized me either gave me a quick, sympathetic smile before they turned away or flat out rolled their eyes and curled up their lip.

I was concentrating so hard my head ached. I took another deep breath. "I can get through this," I told myself. I lifted one of the sweaters up in the air, as if I was showing it to Mike Mike. "Yeah, this is it! I wanna dress you like you'd dress yourself, baby. You know, something that you'd pick out."

The sweater was the perfect blue. I laid it out next to a crisp pair of blue jeans, a button-down, and a bow tie. Louis gave a nod of approval. I gave a half smile. "Yeah, Mike Mike gonna be looking real nice."

August 24, 2014

When they took him away from Canfield Drive, all the cops told me was that he was going to a place called Berkeley. I guess they meant the city of Berkeley, another municipality like Ferguson. The funeral director, Austin Lane, was the only person communicating any real information to me. He told me that the body was at the St. Louis County Medical Examiner's Office.

The funeral home people always tell you that the body is OK, and I don't know why they tell you that, because the body isn't OK. It is as far from OK as it can be. It don't have life in it anymore.

It was the night before the funeral, and it was going to be my first time seeing Mike Mike's body since the day he was killed. It had been two weeks. I'd never been away from him for so long.

When we got to the funeral home, I turned to Louis and said, "I need to see Mike Mike for a minute by myself."

Then I kissed each one of my kids, shut the door behind me, and started walking down the chapel aisle. I felt like I was wading through cement as I approached his casket.

I stood beside Mike Mike, legs feeling like Jell-O. My baby boy looked good. He looked clean and sharp like he always did. I wanted to hear his voice. I wanted to hear him say, "Mama, you did ya thang pickin' these clothes. I look good, right?"

I imagined me telling him, "Mike, Mike, you look real handsome. I love you so much." But I stopped myself from imagining too much, because the reality was that my son was lying there in a casket, and after the next day, I'd never see him again.

My eyes filled with tears. It was just me and Mike Mike in the room together, and seeing him laying there so still, it all settled in and I knew he was never coming back and that my life would never be the same.

I took a deep breath. I just wanted to keep my composure for my other kids.

Big Mike came into the chapel next. He had arrived wearing a button-down shirt, but then he walked out and came back in, and he was wearing a muscle shirt so he could show everybody that he had gotten a tattoo of Mike Mike's face on his back.

As we settled into the pews, Déja wanted to have her own time with Mike Mike. She walked up to the casket and just sort of stood there for several minutes, quiet. Big Mike walked up to Déja and leaned down and whispered something in her ear. Déja said something back to him. Me and Brittanie couldn't hear what they were saying, but all of a sudden, Mike squared off with Déja.

"You need to go sit down and not stand up at the casket like that. You gonna be sick."

"Naw, Daddy, I'mma be fine. I just want to look at him a li'l longer."

"You need to go sit down," he raised his voice.

Then he was shouting, "Do you know how the fuck I feel? Do you? Do you know how the fuck I feel? Do you?"

Stunned, Déja turned around and announced to the room, "Somebody come and get him."

Everyone was standing up, and there was lot of chatter coming from both sides. I rushed up and put my arms around her.

Brittanie put her arms around me and Déja, but Déja pushed us away. She walked back up to the casket and stood looking at her brother. Brittanie walked to her side.

I was in another world, and all I could see was Mike Mike in that casket, Déja, Moo Moo, Jazzy, and my mama. Everything went fuzzy after that.

CHAPTER TWENTY-FOUR

THE LONGEST DAY

August 25, 2014

I woke up about 4:00 a.m. Don't even know if I slept at all. By 6:00 a.m. I had already smoked three cigarettes and I was worn out, like the blood was creeping through my veins. I didn't know how I was going to get through this whole day. I peeked out my bedroom door. The sun was coming through the clouds.

I wrapped my hair up tight and put a shower cap on. I needed to make sure I didn't mess it up. In the shower the hot steam filled my nostrils, and I could feel my head opening up. The water poured over each curve and muscle of my body, and for just a moment everything bad disappeared. The bottle of body wash slipped from my hand and crashed into the tub. In my head I heard the sound of a gunshot. I jumped, and my heart sped up. I looked down at my right hand and traced the same places where Mike Mike had been shot with my left hand. I ran my fingers over my thumb, up my forearm, past my elbow, then gripped my shoulder.

The tears suddenly sprang from my eyes. I tried to wipe them, but now I didn't know the difference between the water and my tears.

I balled up my washcloth and began washing my skin. I thought about all the protesters, news reports, and comments on social media. "They don't know me. They don't know my son." I scrubbed harder. I saw flashes of that killer cop's face, Police Chief Jackson, Governor Nixon, James Knowles, the mayor of Ferguson. White men who didn't see my baby for nothing but a black boy in the hood. What the fuck was he doing today? It felt like the water was pouring with even more force over my body. I wanted it to just wash me right down the drain.

"Oh, God!" I opened my mouth and screamed as loud as I could, dropping the rag.

"Lezley, you OK?" Louis asked, banging on the bathroom door.

"I'm OK," I said, shaking all over. I covered my mouth with my hands.

"Come on," he said, opening the door, handing me a towel. "People gonna be coming soon," he said, turning off the water and wrapping the towel around me.

It took me three tries just to get one leg in my underwear. I slid my dress on, then smoothed it down. I felt a sharp pain in my gut and dry heaved. I leaned up against the wall in the pet room. Even my parakeets weren't chirping this morning.

People just started showing up at my house. All the commotion was too much. It was overwhelming. Why didn't these people just come to the church? Why did they come to my house? I just wanted to have this moment to myself. I wanted to just crawl back into bed. I wanted to say fuck it. I didn't want to go. I didn't want to believe Mike Mike was gone.

There was the loud rumbling of motorcycles outside. Their engines made the house vibrate. The riders who were going to lead the motorcade were zooming up and gathering in the street out front, talking and standing around. Other family members had pulled up and were just parked outside.

I was trying to double-check my makeup and see if the kids were dressed, with their hair combed. The noise from outside was deafening. There was a series of knocks at the front door.

"I heard them! I heard them!" I shouted, my hand trembling again. I was on edge. I looked around the room at Jazzy and Moo Moo's stunned faces. "I'm sorry, y'all. Mama just tryin' to keep it all together."

Jazzy and Moo Moo put their arms around me.

"C'mon now, we gotta go soon," I said, patting each of them on their backs.

"Mama, I look OK?" Déja asked, stepping into the room. She looked prettier than ever this morning.

"You look real nice, Déja," I said, mustering up a smile and hugging her as tight as I could. "We gon' get through this, I promise."

"The limos are here," Brittanie announced.

I was frantically looking for my purse. "How they expect somebody to get ready with all that going on? I need my purse."

"Nette Pooh, I got you," Brittanie said, handing me my purse. We both let out a sigh, and she stepped in and held me close.

Everyone else was out the house and loaded in the limos. I stood at the front door and looked around the room at the shrine that I had created without even realizing it. I had placed each special trinket or candle someone had made with Mike Mike's picture or name on the end tables on each side of the living room couch, which had a large throw with his face printed on it draped over the back. T-shirts with his name and face looking out at me hung over the love seat. The room was bursting with him today.

There were cars and motorcycles everywhere. I just kept my head down and concentrated on getting in the limo. It felt like I didn't take a breath until we pulled away from my little house. I closed my eyes tightly, trying to hold it all in. The limos zoomed down West Florrisant. The sun was shining bright, but when I saw the spray-painted, boarded-up, burned-out buildings and stores left in the aftermath of the looting, I was astounded. It looked like something out of the Middle East on the news, where bombs had gone off. I never thought I'd see anything like this in my life. I closed my eyes again. I just wanted this all to go away.

It was a long drive to Friendly Temple Missionary Baptist Church down in the city of North St. Louis. I looked over at Mama; she was distant, staring out into nowhere. Her sunglasses couldn't hide the tears that rolled down her face. She was hurting. I slid over and grabbed her hand. She looked a little surprised, then cracked a half smile. I just held on to her hand for the rest of the drive.

When we pulled on to the church's street, my body stiffened. I wanted to jump out and run away. My leg began to shake. Louis put his hand on it. News trucks filled the sidewalks. There were cars everywhere, and what seemed like thousands of people, as far as my eyes could see. There were people standing outside on both sides of the street with their hands up. I had never seen anything like it.

A group of kids were holding signs that said: HANDS UP DON'T SHOOT and JUSTICE FOR MIKE BROWN.

I looked back out the window, and it was chaotic. When the driver opened the door, the voices of people chanting for peace, sirens down the block, and news reporters calling my name all stung my ears. I needed my sunglasses to shield my eyes from what seemed like hundreds of cameras and hands reaching out to me. Chevelle swooped in and grabbed me by one hand, and Louis held the other. We all were linked hand in hand, arm in arm, and it felt like a big gush of wind was pushing us all inside.

I was frantically looking around for Brittanie and her family. Where was Bernard? My mouth was moving, but I didn't know what I was saying.

"They OK. Everybody's OK," Louis assured me.

Chevelle and Louis were keeping us all together. We were walking fast, but suddenly it all came to a stop.

I just wanted to get inside, away from all this madness, but we were stuck in a line at the entrance of the church. I heard Chevelle shouting, "This is his mother!"

Then just as quick as we came to a screeching halt, I was whisked inside to join the rest of my family. I saw Auntie Bobbie, Uncle Charles, Key Key, and then all the faces started to blur together.

As we lined up for the processional, everything felt divided. I wanted everyone to wear red, because it was Mike Mike's favorite color. Mike wanted blue. But I couldn't fight at a time like this. We had at least come together and were standing side by side to walk our baby in. His last walk. The last mile. Then he'd be gone.

I stood at the entrance of the sanctuary. The choir's song began to swell.

I shall wear a crown
I shall wear a crown when it's all over
I shall see his face

I shall see his face when it's all over
I'm gonna put on my robe
Tell the story
How I made it over

Louis gripped my hand tight. The church nurses were all dressed in crisp white uniforms and hats, and black men in white tuxedos lined the aisles. Mike Mike's casket was gleaming up ahead. The pews overflowed as folks shouted "Amens" and "Glory, glories." Giant posters of Mike Mike seemed to come at me. It was like I was being swallowed up.

As I sat there rocking back and forth, I was stiffening up again. It was too much, looking at all the people, most who didn't know nothing about Mike Mike.

I looked over at Big Mike. His wife, Calvina, and Louis were between us, but I could see him tending to his baby girl.

My chest tightened. I chewed my gum faster and faster, then turned away. Suddenly, the choir hit a soaring note that surged through my body like electricity. I stood up and walked to Mike Mike's casket and stared at the giant poster that showed him from a baby to a toddler to a young man.

I gave in to my tears. Everything around me began to fade into silence—the choir, the pastor speaking into the microphone, preparing everyone for the service, the chatter that rambled underneath it all. Everyone started to disappear, and then it was just me and Mike Mike's casket in that church. I touched it, rubbing the shiny mahogany wood as if it were his hand. I closed my eyes and began to speak to him.

"I never want this to go unsaid, Mike Mike. There are no words to express how much you mean to me. A son like you I thought could never be. Because the day you were born, I just know God sent me a blessing, and that was you. For this, I thank him every day. You are the true definition of a son in every way. Becoming a mom has shown me a new sense of being. I want you to know that you were the purpose in my life. Out of everything I did, it was you that I did right."

Louis's arm around my waist brought me back to reality. I bent over, kissed Mike Mike's casket, and sat down. I just focused on his picture, his eyes looking directly at me. We were fixed on each other. I could do this. He would be my strength to sit though the tributes, the songs, the speeches, the people, all of it. I wasn't going to take my eyes off him.

When the trail of limos pulled into the cemetery, the funeral directors moved Mike Mike's casket from the hearse to a white horse and carriage.

I couldn't get out of the limo right away, and by the time I collected myself and walked to the grave site, Big Mike released the white doves we had agreed to do together.

I was devastated. I got right back in the limo. For several minutes I couldn't even speak. I waited until everyone had left the grave site, and then I got out of the limo and slowly made my way to the open hole in the ground where his casket sat. I stared at the casket for a long time and then I bent over and started kissing it.

Brittanie got out her limo and rushed to me. I just kept kissing it over and over. "Nette Pooh, c'mon."

"I just cain't, I cain't leave my son here." I lay on his casket and cried a hard cry. Brittanie wrapped her arms around me, peeling me away from the casket and then walked me back to the limo.

I guess it was so hard to let go because I never had gotten my proper time with him. I had to share him even to the end. So this was it. I didn't want to let go, but I knew it was time. This was final. All that was left was to fight. Not like back in high school, not like over on Emma. I could hold my own in the streets, but this was different, bigger, and more powerful than anything I had ever experienced in the hood. I had to fight a system.

CHAPTER TWENTY-FIVE

MAMA GOT FOUR

September 1, 2014

It was September 1st and I was finally sending the kids back to school.

I shot up, sat up on the edge of the bed, and wiped the sleep from my eyes. Today I didn't need my alarm. Louis was still asleep, with his back to me. It was barely light outside. I dragged myself out of the bed. My parakeets were still asleep. The light from the fish tank stung my eyes. I sprinkled some food in the tank, fired up a cigarette, and peeped out the kitchen blinds. The street was empty.

The funeral was over, lawyers were calling, and I was going to let my kids go back at school. Life had restarted, but I was still trying to figure it out. I had made up my mind that I would try to make things as normal as possible around here, even if I was cracking up on the inside.

A few days before, I had sat the kids down at the kitchen table and told them, "Listen, y'all gotta go back to school now. I'm takin' a break from work for a li'l while 'cause I gotta fight for Mike Mike."

Each one of them nodded.

So today I was going to finally send them out into the world. I was terrified that they'd be asked a bunch of questions or harassed. But the school district assured me that they would be taken care of and not interrogated about everything that was going on. I knew I couldn't have them in a bubble, but I had a fierce urge to protect them.

I woke the kids up, put breakfast on the table, and got everybody dressed and into the car. First thing Déja did was turn on the radio. We started bopping our heads as if it were any other morning. Moo Moo and Jazzy were teasing each other in the backseat.

"Y'all got your homework?" I asked.

"Yes, Mama," they all said in unison. Déja kind of smacked her lips.

"Whassup, Déja?"

"I just be gettin' tired of school," she said, picking at her nail.

"Well, it just started, so you cain't be gettin' tired," I said, looking at her again.

I slowed in front of Moo Moo and Jazzy's school, kissed them over the seat, and they hopped out.

At Déja 's school I parked and turned to her, "Déja, we got a long way to go, I know, but we can do this together."

"Mama, it's just so hard with Mike Mike not bein' here. People got so many questions." She opened the door and grabbed her books.

"Look, we just gotta tune everybody else out. And if you need help with your work, we'll get the help. Plus, you a sophomore now! Hey, girl!" I teased.

"Bye, Mama!" She smiled. One of her friends called her name and she waved, running to catch up. Déja disappeared into the school, and I drove off and turned up the music.

Something hit me the moment I walked in our front door and saw Mike Mike's face on the blanket. I marched into the bedroom and found the large shopping bag filled with mail. I took a big swallow, sat down on the floor, and started going through each piece. The first envelope was from Florida. I opened it slowly and pulled out a small notecard.

8/12/14

Dear Parents,

I'm a 67 year old white woman from Virginia. I don't know anything I could say that would make you feel better, but my heart hurts for you and Michael. I'm not going to be "Politically Correct" so here goes . . .

The sorry bastard who murdered Michael should go to the electric chair!!

I would be first in line to pull the switch! I mean that! Most of the cops are just like him! Cowards who use the badge to look tough while 5 of 6 of them are beating one person who is handcuffed! All the time yelling "Stop Resisting" so any witnesses would have to say that if it ever went to court. Very little change of that. Not five minutes before they reported it on TV. I bet $100.00 that the police would say Michael tried to take the killer's gun, and sure enough there it was. We know he'll get away with it and they know it too! If you compared them to any gangs, etc. it would have to be a 50/50 mix of the KKK and the Nazis! I'm so very sorry I'll ask Jesus to ease some of your pain and hold Michael in His arms! I believe He will.

I opened another letter from a union.

August 19, 2014

Dear Sister McSpadden,

Our hearts are breaking as we think of your struggling with the terrible loss of your beloved son, Michael Brown, Jr.

As mothers, daughters, grandmothers, aunts, granddaughters and Union sisters, we grieve with you and for you. We wish you peace and justice as you, your family, and our entire community move through the challenging days ahead.

We hope our words help lift you up and help shoulder your burdens.

Fraternally and in sisterhood,

Coalition of Labor Union Women, St. Louis Chapter

I was feeling stronger with each word I read. Louis brought me an iced tea and a sandwich and laid across the bed. He became my one-man audience as I read and laughed and cried. Letters were from Oregon, California, Mississippi, Atlanta, Oklahoma, even Ferguson. I was reading letters from old people, young people, other mothers who had lost a son or daughter. Some had been shot in the streets, some were victims of police brutality, some just had been sick. I spent hours sitting on that floor opening letters and cards and looking at pictures kids in elementary schools around the country had drawn of Mike Mike and Canfield Drive.

My hand landed on a large plain envelope. I opened it. The words SHAME IS UPON YOU were scribbled across the top.

From Anonymous:

Lesley McSpadden shame is upon you for inciting riots and looting and burning of the business. You have ruined their families. The people have no connection to your son. You are saying in essence that you and your family are the only ones that have a right to life. You failed to teach your son lessons in life. You taught him to disrespect the law and to hate white people. The people of today had nothing to do with slavery. Many things happened in the past. We of today have no connection to. It is wrong to steal and to tread upon the rights of others. Your son stole from a business. He shoved an owner. He prevented people from going down the street. That's a public street. He blocked it.

The policeman was upholding the law as he was trained to do. Your son attacked the policeman and tried to take his gun. If he had been successful the policeman would have been dead. What would you have said about that? Would you have cared? Your son would have been charged with murder! You should pay all the people for the havoc you have reaked upon those people. They are victims of your hatred you should repent of these things you have done. Take a good look at what you and your husband have done. If you have any bit of conscience.

Do you really want the legacy of your son to be that his actions caused to Ferguson and other cities? Truly the blame lies on you. You should stop listening to race baters like Obama, Holder, Sharpton. These are the scorge of America. Listen to your own conscience. The money that is sent to you by the public should be paid to Ferguson you should not profit from your son's death. That is a blight upon you and your husband. I should think that you would feel bad every time you used that money. Think of small children of the ruined business. They will be without homes food and the things you have denied them. Think about it!

I balled it up and threw it across the room and began pacing and punching the air.

"Fuck these racist-ass white people, Louis! I lost my baby. Who would write some shit like that? What kinda person? No, that ain't a person; that's the devil, Louis!"

I was sweating and breathing hard.

"Hold up, Lezley," Louis said, turning me around to face him. "Baby, I know them words hurt. I'm hurt with you, but fuck that racist bastard and his words. He a coward! And they just some fucked-up hate-filled words on a piece of paper. That's all." He pulled me close.

"I just feel like, what if I wanted to go out and just kill some people? Kill somebody's white son! I would be in jail. I woulda been hunted down and killed and thrown under the damn prison!" I shouted, breaking down into heavy sobs.

Louis held me and cried with me for I don't know how long, until finally I was too weary to stand up. Then we sat down on the floor together.

"You ain't that fool; you better than him. Who are you?" he asked, winking at me.

"I'm Lezley Lynette Bingo McSpadden," I said, between wiping my nose and eyes.

"And who else? What you doin' all this for? Why you gotta keep pressin' on?"

I knew exactly what he meant now.

"I'm Mike Mike's mama. And I'm Déja's mama. And I'm Moo Moo and Jazzy's mama!" I knew I had to be better than stooping down to this fool's level. I was mad. Damn mad.

"I liked you the first time I saw you 'cause you was strong, Lezley, strong like my own mama. So you cain't give up."

"But I feel like it, Louis," I said, breaking down again.

"Damn, I didn't know Mike Mike, Déja, Moo Moo, and Jazzy's mama was a punk," he said, raising his eyebrows.

"Boy, don't play," I said, swatting him.

"Just think about all them other mothers that been where you been."

He kissed me and left me with even more to think about.

I sat on the floor alone in the room for a while after that. I started going back through the bag. It was hard. For every ten or fifteen letters that gave me love, there was a hateful one. Then I just got tired of looking at all this shit. I scooped it all up and put it back in the bag.

I checked my watch; it was almost time to leave and pick up the kids from school. I looked outside into the backyard; my thoughts were swelling in my head. The road ahead seemed so dark. The county had opened their investigation. The federal government had opened theirs too. I was behind on reading my e-mails from the lawyers.

There had been too many conference calls to count, and I really didn't remember any of it. But I guessed either I could let everyone else—the police, the lawyers, the media—talk about my son, people who didn't know anything about him or where he came from, or I could pull myself out of this hole and do it myself. I didn't know anything about the law, but I was just going to have to try to understand it if I wanted justice.

It was going to be a hard. I didn't even know how hard, but I'm not stupid and I'm not weak. So it was on.

• • • •

On September 27th, I accepted an invitation to attend the annual Congressional Black Caucus. I never imagined being in a place like this where the most powerful black politicians from all over the country gathered. My head was spinning from all the people offering their sympathy and the politicians pledging to help me fight for justice. By the time I sat down at the table for the big gala I was numb. Here I was all dressed up and feeling emptier than ever. Just then I heard a familiar voice.

"Ms. McSpadden? I'm Attorney General Eric Holder." I looked up and saw Attorney General Holder's kind face. It matched with his voice that I had heard over the phone weeks ago.

I was about to stand up, but he stopped me.

"No, you sit. I just wanted you to know that I'm here to help you in any way that I can." He kissed me on my forehead before excusing himself. I felt that comforting feeling again. I knew this man worked for a big machine, and I was just this little person, but his words helped to keep my hope alive.

CHAPTER TWENTY-SIX

WE DIDN'T START THE FIRE

Each day was a struggle, but I was coping. I was watching the news more, talking to my lawyers more, and just trying to push through the minutes and hours. The attorney general, Eric Holder, had opened his civil rights investigation for Mike Mike back in August and a full inquiry by September looking at the whole Ferguson Police Department.

Governor Nixon's state of emergency had since been lifted, and the National Guard and their tear gas, tanks, and machine guns had gone. But they were now back. The protestors weren't laying down. The county prosecutor, Bob McCulloch, had opened the state's grand jury investigation two months before, and I was trapped in the waiting game.

Meanwhile, the officer who had shot Mike Mike was still on paid leave. It had also taken till September 24, seven weeks after Mike Mike was shot, for Ferguson Police Chief Thomas Jackson to give a so-called apology for what they did to Mike Mike. I got myself all wound up thinking back to the day I turned on the local news and saw him delivering the apology: "I want to say this to the Brown family: No one who has not experienced the loss of a child can understand what you're feeling," he said, facing the camera and standing in front of an American flag. "I am truly sorry for the loss of your son. I'm also sorry that it took so long to remove Michael from the street. The time that it took involved very important work on the part of investigators who were trying to collect evidence and gain a true picture of what happened that day. But it was just too long, and I'm truly sorry for that."

I damn near kicked a hole in the television. I was insulted and disgusted. First off, I'm not a Brown. Second, and most important, he needed to have enough decency to address me and Mike face-to-face. Our lawyers had issued statement after statement on behalf of the family asking for peace and justice. But there was still no justice and no peace. There wasn't even respect.

But today, I wasn't going to focus on Mike Mike's case. I woke up and didn't even have a cigarette. It was Saturday, and Moo Moo and Jazzy had spent the night at Mama's. I had eased them back into staying over there again but didn't really allow Mama to let them go outside and play in the front too much. They were all doing well in school. Moo Moo was appointed to be student security guard, and he was taking his job so seriously that he was even wearing his badge and plastic orange vest at home. Déja was talking about going to college after she graduated. I was just as proud as I could be.

I had picked her and her best friend up from the nail shop. I had decided to treat her to a manicure. Mike Mike's death had made me a lot more sensitive to my kids and making sure I told them and showed them how much they meant to me.

I needed some gas and decided to drive down West Florissant. The city had everything boarded up, and it didn't look like they were going to fix it up around there anytime soon. I honked my horn at a group of peaceful protestors as I turned into the QuickTrip gas station. There were two within blocks of each other; the other one that the looters burned down after Mike Mike was shot was nothing but a burned-out parking lot. They had even torn the charred building down.

I pulled up to a QT pump.

"Mama, can we get somethin' to drink?" Déja asked.

"Yeah, but don't be in there all day, Déja," I warned. "I need to go pick up Moo Moo and Jazzy."

I had filled my tank and was still waiting on those teenage girls to come out. They were going to make me late. An SUV pulled into a spot next to me. Two white women were inside. I glanced over at the car and saw them pointing and mugging me down. The driver started to dial on her cell phone.

I bit my bottom lip, trying to hold back my anger. I went inside to hurry the girls along. Within seconds, the woman driving was inside. I caught her cutting her eyes at me as she went straight to the soda machine and began refilling her jumbo-sized cup. I could tell right away that she was a regular. When you saw white people around there, they were either cops or people who worked for the police department or Ferguson City Hall.

"C'mon, y'all, we need to go," I said, hustling them out of the place.

But then just as I made it to the door, a feeling shot through my body. I wasn't going to let this woman intimidate or disrespect me.

"What the hell are you lookin' at, bitch?"

The white lady twisted her mouth and turned away.

I had rushed Déja and her friend out.

The clerk, a black girl, had come from behind the cash register. She touched me on the shoulder and said, "Ma'am, don't let her get to you. I know who you are, and I want you to know that it's more people with you than against you."

"Sometimes I just don't feel safe," I said, before thanking her.

Then I got back in the car and lit up a cigarette, took a heavy pull, and let out the smoke and my anger.

"Y'all OK?" I turned to Déja.

"Mama, we good. Don't worry about these small-minded people."

Déja was right. Sometimes our kids make a lot more sense than what we do as adults.

I dropped the girls off, and made my way to Mama's street. I tried my best to stay away from West Florissant and Canfield, but of course Mama was there, refusing to move, and as I had gotten older I really enjoyed visiting her. Going down Canfield Drive was always bittersweet. Residents were typically outside in their usual spots, watching over Mike Mike's makeshift memorial of stuffed teddy bears, candles, balloons, and homemade signs stacked in the middle of the street.

Mama's house was further down, but I pulled over and got out. A tall, skinny dreadhead dude was sitting in a lawn chair with a sign propped up against it that read COP WATCH. It had a stick figure–type drawing on it with a cop character standing over a body lying on the ground.

"Hey, you Mike Brown mama, ain't you?" he asked, standing up, extending his hand.

"Yeah," I smiled, shaking his hand. "Somebody added more stuff, huh?" I asked, walking closer to the items piled in the street.

"Aw, they be addin' stuff every day. We got your back, Mama!" he said with pride.

I waved good-bye and got in my car and headed on to Mama's house. I was starting to feel down. Times like that make me feel like I just wanted to leave St. Louis, but where was I going to go? This place was all I knew.

By mid-October, things were on edge on the outside of my household, but it was getting tougher to shield the kids, and even keep myself upbeat. An announcement came out that there would be a "Weekend of Resistance." On my way to Mama's, I saw the protesters revving up.

"What you think about this 'Weekend of Resistance' Brittanie?" I asked, scrolling through my phone.

"Nette Pooh, we should go out there," she said, standing at the stove in Mama's kitchen. "Everything you do is for Mike Mike, you know."

"Ugh, I'm just so tired of waitin'—waitin' on information, waitin' on somebody else to do somethin' so that the lawyers can do somethin'." I jumped up out of my seat and walked into the living room. Mike Mike's picture was staring right at me.

"Nette Pooh, you the symbol of Mike Mike's determination," Brittanie said, giving me one of them so-what-you-gonna-do? looks.

Chevelle and Louis met us on West Florissant. The crowd was greeting me with hugs and smiles, showing me love. Chevelle even took me over to where Dr. Cornel West and Cornell Brooks, the national president of the NAACP, were preparing to lead the marchers. I felt honored they wanted to meet me.

Then, I overheard some of the crowd's comments about Mike Mike's case. I had started to feel anxious and panicked. I wanted to leave.

"That announcement gonna be comin' from the county prosecutor any day, you know. Some shit gonna jump off if they don't indict that cop," a black man said.

"Yeah, well, I just hope we ain't out here for nothin'. You know how these white folks are in St. Louis. They probably won't indict him," a woman replied.

"Well, girl, I ain't gonna stop marchin'. This is part of history! Ain't you seen all them celebrities come out here? I just ain't tryin' to get locked up."

By the time we got back home, the news was playing in the background, announcing that Dr. West and Mr. Brooks had been arrested along with about forty others. I was realizing that even despite some folks who were protesting for the moment, or even in some sick way looking for gain off my son's death, there were a lot more people who were out there with their hearts and souls, risking their jobs and families, just to see us have a victory.

"What if they don't indict, Louis?" I asked, sitting down on the living room couch.

"You can't think like that. We gotta hold on to hope. I'mma go pick up some food. You ain't been eatin' properly, and you need your strength."

I made up my mind that I had to figure out how I was going to do more. All this waiting around for the authorities to "maybe" do the right thing was going to give me a nervous breakdown. It was time, some kind of way, to take charge of my own destiny. I was working hard to get on with my life and make sure my other kids were going to be OK, but I was worn down from everybody else's promises and no results. I was also becoming more and more aware of my power as Mike Mike's mama. I wanted to get justice for Mike Mike and to earn a living again, to provide for my other kids' future.

I scrolled through the messages on my phone and saw that someone had tagged me with a quote from the famous writer Mark Twain. I read: *"The two most important days in your life are the day you are born and the day you find out why."* I have been trying to figure out so many "whys" in my life since August 9th. Why did this happen? Why Mike Mike? Why me? But the longer I sit here in limbo, waiting for someone to decide whether or not my son should get justice, the more anxious I get. I saw something on line about family's starting foundations after a loved one passes. I even recalled Sabrina Fulton talking about her foundation for her son. A foundation would help me keep Mike Mike's legacy alive. I created the Michael. O.D. Brown We Love Our Sons And Daughters Foundation. I wanted it to create programs that advocated for justice and supported families. I'm Mike Mike's mama and if I don't take control of how my son's death is being treated no one will. I thought about how a foundation could help me put my words into action. I knew that fighting for Justice, Education, Health, and Families was the goal, because those were all the things that embodied Mike Mike's life before and now. Now I just had to come up with a way to pull it off.

November 2014

On November 17, 2014, Governor Jay Nixon issued another state of emergency. He ordered the National Guard to patrol the streets of Ferguson. It was rumored the grand jury decision would be coming any day. My nerves were shot. I found myself going back into a dark place again. It hadn't been this bad in a while. I just wanted to lie in bed under my covers and hide. I tried to turn on *Love & Hip Hop* and let reality television drown out my reality, but I couldn't tune the world out. What was happening consumed my thoughts. The lawyers were calling me daily. They were giving me updates on no updates.

I scrolled through social media to pass time. Facebook was on fire. Some reporters were saying that Governor Nixon's latest actions were antagonistic. He was assuming demonstrators would be ready for action, and to me that was outright accusing folks of being violent before they did anything whatsoever.

"My hope and expectation is that peace will prevail," Governor Nixon said, speaking in front of a press conference. "But I have a responsibility to plan for any contingency that might arise."

A week later, on November 24, 2014, I was given a couple hours notification that the grand jury was going to announce the verdict. I wanted to be out in the streets among the people when the announcement came down.

Louis and me stood in front of the Ferguson Police Department on a platform. Hundreds had gathered with us. The cold air was tense and thick, like how it feels when a thunderstorm is about to happen. It wasn't going to take much to send the demonstrators over the edge. I closed my eyes tightly and began to pray for good news.

Thanksgiving was in a few days, and my family needed something to be thankful for.

Everyone huddled around their cell phone or car radio, watching, listening, as Bob McCulloch, the county prosecutor, stood in front of the world, stiff, cold, unfeeling. He peered over his glasses, looking down on all of us, and then rattled off a slew of words that filled up my head so fast I got dizzy. He was aggravated as he rambled about the twenty-four-hour news cycle and its "insatiable appetite for something, for anything, to talk about, following closely behind with the nonstop rumors on social media," he said sarcastically.

Then, finally, he announced, that the grand jury determined that no probable cause existed to indict the officer.

I shook my head back and forth. So many people saw this coming, but I didn't.

I reached for Louis, but he was too far away. The crowd began to chant "Fuck the police!" and "Hands up! Don't shoot!"

Suddenly, someone threw something through the window of an empty police car. The window exploded, glass flew everywhere. Then it went up in flames.

"Burn this motherfucker down! Burn this bitch down!" Louis shouted, raising his arms up and down in the air.

Louis is a peaceful man. He had tried to be strong for me all these months, but McCulloch's announcement broke him. I grabbed him by his shirt and took him in my arms. Next thing I heard was gunshots. We ducked and took off running.

People were outraged. They were not turning back tonight. More police cars were set on fire. You could hear glass breaking in the distance and big crashes and kabooms. Flames had consumed block after block. Louis and me ran for shelter.

I lay on Louis's chest that night, quietly staring at the ceiling. I thought about who those grand jury members were. Were any of the nine whites mothers? What about the three black ones? Was anybody a black man with a black son? Was anybody a black woman trying to raise a black son?

I was numb. Thick black smoke was still hanging in the sky, and you could still see the smoke coming from what used to be small businesses around these parts. But there was something still alive inside me. I know it must've been Mike Mike's spirit, his voice whispering, "Mama, I know you're tired, but you can't give up."

"Physical evidence does not change because of public pressure or personal agenda," Mr. McCulloch said.

Our attorneys wasted no time issuing a statement:

"We are profoundly disappointed that the killer of our child will not face the consequence of his actions. While we understand that many others share our pain, we ask that you channel your frustration in ways that will make a positive change. We need to work together to fix the system that allowed this to happen. Join with us in our campaign to ensure that every police officer working the streets in this country wears a body camera.

"We respectfully ask that you please keep your protests peaceful. Answering violence with violence is not the appropriate reaction.

"Let's not just make noise, let's make a difference."

It was all more bullshit to me. I wanted action, but I was too tired to think about what we were going to do next.

The officer who killed Mike Mike announced his resignation on the Saturday after everything. He said that after the state prosecutor's announcement, he feared for his own safety and for the safety of his fellow police officers. I wonder if he realized Mike Mike had feared for his safety too?

CHAPTER TWENTY-SEVEN

DECEMBER 25, 2014

Christmas 2014

We couldn't even have Thanksgiving and be thankful. Holidays were always big for my family, and I made them big for my kids. But, coming off the Missouri grand jury's decision not to indict, how was I supposed to, just a few days later, sit at the table where he used to sit? Usually the day before Thanksgiving, Mama would spend the night with Brittanie, then we'd all spend the day at her house cooking and hanging out. But I didn't even want to wake up today.

Brittanie cooked anyway, but instead of us spending the day over there, Louis, the kids, and me didn't get there until that evening. At the table, it felt uncomfortable. We all knew the obvious, but no one spoke about Mike Mike, or brought his name up for that matter. It was too painful. Mike Mike loved to eat and that's why this was one of the hardest times to gather. We were sitting at the table looking at all his favorites— ham, macaroni and cheese, greens, chocolate cake, Mama's famous sweet potato pie. I stayed on him about his diet, but I always let him take a break on days like this, because he loved him some ham. He wasn't supposed to eat it because of the sodium, but I let him cheat a little bit. We tried to have something normal, but what was normal about this?

When Christmas came around, I was trying to be in better spirits. I wanted to skip Christmas this year, but I couldn't be unfair to my other kids. After all, they had been through a lot this year. They deserved for me to try to make this holiday season as special as I could.

Everybody in St. Louis was trying to be positive and come together. But the elephant had been let out the room. The lack of an indictment for Mike Mike's killer had left this city with an even bigger bleeding divide. The public knew it was wrong, but that didn't matter. The police were a machine. You can't win, and even when you think you've won—like Wanda Johnson, the mother of Oscar Grant, the unarmed black man who was shot and killed at Fruitvale Station in Oakland, California— you aren't really winning. She went through a trial and everything, got the policeman convicted for murder, and he was out in less than a year.

I was trying to fight the way I was feeling like hell, but I was slowly creeping to a space where I just wanted to lock myself in my room.

I decided to get myself together and accept the NAACP's invitation to their annual jazz brunch.

I had a jittery feeling in the pit of my stomach. The Ritz-Carlton Hotel was just a short distance away from Bob McCulloch's office, where the grand jury chose not to indict Mike Mike's killer. I just wanted Louis to speed up and get us to the hotel as soon as possible. This part of town stirred up too much emotion.

When we pulled up to the Ritz and the valet attendant let me out, I was rushed by a group of people who were going into the event too. They immediately began giving me their "We're so sorrys" and "How do you feels?" It was too much, too soon. Louis got us inside and sitting at our table in no time.

The room was elegant, and I was starting to feel better about being there.

I was in shock when John Gaskin III, the local NAACP youth leader, called me to the stage.

"We want to present you with this small love token, Miss McSpadden, let you know that you are loved and that the county civil rights organization is remaining true to the fight for justice for you and your family. Ever since August, they're saying, 'How can we get this to the Brown family?' There are several things in our office that are being mailed to you, Miss McSpadden, all types of stuff that people want you and your family to have for Christmas."

As I thanked the room, my eyes landed on a chubby white man with glasses. I had to do a double take. When I got back to my seat, I whispered to Louis, "That's the mayor of Ferguson, ain't it?"

It was not only Ferguson Mayor James Knowles III, but also Ferguson Councilman Dwayne T. James. They were sitting at a table on the opposite side of the room from where we were sitting. My eyes narrowed as I looked behind them at another table and saw St. Louis County Police Chief Jon Belmar, whose department had investigated Mike Mike's killing.

I was so angry I wanted to storm out. Instead, I went to the bathroom and splashed water on my face. I dabbed my face dry, put on some fresh lip gloss, and was ready to face the room again.

I walked right past an area where Chief Belmar and Mayor Knowles were being interviewed. I slowed my walk. I wanted to make my presence known to them, so that they were forced to stop and acknowledge me. Ask me for the time. Something!

"I saw coming to the event as a way to help bridge that gap and increase our outreach efforts, because the city of Ferguson has always been committed to being a progressive community," Knowles said. "I think a lot of issues have come to the forefront since August—and those are things the city's going to continue to work on moving forward."

"We can't only see each other in times of hardship," Belmar said. "We've got to see each other in times of joy, otherwise we don't build those relationships."

I stood off to the side and just shook my head. The mayor and the police chief didn't part their lips to speak to me. They didn't have to even give me a condolence or show me sympathy, but they could've at least acknowledged me with a "Hello, Miss McSpadden." Anything. Anything. They were still government officials, and I am a citizen. They showed me their true character and what kind of men they were. They stood for nothing. So I have to keep fighting, even when I get weary, even when I'm scared and confused. I've got to keep fighting.

• • • •

Louis and me came back home with a Christmas tree, and Moo Moo's face lit up. Jazzy was jumping all around.

"Mama, can we make it a *Frozen* Christmas tree?" she screeched.

"Naw, we ain't doin' nothin' like that, Jazzy," Moo Moo said, giving her a playful push.

"Y'all stop playin'! Let's get everything cleaned up so we can decorate."

"Let it go. Let it go!" Jazzy sang a song from the movie, spinning herself right out the room.

We all busted out laughing.

That's just what I decided to do at that point. Even if it was just for one day, I was going to let all the stress and the fighting and the sorrow go and give my family the Christmas we all needed.

Christmas Day, Daddy had already arrived. He was sipping on a beer. Mama and Brittanie and her boyfriend and kids was on the way. Bernard and his girlfriend, too. Louis had the Christmas music going, and I was at the stove doing what I loved. I had my sweet potato pies filled, my collard greens were in the pot, next to the eye with my spaghetti, and my dressing, and mac 'n' cheese was all mixed up and ready to go in the oven. My potato salad was chilled. Even though it was wintertime, Louis was seasoning up some ribs to put out on the grill. My ham was done and the turkey was in the oven.

I pulled out my bowl to start mixing up some cake batter and sat down at the table. I had opened my blinds and was staring out the window.

"Nette, you gon' be able to get through today?" Daddy asked.

"Yeah, Daddy, I'm just thinking about last Christmas when I bought Mike Mike his Beats headphones." I had to stop. I was getting choked up and my eyes filled up with tears. "I had saved my money all year to get those for him. He loved music."

"Baby, it's okay, just let it out. That's why we all here together. We here for Mike Mike," he said, standing up and putting his arms around me.

Everybody had gotten to the house, and we were all in a good mood. It was time to eat, and Daddy gathered everybody in the kitchen. It was tight, but we were going to bless the food together. Louis gave me a nod.

"Well, um, I just want y'all to know how happy I am that we here together. We made it, and some days I wasn't sure." I choked back my tears, but Brittanie couldn't. I looked over at her and they were streaming down her face. "I know this is hard for all of us, but we made it and God blessed us, and He gonna keep on blessing us."

Everybody hugged the next person, and then we got down to the business of eating. We all felt some sadness in our hearts, but today we just wanted to remember Mike Mike's laugh and his smile. Mike Mike loved his family. So I know his gift to us was bringing us together even though he was no longer with us.

CHAPTER TWENTY-EIGHT

SMOKE AND MIRRORS

March 4, 2015

A reporter asked me once if there was anything they could do. I think I shocked him when I said, "Yes, do you have a life that I can give to my son so that he can come back?" He was speechless. That was several months before, when I was still dealing with a lot of denial about Mike Mike being gone for good.

When Mike Mike was put in the ground on August 25, 2014, I knew for sure then that he wasn't coming back. And so I'd been fighting what felt like the world since then. It had taken a lot to keep hope alive, but the Justice Department opening its case seven months before proved to the world that Mike Mike's death wasn't right. I still believed that justice was possible.

The next day the Department of Justice was going to make its decision. My anxiety was starting to build up again. Cleaning up was always good therapy, but I had scrubbed the bathroom twice, fed the fish, mopped the kitchen floor, and vacuumed. Louis was at work, the kids were at school. I felt like I was going to jump out of my skin. I could hear myself breathing. It felt like the walls were starting to close in on me. I fired up a cigarette and looked out the window at the empty street, and it made me think about Mike Mike lying out there alone that day. A firelike feeling shot through my spine. I had to shake off that horrific image of my baby. I jumped into my car with a broom, my mind set on one place: Canfield Drive.

228

When I got out the car in front of the makeshift memorial for Mike Mike, no one was in sight. The dreadhead "cop watch" guy wasn't even sitting in his regular lawn chair. But it was quiet, and I could be alone for a change.

With my broom in hand, I started sweeping the street and straightening up the stuffed animals. Some were dirty and worn, even had started to mildew; others were brand-new. I stood up a candle that had been knocked over. I needed to be here. I needed to feel my son. As I organized the items and swept away the trash, I wondered who all was going to be at the meeting from the DOJ. I had hoped Attorney General Holder would be there. The only other person I knew from the DOJ was Assistant US Attorney Fara Gold. She was my local DOJ contact.

We'd only met in person once, but we had developed a relationship over the phone during the last several months. Our exchanges were often volatile, because I was seeing that as much as she was saying she was on my side, sometimes she didn't have any real answers for me. Our back-and-forth was mainly over text:

> LM: What's goin' on, Fara? Why we ain't got no answers and it's goin' on two months?
>
> FG: Lezley, please be patient. We are interviewing witnesses. I am personally going door-to-door. Please, there is a process . . .
>
> LM: A process? Be patient? With all due respect, Fara, the police wasn't patient when he shot my son in cold blood. You wouldn't be fuckin' patient!
>
> FG: Please try to be calm.
>
> LM: Calm! Are you serious? I'll be calm when this man is indicted! I'll be calm when my son has justice!

We had many more exchanges, but in the end Fara understood that I was just a mother who was refusing to give up. I knew she'd be there the next day. I just wanted to feel like somebody who knew how hard it had been waiting all these days and weeks and months was there. I couldn't talk to Mr. Holder. He was too high up. Fara had been my only resource, and I just hoped she was going to come through for me.

I bent over to pick up a broken piece of glass. I had worked up a sweat sweeping the street and dusting off the still-growing pile of items that were placed there out of love and care from people all over the world, just for Mike Mike. So when I went up in them FBI offices the next day and met with the Department of Justice, I was going to take the spirit of all the hundreds and thousands of people who, even though they didn't know me or my son or my family, felt my pain. I was going to walk up in there with my head held high. I just knew they were going do the right thing. They had to do the right thing.

That night, I removed my Timberland high-heeled boots from the box and placed them by the closet door. I ironed my blouse and hung it up and laid my jeans and suit jacket out too. I carefully wrapped my hair in my scarf. I wanted to look good because I was going to the FBI building to meet with the people who had the real power to finally convict my son's killer.

The day before the decision was to come down, Attorney General Eric Holder and the Department of Justice had released a report from its Ferguson Police Department investigation.

The DOJ findings included the following: (1) a pattern and practice of disproportionate stops and arrests of blacks without probable cause, (2) unreasonable force, (3) racially biased handling of warrants by municipal courts, and (4) a pattern of focusing on revenue over public safety that violated the rights of poor, black residents.

Thank you, God! This had to be a good sign for the next day. At least I could close my eyes and try to sleep.

• • • •

March 5, 2015

On the drive into downtown, Daddy, Louis, and me were silent except when I asked Louis to hand me the lighter. I quietly puffed away, turning up the radio to take my mind off my anxiety. I was jittery and my leg was shaking as Louis pulled past security and into the small arched driveway that was in front of another set of tall iron gates. On the other side was a large white-brick building. You couldn't see a name or address on it. Chevelle pulled up a few seconds behind us, and Ben Crump and Daryl Parks were right behind him.

The wind whipped and cracked past my ears. It must've been the coldest day of the year so far. Everyone saved their greetings for inside. When we reached the door of the building, a tall FBI agent met us and ushered us to a check-in desk. Adolphus Pruitt and Attorney Gray were already waiting inside. I felt like I was on some top-secret mission. A nerve in my right cheek started jumping, and my stomach was on full-blown flip-flop mode.

"You OK, Lezley?" Crump asked, patting me on the shoulder. He had a lazy tongue and talked with a heavy Southern drawl.

"I'm OK. But we needed to be on time for this meeting. "Where's Mike?"

"You know, Lezley, I don't know, but just stay calm." He patted me on my shoulder, and I felt a moment of reassurance. He always cracked me up the way he said my name. That helped lighten the moment.

Thirty minutes later, Mike still wasn't there. Everybody was checking their watches and phones. I felt my heart start to race, and I was pacing nervously back and forth. I didn't want to get upset.

"Gray, can you please go get him?" I asked with a tight jaw.

Attorney Gray was the local attorney on our team, but he had a stronger rapport with Mike. Gray whipped out his cell.

Several DOJ agents and FBI agents, mostly white men, had gathered around. There was one black female agent in the middle of them all. I connected with her eyes, and we had one of those silent sister-girl-hang-in-there moments. I took a deep breath again.

"Crump, can't we just do this without him?" I said, rolling my eyes. I didn't really want to have the meeting without Mike. Crump knew I was just saying that outta anger. Plus, it didn't look good for us being black parents in such an important situation, and the daddy wasn't even there.

Just then, in a cold gush of air, Mike came through the door. He had his regular hard-core demeanor and a stern face. Folks around the room spoke, but he didn't acknowledge anyone except Gray, Pruitt, Crump, and Parks. He ignored my daddy, Louis, and Chevelle.

When he saw me, he looked me in the eye and walked toward me. I was startled at first, unsure what his intention was. I moved closer to Chevelle.

"Hey, Mike." I did my best to keep it civil.

And then he grabbed me in a forceful hug. There was no tenderness there. I didn't understand what the gesture meant. Chevelle's face tightened. I saw my daddy and Louis perk up. I shook my head, letting them know it was OK.

"Seems as if we're all here. So you guys can all follow me!" The tall, slender black female agent motioned for us to follow her.

Thoughts of Mike and his behavior quickly went away. I was trying to concentrate on keeping my balance walking up the cement steps. I held Louis's hand as we were all led into a large conference room. When we entered, Fara was standin' on crutches. I leaned in and gave her a hug. A short, well-groomed white man took over and began introducing himself to everyone in the room.

"Robert Moossy. Great to meet you, Lezley," he said in a friendly, upbeat tone. He was full of energy like he had had too much caffeine.

Mr. Moossy quickly went around to each person. He knew everyone by name and was extra-friendly. But he was getting us in our seats at the same time. We were already late starting, and I could tell they weren't going to waste another minute. My hand was trembling as I opened the bottle of water in my hand.

Mike and his wife sat across the table from Daddy, Pruitt, Chevelle, and me. Crump, Gray, and Parks were next to him. There was a black agent in charge of community relations present, but outside of a friendly hello, he never opened his mouth.

"Well, good morning. We are so glad that everyone could make it," Mr. Moossy said, jumping right in.

Someone handed him a stack of documents, and he started passing them out. It was a large, heavy file:

DEPARTMENT OF JUSTICE REPORT REGARDING THE CRIMINAL INVESTIGATION INTO THE SHOOTING DEATH OF MICHAEL BROWN BY FERGUSON, MIS- SOURI, POLICE OFFICER DARREN WILSON

I was confused. He began to break down what was in the pages in front of us. I was getting fidgety. I didn't care about all this information about Ferguson and their bad policing. I just wanted him to get to the point. His words got faster and faster, and I felt myself crumbling as everything started going in and out.

"As discussed above, Darren Wilson has stated his intent in shooting Michael Brown was in response to a perceived deadly threat . . ."

I was breathing heavy, gripping the arms of my chair. I gasped for air.

"The only possible basis for prosecuting Wilson under section 242 would therefore be if the government could prove that his account is not true. Meaning that Brown never assaulted Wilson at the SUV, never attempted to gain control of Wilson's gun . . ."

I felt like my air supply was being cut off. I needed water. I needed help.

"There is no credible evidence that Wilson willfully shot Brown as he was attempting to surrender or was otherwise not posing a threat . . ."

What the hell was going on here! Then, almost in slow motion, I heard him clear as a bell.

"Because Wilson did not act with the requisite criminal intent, it cannot be proven beyond reasonable doubt to a jury that he violated 18 U.S.C.§ 242 when he fired his weapon at Brown. For the reasons set forth above, this matter lacks prosecutive merit and should be closed."

"What?" Tears exploded from my eyes.

I heard "Oh, nos" and "God, nos," and then Mike pushed back from the table, kicking his chair over. Everyone in the room jumped.

"Fuck this bullshit! Fuck all y'all! I ain't come down here for this shit!" He stormed out.

Agents from around the building ran out in the hall after him.

"Fara! What is this shit? What happened?" I pleaded.

"Lezley, after interviewing all the witnesses . . ."

"Don't tell me that crap! This man killed my son in cold blood!" I didn't give her a chance to say anything.

Meanwhile, Mike was causing an uproar. He stormed back into the room and began pacing wildly. Then he left again.

I was furious at the spectacle he had made. Then his wife, Calvina, got up and left.

I tried to catch my breath, but my mind and heart were moving too fast. I jumped up. "Fara, you owe me a better explanation than this!"

Fara startled, gripping her crutches.

"What are you doin'?" I asked, with a look of utter surprise. "Do you think that I'd hit you?"

"Well, no, no, Lezley. I just want you to calm down."

It was as if all the blood had been drained from my body. My cheeks got hot, and then I collapsed in my chair. She went on to explain and give me so many apologies that my ears overflowed. But I never heard the words I'd been longing for: that Darren Wilson would be prosecuted.

• • • •

I sat in the middle of the bedroom floor. I needed and wanted to escape, to disappear. I was wishing I had something to calm me down, make me sleep, make this all go away. I was weary and broken for sure this time. I mean, how much did these people think a person could take? The lawyers were talking about the next step being a civil suit, but that wasn't going to put the cop that killed Mike Mike behind no bars. It wasn't about no money, never had been. It was about justice. We lost again. I was numb-minded and limp as CNN played in the background. Everyone was commenting on the day, but not Mike Mike's mama. None of these motherfuckers wanted to hear what I really had to say!

I turned to the screen and was face-to-face with Eric Holder. I just kept shaking my head, wondering, *What happened Mr. Holder? You promised me. I thought you had my back. I thought you understood.*

"Michael Brown's death, though a tragedy, did not involve prosecutable conduct on the part of Officer Wilson. Now, this conclusion represents the sound, considered, and independent judgment of the expert career prosecutors within the Department of Justice. I have been personally briefed on multiple occasions about these findings."

The screen cut to the anchor, Wolf Blitzer, talking to Daryl Parks.

"I know the family, the Michael Brown family, is disappointed. But do you accept what Eric Holder said, that he personally reviewed everything and this was his conclusion?" Mr. Blitzer asked.

"Not only do we accept it, Wolf, but we thank the attorney general for his involvement. We also thank the line prosecutors and Fara Gold, who was one of the assistant US attorneys from DC involved, and many other FBI agents. If nothing else, I think that their involvement allowed us to get closer to the truth in this case. I think the truth plays a big role, in that now we know what happened. Whether or not they were able to file a federal civil rights criminal complaint against Darren Wilson is a total different issue. I think that the family, although very disappointed, in that the killer of their son continues to go free, is very disappointing to them and would be disappointing to any person who has lost their child. However, they are, as we said earlier, encouraged by the fact that the Justice Department has found the things that it found within the department. When you think about Michael Brown, think about the first thing that Officer Darren Wilson said to the boys as he approached them. He told them to 'get the F on the sidewalk.' That's just not a way that an officer should greet young men who are walking in their own neighborhood. So we are hopeful that this action by the Department of Justice in Ferguson, Missouri, will lead to some positive change."

I took my shoes off and threw them across the room. "It's bullshit! It's all bullshit!" I kicked and screamed and rolled over on my stomach and let the carpet soak up my tears. Louis cradled me in his arms, and we cried together.

· · · ·

There was a knock at the door at 8:00 a.m. I couldn't imagine who was at my door. I peeked out the front blinds, and there was a FedEx truck, but I wasn't expecting a package. I looked through the front-door peephole and saw that the worker was holding up a letter.

I ran back into the bedroom and shook Louis awake. I had become so paranoid and was too afraid to answer the door.

"You expectin' a package?" I asked frantically. "They at the door."

"Just answer it," Louis said calmly.

I opened the door and there was a FedEx envelope on the mat. I sat on the couch and pulled out a letter that was on official Department of Justice letterhead. I began to read the words out loud. It was from Attorney General Eric Holder.

In between the words, I could see his kind face again. But this time something was different. It was like he was trying to justify why the officer wasn't in violation of Mike Mike's civil rights. At the same time, he had to play his attorney general role and keep things from being to personal. But it was personal, and with each sentence that wasn't formal, I could feel that he was a black man who saw the injustice. He was a black man who knew that my son's civil rights and living rights had been violated, but maybe his hands were tied. I couldn't try to analyze it anymore. I slumped over and my hand fell limp. The letter floated out of my hand and onto the floor.

The Attorney General
Washington, D.C.
March 17, 2015

Ms. Lesley McSpadden
9764 Vickie Place
St. Louis, MO 63136

Dear Ms. McSpadden:

    I am writing to offer my heartfelt condolences and deepest sympathies, both for the loss of your son Michael and for the sorrow and turmoil you have endured since last August.

    It takes extraordinary courage and remarkable fortitude to persevere through a tragedy like the one you experienced. And despite the public attention that has followed, you have held on to your strength, your decency, and your boundless love for a son taken from you far too suddenly, and far too soon. As a parent of three children, I cannot imagine the pain you have endured, or the bravery you must summon each and every day in order to move forward.

    Although the federal investigation into your son's death has come to a close, I want you to know that I am personally committed to doing everything I can to repair the divisions and heal the rifts that were uncovered in the aftermath of this tragedy. Our investigation into the Ferguson Police Department, which revealed the toxic law enforcement environment surrounding Michael's death, is just one step in our ongoing work to build a brighter future for all Americans, and to create a society that protects and values the lives of all young people. Your son will live on in the work that we do together.

    Again, please accept my condolences for your loss. You have experienced pain that no parent should ever have to bear. And while I recognize that no words can ease the grief that inevitably remains, I want you to know that my thoughts and prayers will continue to be with you and your family.

                          Sincerely,

                          Eric H. Holder, Jr.

CHAPTER TWENTY-NINE

RAINBOW OF MOTHERS

May 2015

I grew up with my granny doing spring cleaning, and all the kids would have to get a rag or a broom or a mop, something. You weren't going to be at her house and not doing something. Even with us moving a lot growing up, my mama was all about throwing out the old to make room for the new. I do it with my kids too. But I was also doing it with my life.

I read that there are five stages of grieving that help us learn to live without our loved one: denial, anger, bargaining, depression, and acceptance. A lot of days lately, I feel like I'm in the bargaining phase, feeling like *what if* I devote the rest of my life to helping others; or *if only* I could go back and stop that cop from pulling out his gun and shooting Mike Mike. Then sometimes I just feel straight depressed and ask myself, *Why go on at all?* So I was stuck and I knew I needed to get some help for real.

I just wasn't feeling the church thing yet. I was praying more, though, and I was now open to therapy. I had to get to this place of admitting that I needed help. With black people, you just don't hear us talk about therapy. It's kind of taboo.

One of the experiences I've had that made me more open to even just having a support system outside of family was meeting Sybrina Fulton, Trayvon Martin's mama. We had the same lawyer, and we were called to do an interview for CNN with Don Lemon. Valerie Bell, the mother of Sean Bell, was with us too. Sean was the unarmed young black man killed in 2006, on the morning of his wedding day, in Queens, New York, after five police officers unloaded fifty rounds of bullets on him and his two friends. The officers were all found not guilty.

When I first met Sybrina, everything was just too fresh and my spirit wasn't as open. These ladies were nice, but what did they really know about me? They had lost their sons senselessly like me, but my life was different than theirs.

I was so nervous my feet even were shaking with each step I took. Don Lemon opened the door to the room we were interviewing in, and Sybrina rushed toward me.

"Hey, mama," she said, throwing her arms around me. "God Bless you, mama," she said, pulling back and stepping to the side. Sybrina was so full of life, and that inspired me. I couldn't believe she could be that upbeat with all she had gone through.

Valerie Bell was a little older and had been on this journey longer than the both of us. She was more reserved. She was dark-skinned, attractive, dressed conservatively, and very gentle. Her smile made me feel like I could drop my guard.

"We got you! We got you!" Valerie said, hugging me tightly.

"Yeah, we got you!" Sybrina nodded, and the two of them just took me in their arms.

That afternoon, Don Lemon thought he was just getting an interview, but I think what he witnessed was the power of the love.

"I was scared to come here, y'all. I almost said no. But I know y'all are speaking to me from experience. You know? You offerin' me somethin' right now that I cain't tell you what it is. But it's somethin'. And somethin' is more than nothin'."

Valerie touched my hand, "Keep the memories in your heart; that's going to help you to continue to carry on with your son, and believing and having faith in God will also help you and the close family members. That's what keeps me, the memories of my son. He always did tell me, 'Ma, I got this.' So I'm telling you, 'Ma, you got this.' It's OK to cry, scream . . . I still do. It's eight years, but you got this."

"You have to focus on when he was smiling. You have to focus on his first day of school, and you have to focus on Christmas Day and things like that. The happier times. Put a picture up when he was happy. And you have to focus on those. Just don't focus on the death, because that's going to eat away at you," Sybrina said.

When I flew home after the interview, Valerie's words kept coming to me as Tamela Mann's "Take Me to the King" played softly in my headphones: "Losing my son was like losing a part of your body. But you remember, you remember what that part of your body has done for you. Like if you lose an arm, you knew what that arm did. So my thing is keeping the memories that will keep you and carry you on."

That day I began to wonder how mothers like us all over the country could connect with each other and build a unified support system. Maybe then we could stop the violence against our babies.

· · · ·

A new season meant shedding the winter coats and hats for some people, but for me it had a new meaning. It meant cleaning out my mind to make way for new ideas. After a heavy storm one day, I opened the front door and looked up in the sky and saw a rainbow. I hadn't paid attention to much of anything in months, let alone nature. But the storm had really affected me and made me cry because Mike Mike loved it when it rained. I stood outside, fascinated by the rainbow, and rushed back in to get my phone.

I was acting more and more like Louis, going to Google every time I saw or heard something and wanting to know more about it. I quickly typed in the word *rainbow*.

rain·bow/ˈrānˌbō/
an arch of colors formed in the sky in certain circumstances, caused by the refraction and dispersion of the sun's light by rain or other water droplets in the atmosphere.

The definition stuck in my head, and I thought about chasing rainbows and never catching one, but it was always beautiful up in the sky. That's what it's like when you have a kid that you lose. You know they are up there and may even see a beautiful image, but you'll never be able to physically hold that child again.

I started posting rainbows in text messages and found pictures of everything from rainbow-colored Christmas trees to bagels.

After Freddie Gray, an unarmed young black man in Baltimore, was killed when the police broke his neck, I was invited to attend a special concert on Mother's Day in Baltimore. I thought I had been nervous about these kinds of events before, but this time it was Prince and Beyoncé who wanted to meet me and a couple other mothers who had had son's killed in nationally publicized cases, backstage.

So here I was at a Prince concert, and now meeting Beyoncé, and she was so down-to-earth and kind. She cried with us and embraced me. I've never been a person who got starstruck, but I didn't know how much of a diva she'd be. She wasn't like that; she was just a regular woman, a black woman who was a mother now herself. She shared her Mother's Day with us.

As I stood off to the side, taking in the moment of how a little black girl from the hood could have become a world traveler as a result of her son getting killed, more tears filled my eyes. I was sad yet thankful that I was working through the grieving process better now. Thankful that I hadn't given up.

I felt a light tap and turned to see Beyoncé's mama, Tina Knowles, standing there. She immediately wrapped her arms around me. She wasn't an old woman by any stretch of the imagination. In fact, she looked fabulous, better than a lot of women my age, but she still had that experienced "mama" vibe. For the next few minutes she shared something very special with me.

"What are you going do now? You have to do something," she said, looking me in the eye.

"I know. I started a foundation, but I'm still figurin' it all out," I said.

"Listen, Lezley, there was an organization that started back in the 1980s called Mothers Against Drunk Drivers, MADD. You should look it up. It could inspire you."

"Thank you, Ms. Tina, for being an inspiration yourself. I have been working on getting my foundation set up and it's almost ready, but I definitely think a new movement for mothers is what the country needs," I said. The wheels in my head were spinning.

I took that moment to heart. I was seeing that God gives us little messages when we least expect them. I didn't waste no time looking up MADD. Those mothers had gotten together to fight drunk drivers because too many of their babies were getting killed with a drunk driver behind the wheel, or they were underage getting alcohol, getting drunk, and killing themselves. Their mothers created a movement.

I got back to St. Louis on a mission. I already had my foundation name, but I wanted my first program to be the Rainbow of Mothers. That name came to me in the middle of the night. I hadn't been this excited in months. I was smiling again. I wanted to use my voice to bring together a rainbow of mothers from all races and backgrounds who had either lost a child to street violence, gun violence, excessive police force, or just untimely death due to illness. I saw services for counseling, programs for our surviving kids, physical activities so that we could keep our bodies and minds occupied. I wanted this to be a support network for mothers across the country, maybe even the world one day.

Sometimes when you have a dream, you just have to step out there. I was stepping out on faith. I just prayed I could make a difference.

August 7, 2015

As me and Louis turned onto Washington Avenue, the street was jam-packed. Women were lined up at the door with their after-five best, dressed to the nines, hair whipped. Butterflies danced in my stomach.

I was relieved to see that the police had everything under control. I spotted Captain Ron Johnson, waved and mouthed "thank you." The day before, after I was finishing up a local TV interview to promote the event, I looked up and Captain Ron Johnson was standing near the front door, waiting to talk to me. A year ago, on August fifteenth, after tear gas and riot police in Ferguson set off criticism from all over the country, the state sent Missouri Highway Patrol Captain in to oversee the police presence there. Captain Ron, as we all call him, was African-American and had grown up in north St. Louis County. So when the governor put him in charge, we all knew he was the police, but we was proud at the same time, 'cause he was one of "us." He had to do his job, but he brought understanding to the situation in his role. Captain Ron even marched with the peaceful protesters.

So, I was speechless when he had called and offered to support the event by making sure we had proper police presence to secure the event. Before I could get a word out, he had reached out and gave me a warm embrace.

"You okay?" He asked with a smile.

"Yeah, I'm doin' pretty good. I really thank you for offering to take care of things for the event."

"Look, I know you've suffered a lot, and I just want you to know that I'm here for you."

We finished going over the logistics for the event and I even cried a little bit. It was a huge moment, because when everything happened with Mike Mike, the public perception was that me demanding justice and for the officer to be prosecuted, was me being anti-police. First off, I got police officers in my family. We need the police, but what we don't need is no more bad policing. Captain Ron was real and compassionate. Before he left he vowed not only his support, but the support of the St. Louis City Police Department for the event. That was the kind of respect that I had been asking for all this time. It wasn't too much to ask for either. Finally, somebody in a position of authority was doing the right thing. I quickly made my way to the back entrance of the building. Suddenly, I closed my eyes and could see Mike Mike's face, smiling. He was my oxygen tonight. I reopened my eyes and looked around in amazement at the room.

Wanda Johnson, the mother of Oscar Grant, who had been killed by police at the Fruitvale Station subway stop in Oakland, California, took the mic and gave us the opening prayer, and the mothers gathered in a circle with candles and photos of their lost children, calling out their babies' names.

Congresswoman Maxine Waters, Ben Crump, Anthony Gray, Daryl Parks, and Reverend Al Sharpton were all there to stand with me. I had been dreaming about all this since the beginning of the New Year, and with the help of my gala committee and board members, I had made it happen.

It was August 7, 2015, two days before the anniversary of Mike Mike's death, and as I was celebrating my son's legacy with all the other mothers in the room, I thought about the fact that it had been a year, and still no justice for Mike Mike. In fact most of the mothers in the room were still in desperate need of justice for their beloved son or daughter. Tonight was the fuel I needed to take my fight to the next level.

Making it through the one-year anniversary of Mike Mike's death was one of the hardest things I'd ever done. But somehow, whether it's a pep talk from Louis, Brittanie, a board member, or my therapist, or just seeing my other kids smile. I push past it. Also, when I saw the turn out at the gala, I understood that I did have a voice that could reach people.

I had been talking with other Rainbow Mothers, more recently like Lucia McBath, mother of Jordan Davis, the unarmed seventeen year old boy, shot by a white man at a gas station in Florida in 2012 because he and his friends were playing their music loud. Lucia is an advocate for gun legislation. So, when I see her speaking in front of Congress, or on panels, I'm amazed how she is still fighting, regardless of the pain, and I know I can do it, too.

Now, I'm determined to make real change through the Michael O. D. Brown We Love Our Sons And Daughters Foundation. One of the big things that legislators like Missouri Congressman William Clay, Jr., and Missouri State Senator Jamilah Nasheed had all begun pushing for is the mandatory use of body cameras. If the officer had had a body cam on the day he shot Mike Mike, we'd know the truth.

I had never even been active in politics, but now was my chance. If I had to bang on every Missouri politicians door, that's what I was going to do. Luckily, both Congressman Clay and Senator Nasheed have opened their doors to me, and also my goal to get a bill in Mike Mike's name.

Some hater might say I'm never going to be successful 'cause I don't have the education or background, or even the right connections, but I look back at my Granny's life. She came up to St. Louis from Mississippi, and she didn't have any connections or a lot of resources, but she made a way anyway. So, as I sat down to write to the powers that be, I was confident that if I could just get one legislator, the rest would follow.

Michael Brown was not some made up character like Hulk Hogan, but the cop who shot him tried to paint him that way. On August 9, 2014, there is no recorded account of Michael Brown's last moments in life. I still do not have closure or the solid truth of what really happened that day.

But police worn body cameras are only a piece of the puzzle when it comes to the whole picture of police accountability and transparency. But body cameras are not a substitute for good policies, good training or good community policing programs.

I want lawmakers to think about me and my family, and other families that need closure and the truth. The death of my son and all the other unarmed victims to police involved shootings whose deaths must not be in vain. Their blood cries out for answers from the streets. And this isn't a black versus white issue. This is an issue about Right versus Wrong. And anything done in the dark will always come to light.

CHAPTER THIRTY

STILL WE RISE

December 5, 2015

On the eve of December fifth, I stood in the middle of my kitchen surrounded by a sea of grocery bags, wondering what in the hell I had gotten myself into. The clock on the microwave read 10:35 p.m. I had twelve hours before my second public event for my Rainbow Of Mothers Program.

The name Body, Mind, and Spirit had come to me clear as day while I was driving home from therapy one evening. I started to smile. Through my counseling, I was learning that a person couldn't get better unless they start from the inside. This holiday I didn't want to be all down and depressed. I needed to be lifted up, and I wanted to help lift up my fellow Rainbow Mothers. The idea was to give fifty mothers who had lost their children, a day of counseling and activities, holiday food bags, and a reminder that they weren't alone.

The gift bags had been hard enough. Everyone the foundation team and I called to donate turkeys and other holiday fixings turned us down. Just hearing the word "no" made me start to doubt myself. I didn't know how I was going to pull it off, but that's the story of my life.

Then, my cousin and board member Sandra got her church to give us the turkeys and things started to fall into place. The only thing left to figure out was the luncheon we wanted to close the day with. After several dead-end attempts to get a sponsor, I found myself pulling out my old catering apron.

I got busy unpacking bags and before long, I was in my zone. I pulled out my cutting board and started chopping onions and celery, then the tender white breast meat from the chicken I'd just taken out the pot. I pulled out a huge bowl, poured everything in, added some scoops of mayonnaise and relish, salt and white pepper, and began to mix it all together. I carefully folded deli meats and cheeses and arranged them on platters. Next were my relish trays, my fruits, and veggies.

I don't even know when I crawled into bed, but it seemed like no sooner than I had shut my eyes, I was waking up. Louis loaded up the car with everything, and on the ride, I was a nervous wreck. I had to keep shaking off disastrous thoughts. Today was another huge leap of faith and was praying that God had a safety net for me.

• • • •

Scented candles burned, soft music played, and the dance studio inside the Better Family Life building had been transformed into our own private sanctuary where we could all lay our burdens down. Twenty of us, sitting on yoga mats, the instructor coaching us to breathe in through our mouths, slowly, letting the air fill up our lungs, becoming still and one with breath, then releasing it slowly. When you lose a child it isn't something that just sits in your heart. It's in your mind. It darkens your spirit. So today was about healing.

The pastor who was also a Rainbow Mother walked up to the front of the dimly lit room. She gave a short opening prayer, every eye was closed and head bowed. A Rainbow Mother twice over, she lost one son, Jason, when he was in college after he was fatally stabbed and murdered by a white supremacist. Her second son had had a pulmonary embolism and died suddenly.

"God took me out of the mode of hate and guilt. I searched myself to see if this had happened as a result of something I had done. Know that if God can forgive us, then who are we to hold on to the guilt?"

While the yoga instructor tiptoed through the room, reminding each of us to continue breathing, mothers started weeping, and then, they started comforting each other. Some just sat in silent reflection. My whole body shuddered, from a chill that shot up my spine, my eyes filled with tears.

Everybody up in here was a Rainbow Mother, most of us had lost sons to black on black street violence. There were two women who are best friends, whose sons were killed together.

Another mother's son had been shot. The killer was never arrested and is still living in her neighborhood. The police simply closed the case because they said no witnesses came forth, or no evidence. But she knows who took her baby. The whole neighborhood knows.

There was one young mother who reminded me of myself so many years ago. She couldn't have been more than twenty-five; she had three babies and had been left to raise them after her boyfriend was shot and killed.

All of us have a story and moments like this get me a little too full still. I got up and slipped out the room, into the hallway where I could take a quiet minute to myself. I leaned up against the wall and tried to do like the instructor had just told us—breathe in slowly, exhale, connect with my breath.

While the rest of the world has Christmas celebrations and parties to line up and shopping to do, most of us would rather skip over Christmas. That's the time of family and gathering for good times and good food. But it is hard to enjoy any of that when your child isn't here anymore. Holidays are days that Rainbow Mothers struggle through. So, I figured if I can help somebody feel better, even if I'm still trying to get help and feel better myself, then this is a testament of me planting that mustard seed of hope.

Around this time last year I went on CNN again, because yet another black boy had been killed by the police. Me and Sybrina Fulton were now embracing Gwen Carr, the mother of Eric Garner and Samaria Rice, the mother of unarmed twelve year old Tamir Rice, the boy who had been shot and killed while playing in the park, by a white Cleveland Police Officer. I connected powerfully with Samaria, because we were not only close in age, but we had both been young single mothers. When

Samaria sat down in the same seat I had sat in when I first met Sybrina and Valerie Bell months before I was struck again by the unending chain of mothers suffering the loss of their children at the hands of violence.

Louis saw me and walked over to check on me.

"You good, baby?" he handed me a Kleenex.

"Yeah, yeah, I just needed a break. It got kinda emotional in there."

"Well, we need you to set the food up when you get a chance," he rubbed my back, before walking back down the long hallway to the main room, where lunch was going to be served.

I collected myself and headed over to get lunch ready. Board members were talking to Rainbow Mothers who had just arrived and checking people in.

Felice McClendon reported, "Lezley, the kids have started their arts and crafts session downstairs. The counseling sessions are starting next."

I was still in amazement that the event was actually happening. She put her arm around me and led me over to where Sandra and Chevelle were gathered with a small group of people.

Better Family Life had helped us get to a network of black therapists who had agreed to donate their entire afternoon to us. I was so moved that they would give their time to help us. They saw us, the Rainbow Mothers, and they saw our need.

When I got into the main room there were more mothers gathered, they walked over to me.

"Thank you for havin' us," one mother said, holding my hand tightly.

"No one ever thinks about us and how hard it is. We were at your event in August and we wasn't gonna miss this one," another one who was older said with tears in her eyes.

I threw my arms around her and we both rocked back and forth.

Back down the hall, the kids were happily doing Zumba moves and the counseling sessions were in full swing. Each counselor was talking to groups of two or three mothers. I saw women laughing and some crying real hard. I walked through each room checking on everyone and even joined in a few of the conversations.

I overheard a mother sobbing in a corner where she was in a one on one moment with a volunteer counselor. Her young son was shot walking to school.

I unwrapped the food and Louis helped me arrange it on the table. Déja and Brittanie were double-checking the food and gift bags. I suddenly got choked up looking at my daughter working her butt off.

It was time for lunch and the women gathered in the main room. We gave the blessing and then lunch was served. Folks were eating, having fellowship. Feel good music was pumping through the speakers and it was a good time.

At the end of the day, something came over me and I suddenly grabbed the microphone. I tried to keep my words slow and steady so that I didn't mess up. Talking in front of people like this always made me a little shy.

"Um, I just, um, want to tell each of you how much I appreciate you being here today," I took a deep breath before continuing. "I feel like I go to a lot of cities, and you see the mothers come out to these events for kids that have been killed, and they all together. But I get sad when I come back home, because I haven't really seen a group of mothers do something collectively here."

I was starting to get charged up. Some of the women began to shout out, "Amen!" and "That's right!"

"For real, ya'll we got one of the highest murder rates in the country, and it's time for us to stand up for our babies!" The room erupted in applause.

"I'm just saying we've all suffered a loss, and even though my son, Mike Mike, got a lot of media attention, don't think that I'm not out here telling the same media that there are others just like me right here."

Pretty soon the room sounded like a down home Baptist church on a Sunday morning.

"So, if I can get media here, then if we riding together, all our children are going to be talked about. Let's stand together and have each other's backs. And if one of ya'll got an event I'm going to be there for ya'll ten toes down! Let's show up and show out at political rallies and in these streets! Thank you and I love each and every one of ya'll!"

Today was a testament of the power of mothers. But, one day, I want there to be an end to the rainbow. I want to run out of Rainbow Mothers. I want our sons and daughters to live. I don't wish this pain, this struggle, this hurt, this void, this guilt, or this grief on anybody.

After Mike Mike died, I believed we would have justice. I waited for the police to right the wrong, I waited for the county to bring justice to Mike Mike, I waited for the DOJ to discover the truth. The system has failed my son. It has failed me and it has failed all of us. But, now, I know that I can't wait for anybody else to make change. I must make change, myself, that will be Mike Mike's legacy; that will be his justice. That's the truth of it.

EPILOGUE
MOTHER TO SON

I felt like visiting Mike Mike's grave site today. The sky was clear, and for February in St. Louis, the weather was mild. Usually we got snow and ice, but it was almost 60. I guess I don't really like coming out here to the cemetery. I put a hat on so nobody recognized me, and I tried to pick a morning when I thought fewer people would be around. I mean how many people would be at a cemetery on a Wednesday at 11:30 in the morning? It was actually peaceful.

I kneeled down and brushed the dirt off the cement plaque that simply read MB. I felt myself start to tremble. "Everybody got somethin' to say about why I don't have a headstone for you yet, but it isn't their business that I wanted the perfect stone, design, and words. I finally got everything the way I want it." I kneeled down, closed my eyes, and imagined him sitting out here with me.

Dear Mike Mike,

It's been almost two years, and it still feels like yesterday that you were stolen from me. I'm working on myself, though. Brittanie misses you. Déja misses you. You were her best friend. She figuring out her way in life. She's going to be a senior in high school next fall. I want her to do everything I couldn't do

252

when I was her age. Maybe she'll go to college, too. Moo Moo is a preteen now. I have to keep him on track. I get scared 'cause he a black boy out here, but I got to believe you up there helping to watch over him to make sure he doesn't get caught up with the wrong crowd. And Jazzy is her sweet self. She always says to me, "Mama, Mike Mike didn't have no weapon." And I say, "You right, Jazzy."

This is real hard, Mike Mike, because you were supposed to be here with us. But I'm going to be strong. I have to be for you. I just got so much I should have said before you left. Then part of me feels like there's nothing that I could say to you that I haven't already said. I was always telling you that I loved you and I was there for you. I know you knew that.

At times, as much as I pray, things aren't changing fast enough. That's why I have to keep reminding myself to look at everything that's happened from a spiritual place. I guess I learned that from you. It's hard to go to the beauty shop. It's hard to go to the grocery store. It's still hard to get outta bed some days. It's hard to go over to your Gun Gun's 'cause she won't move from Canfield.

Life now is so different and new to me. It's funny, I'm not even the type of person who really wears makeup. But I try to keep in mind how things are now, and every time I leave the house, I try to look presentable, because I don't know who might be watching me.

So there isn't a day that goes by that I don't think about you, Mike Mike. I've accepted that you were God's before you were mine. He just let me borrow you for eighteen years. Eighteen of the most incredible, tough, beautiful years of my life.

People always say they OK when tragedy happens and some time passes. Well, I'm not OK, and the way you died wasn't OK. So I'm not going to say that any of this is OK. I'm confused and lost about why this had to happen to you. Why this happened to me, us. I don't get it. So what I have to say is really more like a list of wishes.

I wish you were still here. I wish you had been around the house with me. I wish I had been off work. I wish we had been together. I wish you'd been at the house for me to fire up the grill and put you some chicken breasts out there.

I wish, I wish, I wish . . .

There were three people out there on Canfield that day. So there are three sides to the story. The truth hasn't ever been told. Your truth. You're not here to tell the world what happened. So I'm gonna represent, baby, as best I can.

Sometimes, when I'm laying in my bed awake because I can't sleep, you come to me. I see you so vividly, and I know that you are just watching out for Mama, I know. And I know I'll see you again one day.

I love you,
Mama

ACKNOWLEDGMENTS

Lezley L. McSpadden-Head wishes to thank: My family the Ewings, and my extended family the Browns and Hathaways, and a host of cousins, friends, and supporters; special thanks to my God, who has covered and kept me thus far; my parents Desuirea and Leslie, without them who am I; my husband Louis who has showed me love without a limit; my sister Brittanie for her sweet, kind, and gentle personality; my #FAV Keyanna for her warrior spirit and keeping me grounded; my hairstylist Lanetha "Necie" Quinn for her positive words and anointed hands; board members of Michael O. D. Brown We Love Our Sons & Daughters Foundation. S/O Eric Chevelle Davis, Sandra Tolbert, Felice G. McClendon, and Lyah B. LeFlore for making my mission and vision a priority and helping keep the legacy of my son alive while fighting for justice. *"Truth hurts" is a saying for the guilty. "Truth heals" is a fact for the hurting. . . .*

Authors' Acknowledgements: Special thanks to our agents, B.G. Dilworth of the B.G. Dilworth Agency, and Amy Schiffman, of Intellectual Property Group for your belief, tireless support, and for being fearless champions! Very special thanks to our brilliant editor, Alexis Gargagliano, for your passion, vision, guidance, the many all-nighters that helped us get this beautiful journey to the finish line. And, thanks to the entire Regan Arts family: Judith Regan, Gregory Henry, Richard Ljoenes, Lynne Ciccaglione, Nancy Singer, and Mia Abrahams.

Lyah Beth LeFlore wishes to thank: My loving husband, Eno, for your undying support and unconditional love, and pushing me to keep my eyes on the prize; Bella Grace, my angel, my muse, you are a gift from God and all I do is for you; Mom, Hope, and Jacie, each of you is the wind beneath my wings, your all are my biggest cheerleaders, and its your strength and prayers that have kept me afloat; Daddy, for your watchful eye from above, and being my guardian angel; Cousin Lita, for your spiritual guidance, love, and support; my close circle of girlfriends and cousin friends for having my back; my producing partner and sister, Takia "Tizzi" Green; Rachel Weiss of IPG; Eric Davis, thank you for your support and bringing Lezley and I together; Lezley, for your honesty and strength, and allowing me to capture the powerful journey you shared with your son; and Al Haymon, my longtime mentor, who has always encouraged me.

LEZLEY McSPADDEN is the mother of Michael Brown, and founder of The Michael O. D. Brown We Love Our Sons & Daughters Foundation. The organization advocates for justice, improving health, advancing education, and strengthening families. McSpadden also founded its signature program, Rainbow of Mothers, which was established to support mothers who have suffered the devastating loss of a child. She lives in St. Louis, MO with her family. Visit michaelodbrown.org.

LYAH BETH LeFLORE is the author of eight books, including the novels *Last Night a DJ Saved My Life* and *Wildflowers*; the teen book series *The Come Up*; the *New York Times* bestseller *I Got Your Back*, and NAACP Image Award-winning *The Strawberry Letter*. LeFlore is also a television and film producer who has been profiled in the *New York Times*, *Essence*, *Ebony*, and *Entertainment Weekly*.